Language and Revolutionary Magic
in the Orinoco Delta

Bloomsbury Studies in Linguistic Anthropology

Series Editors

Sabina Perrino, Paul Manning, and Jim Wilce

Presenting and exploring new and current approaches to discourse and culture, Bloomsbury Studies in Linguistic Anthropology examines the most recent topics in this field. Publishing contemporary, cutting-edge research, this series investigates social life through everyday discursive practices, making these practices visible and unveiling processes that would remain concealed without careful attention to discourse.

Titles in this series focus on specific themes to advance the field both theoretically and methodologically, such as language contact dynamics, language revitalization and reclamation, and language, migration and social justice. Positioning linguistic anthropology at the intersection with other fields, this series will cast light on various cultural settings across the globe by viewing important linguistic ethnographies through an anthropological lens. Standing at the frontier of this growing field, Bloomsbury Studies in Linguistic Anthropology offers a balanced view of the current state of the discipline, as well as promoting and advancing exciting new directions for research.

Forthcoming Titles in the Series:

Graphic Politics in Eastern India
Nishaant Choksi
Language Revitalization and Indigenous Remaking in Amazonia
Michael Wroblewski
Saying and Doing in Zapotec
Mark A. Sicoli

Language and Revolutionary Magic in the Orinoco Delta

Juan Luis Rodríguez

BLOOMSBURY ACADEMIC
LONDON • NEW YORK • OXFORD • NEW DELHI • SYDNEY

BLOOMSBURY ACADEMIC
Bloomsbury Publishing Plc
50 Bedford Square, London, WC1B 3DP, UK
1385 Broadway, New York, NY 10018, USA

BLOOMSBURY, BLOOMSBURY ACADEMIC and the Diana logo are trademarks of
Bloomsbury Publishing Plc

First published in Great Britain 2021

Series design by Ben Anslow
Image © DEA / G. SIOEN / Getty Images

A catalogue record for this book is available from the British Library.

Library of Congress Cataloging-in-Publication Data
Names: Rodríguez, Juan Luis, 1974- author.
Title: Language and revolutionary magic in the Orinoco Delta / Juan Luis Rodríguez.
Description: London, UK; New York, NY: Bloomsbury Academic, 2020. | Series: Bloomsbury
studies in linguistic anthropology | Includes bibliographical references and index.
Identifiers: LCCN 2020026389 (print) | LCCN 2020026390 (ebook) | ISBN 9781350115750
(hardback) | ISBN 9781350115767 (ebook) | ISBN 9781350115774 (epub)
Subjects: LCSH: Anthropological linguistics–Venezuela–Orinoco River Delta. |
Warao language–Social aspects–Venezuela–Orinoco River Delta. |
Warao language–Political aspects–Venezuela–Orinoco River Delta. |
Bilingualism–Venezuela–Orinoco River Delta. | Warao Indians–Venezuela–
Orinoco River Delta. | Orinoco River Delta (Venezuela)–Languages.
Classification: LCC P35.5.V46 R63 2020 (print) | LCC P35.5.V46 (ebook) |
DDC 306.440987–dc23
LC record available at https://lccn.loc.gov/2020026389
LC ebook record available at https://lccn.loc.gov/2020026390

ISBN: HB: 978-1-3501-1575-0
ePDF: 978-1-3501-1576-7
eBook: 978-1-3501-1577-4

Series: Bloomsbury Studies in Linguistic Anthropology

Typeset by Deanta Global Publishing Services, Chennai, India

To find out more about our authors and books visit www.bloomsbury.com
and sign up for our newsletters.

This book is dedicated to my family

Contents

Illustrations

Figures

Tables

Acknowledgments

I am in profound intellectual debt for this work. First, I would like to recognize the Warao people of the Orinoco Delta, the community of Morichito, and especially Tirso and Amalia Rivero who so kindly opened their homes for me to do this work. The seeds of this book were planted in me during my undergraduate work at Universidad Central de Venezuela where I found teachers and friends who profoundly shaped my intellectual path. For a brief but fruitful time I also had the good luck to partake in the doctoral program at the Venezuelan Institution for Scientific Research where Dr. Werner Wilbert was a generous mentor, and the late Dieter Heinen shared his lifetime experience of research in Orinoco Delta with me. In 2003 I received a Fulbright-IIE fellowship to come to the United States as a graduate student. I had the good fortune to join the graduate program at Southern Illinois University, Carbondale. At SIU I found myself at an intellectually challenging program, and found in Jonathan D. Hill and Anthony K. Webster mentors and friends like no other. I also enjoyed the intellectual rigorosity of conversations with Yuki Tanaka-McFarlane, Matt Nowak, Aimee Hosemann, Jackie Prime, Monrico Brown, Zach Gilmore, and Val Solomon. While at SIU I received funding for my dissertation from the Wenner-Gren Foundation for Anthropological Research, which funded the bulk of the research that sustains this book. This book would have never been possible without all the intellectual help and encouragement of Chihiro Shibata whose patience with me had no parallel during trying times.

This book developed while I am an assistant professor at the Department of Anthropology at Queens College, City University of New York. Here I have been fortunate to enjoy the intellectual support of the entire faculty and especially Miki Makihara and John Collins who have been real mentors to me since I joined the department. I want to also thank Jose del Valle and the entire *grupo de glotopolitica* at CUNY Graduate Center who have provided me a nurturing intellectual environment for thinking about language and politics. I am very grateful to the students of my first graduate seminar at CUNY. Carmin Quijano, Anthony Harb, Tania Aviles, Lara Alonso, and Jorge Alvis were the best first-year group any new assistant professor could ever hope for.

Some of the materials presented here had some form of previous iteration. Chapter 2, "From Spanish to Warao," is a slightly modified version of "The Translation of Poverty and the Poverty of Translation in the Orinoco Delta" which appeared in *Ethnohistory* (55, no3: 417–38). Chapter 3, "From Warao to Spanish," is a modified version of "The National Anthem in Warao: Semiotic Ground and Performative Affordances of Indigenous Language Texts in Venezuela" in *Journal of Linguistic Anthropology* (26, no 3: 335–51). Chapter 4, "Greetings and Promises," appeared previously as "The Interplay of Greetings and Promises: Political Encounters between the Warao and the New Indigenous Leadership in the Orinoco Delta, Venezuela" in *Pragmatics* (22, no 1:167–87). A previous, modified, version of Chapter 5, "Frames and Revolutionary Magic," appeared as "Ordeal of Language and Political Agonistic Exchange in the Orinoco Delta Venezuela" in *Journal of Anthropological Research* 68(3): 357–72.

Introduction

This book is about the distribution of political gifts and the changing linguistic practices that mediate the relationship between the Warao of the Orinoco Delta and Venezuelan politicians. In a broader sense it sheds light on the interpenetration of the linguistic, performative, and gift-giving practices underlying current Venezuelan politics. This work focuses on the ways the Warao try to understand semiotic communicative practices in the context of a self-identified socialist revolutionary government. It analyzes how and why the Warao found themselves involved in electoral politics in the twentieth century and the consequences of such integration. The book argues that the challenge of understanding this relationship calls for an ethnographic exploration of acts of translation and transduction, and of meaningful correspondences between semiotic mediums. I focus throughout the book on publicly available text, discourses, and practices (Sherzer 1987; Urban 1991), and how they can be translated and transformed into other semiotic forms. These translations and transformations depend on a conceptualization of language as material social action, and of gifts as part of a general process of sign interpretation. My analysis is ultimately about the importance of processes such as translation, transduction, and co-naturalization of semiotic signs (Rosa 2019) for the construction of political reality in Venezuela.

I take as a background for my analysis perhaps the most important process of transformation and translation at work in Venezuela, that of oil revenue into state resources and ultimately into meaningful social/political relations. Venezuela became a "magical state" during the twentieth century (Coronil 1997). What makes it magical is that the state situates itself as a mediator between the social body of the nation, oil as the main product of export extracted from the nation's natural body, and foreign capital. In this position the magical state mediates the relationship between international capital and the natural resources of the state on the one hand, and the social and political body of the nation on the other. The Venezuelan state has at its disposal a source of financial funding that allows it to take on a role independent from the people, and makes it capable sometimes of

creating a clientelist relationship between politicians and their constituents. The state does not depend on taxes or any other form of public financing, and, at the same time, is capable of providing for the people with resources that seem to come straight from nature. Such a state is then capable of producing spectacular acts of development that seems to come out of nowhere. The magical state must be able to also produce the signs of a modern way of life. It, in Coronil's interpretation, "'captivates minds' through highly rhetorical forms which seek the public's compliance by leaving it, in Godzich's words, *boquiabierto* (dumbfounded; literally open-mouthed)" (Coronil 1997: 4–5).

This book is an exploration of these rhetorical forms not as an abstract idea but as a matter of naturally occurring instances of language use and actual performances by politicians in their interactions with the nation's social body. I take here a discourse-centered approach to language and culture (Urban 1991; Sherzer 1987), which requires paying attention to actual instances of language use to understand how the magical state is produced and sustained in the Orinoco Delta and what other semiotic forms, such as campaign gifts distributed during elections, play a role in captivating people's political imagination.

Hanks and Severi (2014) have argued that translation should be central to understanding all cultural and social processes. I take that point to heart at multiple levels by paying attention to actual processes of linguistic translation, as well as the transformation of state resources available to politicians into meaningful performances for their constituents. Thus, both narrowly defined linguistic translations and broader semiotic processes of transforming oil into public performances are central to the creation of democratic publics (Warner 2002; Gal and Woolard 2001) and the Venezuelan political system.

The Venezuelan state is in a translating/transducting position. The state transforms natural resources into revenue, and rent into performances and gifts for the people. This is also a performative (Austin 1962) process that affects electoral politics in Venezuela as a whole. Venezuelan politicians are then forced by this structural dynamic to use the natural body of the nation to "promise paradise," as Venezuelan playwright Jose Ignasio Cabrujas (1987) would put it. The money obtained through oil is used to enchant the political body, which in turn expects nothing but the promise of instant reward from its political leaders. This has resulted in an extreme personalization of politics in Venezuela. Those leaders who have benefited from an oil boom are remembered as magicians who fulfilled the country's fantasies, but those who could not use the natural body in this way have been rejected and at best forgotten in Venezuela's history. They have been lost in translation, so to speak.

Coronil's analysis of Venezuela's history is important as a point of entry into the mediated dynamic between the political body of the nation and the resources of the state. But, in this book, I want to argue that there is more to it than meets the eye in this process. While the political body of the nation is taken as already existing in Coronil's analysis, I trace the incorporation of an indigenous people into this body as a particular kind of public. By this I mean as a kind of interpellated subject organized around text and discursive practices (Warner 2002). The Warao were not part of the political body of the nation in Coronil's sense for most of the twentieth century. Rather, the magic of the Venezuelan nation-state is something that surrounded them but that they did not participate in until very recently. One has to ask what kinds of linguistic strategies need to be put in place for the magical state to take hold among indigenous communities. This implies a particular historical trajectory that sheds light into how forms of political speech are translated and how these forms come to craft the kind of publics that become, in turn, part of Venezuela's political body. Such is the problem this book attempts to tackle, to add complexity to our understanding of how indigenous peoples are integrated into Venezuela's political public sphere.

Ethnographic Setting

It takes ten to fourteen hours by bus or car to get from Caracas to Tucupita, the capital of the state of Delta Amacuro, and some four to five hours by boat to get to the Winikina River in the lower Orinoco Delta in eastern Venezuela (see Figure 1 in Chapter 1). I have repeated some version of this sentence many times over the years in casual conversation, even though it always makes me feel uncomfortable. I am aware that it makes my interlocutors imagine a remote Amazonian frontier where indigenous peoples (those who identify themselves as Warao) live in an untouched landscape of rivers and islands. They imagine the Delta as a faraway place where exotic plants and wildlife match an equally exotic culture and language. These are stereotypes imposed upon the Warao—as they are imposed upon other indigenous peoples in Venezuela—and are tacitly confirmed by ready-made sentences like mine. Isolated, exotic, traditional, these are the adjectives that Venezuelans have in mind when they think of the Delta, if they even think about it at all.

The early ethnographic and missionary accounts about the Warao also reflect the idea that they inhabit a separate world. We are told that they were notoriously reclusive people who retreated into the maze of rivers of the Orinoco Delta to

avoid their more violent indigenous neighbors and the perils of the colonial world (Wilbert 1972; Heinen 1988, 1992; Heinen and Castro 2000). Their language has no clear connection to any of the major linguistic families of South America or the Caribbean (Heinen 1988). Even their blood type seems to isolate them as one of the first peoples to inhabit South America (Wilbert and Layrisse 1980). This remoteness becomes more puzzling when I explain that my research is about how Venezuelan politicians communicate with their constituents and voters both through discursive practices and by giving away state resources as political gifts.[1] Indeed, this topic is so close to many Venezuelans' everyday life that I was told I didn't have to go that far to study it. I could see it right there in Caracas.

It is at this point in the course of casual conversation that I always feel I have the first chance to burst the bubble of exoticism and isolation that my initial comments about the Delta create. Yes, the Warao have their own language and culture, and a great number of them live in the remote rivers of the Delta, but they are by no means living outside of Venezuela's historical reality. There is an unknown, but clearly important, number of multi-/bilingual individuals, and a great deal of local politics of the electoral kind is conducted in Spanish. The Warao have lived for a long time in this multilingual reality, and although the numeric importance of their own language is obvious—over thirty thousand speakers, especially in the lower Delta—their involvement in politics, and, in some cases, their very livelihood depend on social interactions conducted mainly in Spanish. Their everyday life contradicts any notion of isolation. They live in a complex political and social situation that I try to do justice to in this book by addressing the linguistic and semiotic challenges that becoming citizens of the Venezuelan nation-state entails for the Warao.

What interests me about this dynamic is that more often than not political actors involved in electoral politics in the Orinoco Delta use performative forms and state resources that are neither Warao nor Venezuelan exclusively. Warao and non-Warao politicians give speeches, promise gifts, and give those gifts away, in ways that resemble other politicians in Venezuela, and indeed around the world. This dynamic is often taken for granted and is also often depicted as simple political clientelism, or populism.[2] I am deeply suspicious of how obvious the relationship between language and political gifts seems to be for the people involved in this dynamic. In Venezuela I was always confronted with some version of a story in which politicians give away things, usually money and favors, and then the Warao vote blindly for them. This was always related to me in a matter-of-fact tone and as the most logical conclusion there is. That is

how they (the politicians) win elections, I was told again and again. Every time I voiced any sort of challenge to this idea, I was rebutted. After a while I started wondering if I was just another naive anthropologist asking the wrong questions. First, the adecos and copeyanos—the two political parties more representative of the so-called Venezuelan fourth republic—and now the chavistas, during the fifth republic, were all equally guilty of this populist vote buying. So, why should I be looking into something so obvious and self-explanatory?

These are meta-cultural (Urban 2001) statements that seemed to give people a sense of knowing the situation they are dealing with. They are infused with a deep ideological sense of truth that produces an ethical stance difficult to shake. Just as interesting is the fact that politicians adopt these stereotypes and act accordingly. They embrace these registers (Agha 2007) that they have learned how to perform and interpret for their own messaging strategies (Silverstein and Lempert 2012). I am not interested in proving these politicians wrong. Instead, I am interested in how the register itself, as an ideological semiotic form, shapes political life for the Warao and becomes their political reality. I do not assume that there is a deeper truth hidden behind these ideological registers, but seek to account for what is publicly available in naturally occurring instances of social interaction and how it becomes meaningful and consequential. This goes for discourse as well as for any other meaningful activities performed in the course of political life. What I intend to do in this book is to understand the Warao and Venezuela's politics not as separate entities but as part of a single historical process that does not belong to one or the other exclusively. It encompasses both at once in very unequal linguistic, performative, and economic conditions.

The supposed simplicity of the meta-cultural ideas about political clientelism that I address in this book is better conceived as the result of a semiotic process that mediates particular forms of social interaction. I pay attention, then, to semiotic forms in the sense of naturally occurring instances of language use and electoral gift giving because they go hand in hand making each other seem natural. Thus, it is my contention that in the Orinoco Delta (and perhaps in many other places in Venezuela) political gifts and political speech are ideologically placed in a co-naturalizing[3] position, acting and speaking as if gift and speech intrinsically need each other to make sense. These two has become interacting communicative systems (Jakobson 1970; Keane 1994). The relationship between gifts and speech becomes intrinsically natural over time by a process of semiotic erasure (Gal and Irvine 2019) that allows people to hide or explain away the contradictions that make it seem so. Politicians make promises, and people see in the political gifts the realization of such promises even when the origins of

such an interpretation are buried behind complicated processes of transduction (Jakobson 1960) and reimagination.

During my fieldwork I started by considering the distribution of political gifts and the performance of all kinds of related linguistic interactions in the Delta. This included politicians both indigenous and criollo (nonindigenous), as well as Warao people whose lives are dependent on the local government in the states of Delta Amacuro and Monagas. I wanted to explore how politicians made promises and gave people what they thought they wanted—and how people gossiped about these things. I also wanted to understand how political gifts were manipulated or twisted (Aragon 1996) to gain power and create hierarchies. It seemed to me that taking a look at this communicative whole complicates enormously our apparently commonsensical ideas about political clientelism.

Since the beginning of my research in 2007 this relation proved to be far from straightforward, and much more than merely pragmatic. To understand this process is not just a matter of numbers and statistics. How much money is given away? How many people received things? How many votes are gained by the gifts? Do politicians actually win the elections by giving things away? Do politicians win by making promises and delivering good political speeches? These are questions that have no evident answer. In doing ethnographic research in Venezuela it became clear that politicians do not carefully plan the distribution of resources, or engage in rational calculations as part of their electoral strategies. Politicians in the Orinoco Delta do not engage in any kind of rational calculation when performing a political speech, or when giving away state resources during election time. What is clear is that they want to show their generosity, to appear magnanimous and to create a public image as ethical moral exemplars. State resources, then, become gifts because they are not distributed just to solve a particular problem or out of the calculation of government agencies around tackling important issues. Instead, these gifts create moral/ethical entanglements between politicians and their voters, which is the defining characteristic of a gift (Mauss 1967).

Politicians in the Orinoco Delta are also much more interested in constituting the Warao into a public in Michael Warner's (2002) sense than in devising a strategic electoral plan. They use both political oratory and gifts as texts to interpellate the Warao and allow for that form of autotelic organization that Warner (2002) describes as a public to take shape. Becoming organized around political texts (or semiotic forms coming from the state in this case) has nothing to do with an intrinsic cultural logic among the Warao, but it is a characteristic of a particular historical dynamic that developed over time in the Delta. The reason

gifts and political discourse can create and captivate a public among the Warao is that a particular form of public sphere has developed during the twentieth century in the Delta around the Warao without including them completely until very recently (see Chapter 1 for a discussion on this surrounding public sphere). It is this particular historical context that helps us understand how the Warao have become a kind of public in modern electoral politics in Venezuela. Political speech and gifts produce inter-animating texts around which the Warao have come to be interpellated. I further make the case that in Venezuela these texts are only made possible by the transformation of oil rent into state resources, which in turn are interpreted as semiotic forms which sustain related public performances. Thus, oil rent is the material historical circumstance and background that allows the conformation of political texts in the form of co-naturalizing political speech and gifts, and the economic circumstance that therefore allows the emergence of a modern political public among the Warao.

The Warao who receive these gifts and hear these speeches do not take them at face value. They are not naive about the politician's intentions. They interpret the gifts in the context of their own political interest. For them, political gifts are not numbers or statistics. It is as much about building meaning and social relationships as it is about economic benefits or solving immediate problems. For them, this is not just a cynical game of getting what you can out of the government. It is also about accepting those gifts and speeches to build moral/ethical stances in their own communities. This is why gifts and speech are inseparable. They are part of public ethical practices, and my goal is to understand these two as ethical semiotic interpretants (Pierce 1955; Parmentier 1994; Singer 1986) of each other. I take a semiotic approach in this book that privileges the role of mediation. I conceive of speeches and gifts as semiotic forms and interpretants (semiotic consequences) of each other. In other words, I take speeches to stand for the gifts they represent and as the result of events of political gift giving. Similarly, gifts stand for political speech and are the result of political speech acts and events. This is a processual meaning-making dynamic in which speech is transformed into gifts, gifts are made into speech, and these two are conceived at one point or another as semiotic forms.

When I first arrived in the field, I wanted to be at the center of political action in the Delta to follow this semiotic process. I rented a room in Barrancas del Orinoco because some of my Warao acquaintances were living in this town. More importantly, my main contact in the Delta had moved there and became the president of a communal council. Barrancas seemed like the ideal place to follow his comings and goings and the development of this political organization.

I shadowed Benito and other political leaders in meetings and public gatherings with state and national politicians. My purpose was to record all forms of public political discourse and displays of gift giving. Since the beginning, I knew that this kind of fieldwork would be a rollercoaster of frantic recordings and interviews followed by very long periods of tedious waiting for some meeting to happen. To better use my time in the Delta I set up a plan with Benito to study Warao and gather linguistic data. We collected countless hours of elicitation on vocabulary items and grammatical examples that I kept in digital files. In hindsight I might have been walking the path between grammar and politics in the opposite direction as Alessandro Duranti (1994). In his book *From Grammar to Politics*, Duranti describes going to the field in Samoa to describe ergative grammatical marking in adults as a target description to understand the acquisition of ergative marking by Samoan children. In the process he became interested in local politics by way of trying to understand the use of grammatical particles in a particular speech event, the fono. In the field I was somehow doing the contrary, starting with politics and proceeding to find grammar. Admittedly, I never found the balance that Duranti did. I started with a discourse-centered approach to culture and I stuck to it. I never produced a detailed account of grammatical choices, or any other kind of technical linguistic account, but focused my attention on performative practices, discursive events, and, most importantly, practices of translation.

My preoccupation with political life was as strong as my concern with language. I wanted to understand political life of the electoral kind in the context of profound socialist revolutionary transformations in Venezuela. Much has been written already about this revolution (e.g., Ciccariello-Maher 2013; Fernandes 2010; Samet 2019; Schiller 2018; Smilde and Hellinger 2011; Velasco 2015), but so far it has escaped the attention of linguistic anthropologists with a semiotic inclination. The reason why this approach is appealing is because revolutionary processes, especially when they are about constructing new publics as "the people" (Warner 2002; Gal and Woolard 2001), imply public, sometimes spectacular, displays of language use alongside spectacular public displays of material generosity. What does it mean, then, for people like the Warao, who live at the margins of the nation-state, to be integrated into this kind of politics? And what does it mean that this integration happens by linguistic means and by way of gifts controlled by state representatives? The overarching argument in this book is that translation and semiotic transduction (Keane 2013; Silverstein 2003) are behind the development of Venezuela as what Fernando Coronil (1997) called a magical state.

The Road to the Socialist Revolution

In December 1998, after forty years of the hegemonic control of Acción Democrática (AD) and Comité de Organización Política Electoral Independiente (COPEI), the Venezuelan electorate was tired of a de facto bipartisan system. AD and COPEI had been the only two parties that really benefited from the Pacto de Puntofijo (the Puntofijo Pact), as the pact between the political parties that overthrew Colonel Marcos Pérez Jiménez in 1958 was known. This pact was meant to guarantee the respect and recognition of fair and open elections for all national political parties. In fact, after 1958, Venezuela became one of the most stable democracies in Latin America during the Cold War. This stability came at the cost of excluding all communist and socialist parties and creating a centrist liberal bipartisan system. But at the end of the 1980s, after more than thirty years of this political experiment, AD and COPEI were perceived by the Venezuelan public and media as corrupt. Furthermore, they had lost touch with their constituents. They depended more and more on the popularity of charismatic leaders such as Carlos Andrés Pérez (AD) and Rafael Caldera (COPEI) who still had some political clout based on the memories of their previous administrations. But Venezuela's economy in 1989 was very different from that in 1976, when Carlos Andrés Pérez led the country to zero unemployment and the fastest economic growth in its history, thanks to a global oil crisis that allowed him to nationalize the industry. Low oil prices were the rule since 1983, when lack of money produced the financial crisis that pushed the government to devalue the bolivar (Venezuela's currency). Oil prices did not recover during the next decade, and Venezuela's foreign debt made public spending very difficult to sustain. Inflation was out of control and unemployment remained high, producing a sense of despair in a generation that used to believe in the dream of "the great Venezuela" (as Carlos Andrés Pérez called it during his first administration in the 1970s). Carlos Andrés Pérez was reelected in December 1988 promising that the "good old days" of the great Venezuela would come back. His inauguration took place on February 2, 1989, with a ceremony that was referred to as "the crowning" in the international press (Bastenier 1989). He took power from President Jaime Lusinchi, also from AD, and soon realized that he had inherited a monstrous debt and an economy in ruins. He turned to the International Monetary Fund (IMF) and the United States, especially his fellow President George H. W. Bush, for help. The IMF and the Bush administration advised the Venezuelan president to follow a neoliberal economic shock therapy that came to be known locally in Venezuela as *el paquetazo* (the big package).

The president announced the structural economic reforms as *el gran viraje* (the great turn around).

In a country dependent on oil revenues, lack of international currency resulted in high inflation. Carlos Andrés Pérez's decision to raise the price of gasoline in the internal market, which he did following the IMF and Bush's advice to "balance" that market, struck a raw nerve among the population. Higher gas prices made transportation much more expensive overnight. This situation produced spontaneous, and some not-so-spontaneous, protests that started in Valles del Tuy and other peripheral towns in the outskirts of Caracas, especially in strongholds of socially and politically mobilized communities that had been active at least since the 1960s (Cicarello-Maher 2013). Suddenly, the cost of commuting was unsustainable for workers. It was also impossible to pay for living expenses with the same salary. People found themselves wondering as to how to commute to work. How to buy groceries next month? What to do? This desperate situation sparked a popular insurrection known as *el Caracazo*.[4] People started by blocking roads and marching without direction. But soon they identified targets for their rage in local commercial businesses, mainly those owned by Portuguese and Chinese immigrants, who they blamed for the high prices. The looting started on February 27, 1989, and extended throughout all of the poor sectors of Caracas. President Carlos Andrés Pérez, fearing for the safety of his administration, called in the National Guard and the army to implement the *Plan Avila* (a special plan against coup d'état). The minister of defense, General Italo del Valle Alliegro deployed troops in Caracas to restore public order. The president called a cabinet meeting after generalized looting spread to other cities. He suspended constitutional liberties, and instituted a curfew restricting freedom of movement and public gatherings. Under the 1961 constitution, when the president suspended constitutional liberties a green light was given to all law enforcement agencies to take control of the streets by any means necessary. That February this executive decision resulted in mass killing on the streets of Caracas. The actual number of deaths is a matter of contention in Venezuela—estimates range from 396 to a few thousands (López Maya 2003). Regardless of the actual number of deaths, one thing was sure: the down payment for the neoliberal package was paid with the blood of the poor. The policies advised by the IMF and the Bush administration, followed by Venezuelan politicians, resulted in a national economic crisis. This spectacular failure produced a widespread desire for political change in the country.

Furthermore, the shockwave of February 27 did not only influence civilians. The Venezuelan military, especially the army, was confronted with one of its

biggest ethical dilemmas in the twentieth century. They were responsible for the most horrendous mass killing in the country's recent history. This ethical and moral failure haunted a group of officers who then founded the *Movimiento Bolivariano Revolucionario* 200 (MBR 200). The young, middle-ranked officers who felt impotent at the sight of their commanders during the February 27 massacre led this organization. Among these young officers was Lieutenant Colonel Hugo Rafael Chávez Frías, who was serving in the presidential guard when Carlos Andrés Pérez was inaugurated. On February 4, 1992, the officers of the MBR 200 decided to rebel against Carlos Andrés Pérez and the neoliberal measures that he represented.

Lieutenant Colonel Hugo Chávez Frías, or *Comandante* Chávez as he was known during the coup, took the lead of the operations in Caracas, but the coup against Carlos Andrés Pérez failed. Hugo Chávez then famously pronounced the coup attempt as unsuccessful *por ahora* (for now). This "for now" became immediately ingrained in popular imagination and was repeated and used to refer to the desire for political change that had been delayed for too long. The old political guard was in power "just for now." All the officers involved in the coup were arrested and sentenced to prison by military courts. Two years later, in 1994, the Supreme Court impeached Carlos Andrés Pérez for unlawful use of public funds. He moved to Miami, Florida, and spent the rest of his life in the United States protected from extradition to face trial in Venezuela. New elections were called and Rafael Caldera was elected president. As a sign of national reconciliation, he signed a pardon for the highly popular commanders of the failed coup of February 4, 1992. The commanders of the military insurrection became a symbol of the rage against the old political establishment. The country was ready to support them in elections against the corrupt governments of AD and COPEI.

In December 1998, Venezuelans had for the first time the opportunity to vote for a political group completely unconnected with the old establishment created by the Puntofijo Pact. In that election Hugo Chávez Frías won by a landslide of votes. The president-elect's first appearance in front of the Teresa Carreño theater in Caracas was attended by thousands of followers, and there he repeated the promise of his campaign to change the old social and political structures of the country, and invited the people to write a new constitution. He wanted nothing less than re-founding the nation in a new moral and ethical light. Importantly for this book is the fact that Chávez envisioned the future of Venezuela as a participatory democracy and pushed for the inclusion of indigenous representatives in the drafting of the new constitution. This opened

for the first time the gates of political representation of indigenous groups as a politically recognized group. In 1999 Chávez called a referendum to approve the new constitution, which was subject to a popular vote the following year. After its approval, the representatives of the Old Regime formed an opposition front against Chávez simply called *la oposición* (the opposition). Ever since these events in the early 2000s, the country has been divided into *chavistas* and *opositores*. The vast majority of indigenous peoples became loyal *chavista* followers.

The events described so far are the starting point of the historical period in which this book is situated. Most analyses of this process (e.g., Caballero 2000; Jones 2007; Marcano and Barrera Tyszka 2007; Valencia 2005, 2008, 2015; Cicarello-Maher 2013; Fernandes 2010) follow the rise of Chávez to power and the subsequent ten years which included referendums, attempted coups, mass demonstrations, national strikes, accusations, and counteraccusations between the United States, Venezuela, and sometimes Colombia, the struggle with the media and the universities, and the expansion of the influence of this revolution to other countries in Latin America (Cusack 2018). Most recently, after Chávez's death in 2013, it has also been dominated by the failure of his successor Nicolás Maduro to stabilize the national economy and by the first major electoral defeat of chavismo since the start of the revolution in the elections for congress of December 2015. These analyses of Chávez's Bolivarian revolution have largely focused on the spheres of high national politics and the city of Caracas.

In this book I situate my analysis at the margins (Tsing 1994), both geographic and social, of this process in order to produce a depiction of how politics is played out in a place other than Caracas and among an indigenous group, the Warao of the state of Delta Amacuro in eastern Venezuela (see Figure 1 in Chapter 1). I also want to understand how the populist socialist Bolivarian revolution that Hugo Chávez started takes for granted the connection between public rhetoric, distribution of services and political gifts, and the creation of patron-client relations with the electorate: in other words, how, despite promoting revolutionary change, the Bolivarian revolution resorted to the same mystification of the state and the figure of the president deepening the reliance on oil and political personalism. This is a continuation of the Puntofijo Pact-era political practice, which has taken a socialist rhetorical turn during the Bolivarian revolution. This in turn has also reproduced in the Venezuelan opposition a common ideological depiction: poor people, especially from the countryside, and even more so if they are indigenous, are subjects of political bribes in times of elections. Local and regional problems such as health care,

education, crime, and the like are temporarily solved with the outpouring of state money coming from the country's huge oil revenue. These short periods of public spending enhance the image of politicians who, as soon as they are in office, stop the distribution of public funds thus keeping up only a minimum of functional government activity.

This depiction prevails among most Venezuelans when they imagine the effects of socialist revolutionary politics among indigenous populations. It is probably a contemporary version of the myth of the colonial exchange of mirrors for gold. The naive Indian accepts an alluring object and gives away something whose value they are not aware of. This narrative is accompanied with accounts of rhetorical practices used by politicians to persuade and deceive the electorate. The aim of this book is to challenge these stereotypes describing how meaningful practices mediate these forms of political communication.

The kind of relationship between political gift giving and discursive practices that I am proposing has its roots also in the idea of intertextuality (Briggs and Bauman 1992; Silverstein and Urban 1996). In this view, an utterance is never produced in a synchronic or diachronic vacuum; there is always discourse that proceeds, discourse that is used in tandem with, and discourse that follows that utterance, an idea in turn inspired by Bakhtin (1981). In intertextual relations texts become text-objects and then circulate. They are embedded or are referred to in other instances of discourse. Intertextual relations begin with the transformation of an utterance into a text-object by making it a piece of discourse that can be moved around. This is a process of objectification that highlights the material qualities of the text. Then, these texts can be decontextualized or taken out of their original contexts. A process of recontextualization, in which texts are embedded in new contexts and become part of other utterances, follows decontextualization. Needless to say, this is a mediated process.

Inspired by Silverstein's (2005b) and Keane's (1997) ideas about the materiality of language and semiosis, I take the idea of intertextuality to encompass processes of interaction between multiple semiotic modalities. I will refer to this process as transduction (Keane 2013) or the process through which a sign system interacts with and depends on other semiotic modalities to produce meaning. Just like no text is ever produced in a vacuum and depends on intertextual relations with previous and future texts, discourse also depends on a set of relations with other meaningful activities. This interaction extends over time and space, producing a cycle in which talk about future gifts is followed by acts of political gift giving, and acts of gift giving are followed by discourse about past political gifts. This process is often curtailed by hazards and inconsistencies. Furthermore, this interaction

between discourse and gift is the product of historical circumstances. More importantly, this process is crucial in the development of new publics organized around these intertextual chains.

This approach is also similar to other approaches in linguistic anthropology that illustrate how different genres of political discourse inter-animate (Jackson 2008) each other. In this case, it is not genres but speech acts and gifts that are the elements interacting. This approach depends on conceiving of language as material. Judith Irvine (1989) proposed seeing discourse as an object of exchange subjected to political economies in the same sense as other supposedly more material objects. For her, discourse can enter the exchange market much as any other material item (see also Bourdieu 1977, 1991). Therefore, discourse not only is indexical of social positioning but can also be possessed and entered in a generalized political economy of semiotic objects. I will seek to complement this kind of analysis with a different form of indexicality that links discourse and material objects as part of a single process of constructing political reality. Therefore, I look for ways in which people use language and gifts as two complementary elements to be deployed and used at different points in time to make sense of political interactions and to construct a political following.

Likewise, I follow Sherzer (1987) and Urban's (1991) idea that both discursive and cultural phenomena are primarily found and deployed in public signs. Their discourse-centered approach to culture allows us to explore the realm of contentious social relations and political mobilization by paying attention to naturally occurring instances of language use that circulate in public. Sherzer (1983, 1987) has shown that a discourse-centered approach to culture is a powerful tool for the analysis of micro-political situations. Briggs (2016, 2008, 1998, 1996a, 1996b, 1993, 1992) has also shown how useful this approach is to understand the power-laden discursive relations among the Warao. This book expands these analyses into the realm of state politics and the encroachment into Warao political life by Venezuelan politicians. It is also an attempt to understand Chávez's Bolivarian revolution from a semiotic point of view and gain a fresh view into Venezuelan populism.

I focus on the Orinoco Delta to complete this depiction of the magical state. The Delta is an area whose Warao population has always been stereotyped as quintessentially backward, peripheral people in Venezuela. The Delta was previously only a national territory and just recently achieved political autonomy as a state. In 1991 its population gained the right to elect their governor and local authorities. Hence, I discuss just the second generation of Warao participating in the election of local political leaders other than the municipal councils.

On the other hand, the main source of employment for the Warao is the local government (OCEI 1993). Despite living on the largest natural gas reserve in the country, the Warao have never been participants in economic activities related to its extraction because oil companies systematically exclude them from their labor force. Due to these circumstances (the Waraos' dependence on local government jobs, the extensive use of government resources to foster political agendas, and the newly acquired rights to elect their governor), this area presents a clear opportunity to observe the use of political gifts and political speech as textual strategies in the creation and perpetuation of revolutionary politics in Venezuela.

Book Plan

This book is divided into six ethnographic chapters and a conclusion. Chapter 1 describes the expansion of national politics into the Orinoco Delta. It is an attempt to give historical context to the forms of political discourses and patterns of political gift giving that we currently encounter in this region. The main purpose of this chapter is to show how what Habermas called the public sphere, or the creation of spaces for free political expression under the tenets of liberal democracy, expands into geographical areas following specific economic processes, creating forms of communicative inequality. These forms of inequality arise because the means to participate as a full member of the public sphere are not necessarily open to the new populations included in such expansion. Instead, indigenous peoples are only allowed to be surrounded by and be witness to the political system being developed around them. The Bolivarian socialist revolution has changed this exclusion to an extent, and the rest of the book is an attempt to show what this new inclusion means.

Chapter 2, "From Warao to Spanish: The Translation of Poverty and the Poverty of Translation," discusses contending language ideologies in the early twentieth century. Its main focus is on the Catholic missionaries' production of dictionaries, grammars, and other forms of linguistic descriptions, and the Waraos' own interpretation of the language encounter. At the beginning of the twentieth century, the Warao language was regarded by the missionaries as incompatible with modernity and the political developments of the new century. It was considered too underdeveloped and illogical to be the language of Venezuelan citizens. Hence, the goal of the missionaries was to give the Warao the tools for interpreting modernity. Making the Warao into Spanish speakers

was at the heart of this project. At the same time, the Warao interpreted the encounter with the nation-state as a mistranslation. This lack of communication with the new nation-state was expressed in Warao narratives and general discursive topics. From their standpoint, the encounter with missionaries and modernity was full of confusion and misunderstandings. This chapter argues that a raising consciousness of subordination as Venezuelan citizens among the Warao parallels the naturalization of semiotic/linguistic misunderstandings at the moment of the encounter with the state. The analysis of the linguistic ideologies that this situation produced is useful to illustrate how the Warao internalized their subordinate position within the structure of the state and in Venezuela's democratic system.

Chapter 3, "From Spanish to Warao: Translating the National Anthem," analyzes the translation of the Venezuelan national anthem from Spanish to Warao. This translation practice moves in the opposite direction to the one analyzed in Chapter 2. If in the early twentieth-century translations from Warao to Spanish were meant to transform the Warao into citizens, here I ask what is to be gained by translating the symbols of the Venezuelan state from Spanish to Warao. The chapter focuses on publicly available videos and written versions of the lyrics to understand the material dimensions of this translation and its role in the reproduction of revolutionary politics. The chapter argues that the transformation of the linguistic materiality of the anthem resulted in a parallel break between types and tokens in the oral and written versions of the anthem. This break gave the anthem new semiotic affordances making possible seemingly contradictory ways of using it. The anthem in its translated form affords indigenous peoples a strong political stance. At the same time, it also affords nonindigenous peoples a chance to produce stereotypical depictions of indigenous languages and cultures. This openness is part of a changing ideological landscape in which overt political exclusion has been replaced with open-ended and contradictory inclusion of Venezuelan indigenous peoples into an imagined socialist society.

Chapter 4 focuses on the specific greeting and promises used by prominent political personalities form the Orinoco Delta and the Venezuelan government addressing Warao audiences to make promises of political gifts. The chapter shows the disparate use of these strategies by politicians. Even more importantly, it argues that the strategies of greetings and promising are the connecting points of transduction. Greetings frame political discourses as a legitimate political text in relation to gifts, and they are both meant to produce a particular form of political electoral public. Greetings establish a connection with the public and set the ground for promises. From the Warao point of view public promises are

absolutely expected in public performances coming from national politicians. Nevertheless, the chapter shows that the new leaders in the Delta are susceptible to failure in performing what is regarded as proper political discourse because they are not always in the position to promise. In other words, they can fail at promising even after framing their discourse with what they think is an appropriate greeting.

I propose that there is a semiotic ideology in which a political promise is regarded as a connection between the here and now of the discourse and there and then of the delivery of political gifts. The promise is the first step of a transduction process in which the Warao create expectations of material benefits and a connection with future distributions of promised state resources. This chapter shows that the expectation of a promise is not necessarily fulfilled (politicians do not always make promises), putting in question the all-encompassing nature of the magical state.

Chapter 5 focuses on the delivery of political gifts. In this chapter, I analyze the gift of a power plant to the community of Morichito and its unintended political consequences. This is a gift delivered unexpectedly and not previously promised to the community. I argue that the conflicts that the delivery of this gift brought to the community point to the importance of political promises in the transduction of state resources into political performance. The conflict produced by this gift shows how material signs and acts of gift giving are in intimate relation with linguistic signs and speech acts. This gift was contentious because its delivery left its relation to past promises and discourses unclear. In other words, a semiotic disconnection was produced by the lack of necessary and proper political speech.

In Chapter 6, I show how politicians harness the dialectic relation between gifts and discourse to construct their political selves and a Warao imagined public. Through analysis of press releases in *Notidiario*, the only local newspaper in the Delta, I analyze how discourses and gifts are deployed and used for this construction, and what the circumstances are for the circulation and constructions of these political images.

Finally, I explore the theoretical consequences of this process of translation, transduction, and gift giving for politics in Venezuela. By paying attention to the materiality of language and the exchange of gifts, I hope to highlight how the magical state can be conceived as resulting from a process of translation of linguistic forms and gifts into political performances. This, I argue, produces particular historical instantiations of the magical state in Venezuela, and the latest of such instantiations is the magical revolutionary state of Chávez's magical Bolivarian revolution.

The Surrounding Public Sphere

The main purpose of this chapter is to describe the historical process by which the Warao were surrounded by the Venezuelan public sphere in the twentieth century. I prefer the term "surrounded" because for most of the twentieth century, the national public sphere was something that grew and expanded around the Warao without including them. All of the institutions on which this public sphere depends were out of reach for the Warao, and all the communicative means that are fundamental for this kind of political environment to develop were also created by and for the nonindigenous population. The only ones trying to integrate the Warao into the criollo world were the Catholic missionaries working in the Delta. Yet, they envisioned the Waraos as laborers but not as participants in any form of political activity. The Warao began some form of political participation in state matters only recently, which does not mean that they have been passive subjects of their own history. My purpose in this chapter is to show how the criollo public sphere was created in the state of Delta Amacuro in a process that purposefully excluded them until very recently.

Habermas's (1989) genealogy of the European bourgeois public sphere has captured a great deal of the academic imagination. According to his account, the eighteenth-century development of commodity exchange and the rise of capitalism in Europe created a new class of private individuals (the bourgeoisie) liberated from the royal courts and the demands of the monarchic state. By virtue of their economic independence from the state, sophisticated education, and taste for rational thinking, they were able to construct an independent political space in which individuals interacted as free men, and in which the power of the better argument was more important than social status in matters of public opinion. The starting point of this process was the public-but-restricted space of the salons, the coffee houses, and the table societies that replaced the European courts in attracting writers, intellectuals, and businessmen. These interactions produced opinions and arguments that grew in number and importance, and

were disseminated by the new forms of information exchange created by the need for knowledge about economic activities. When the need for information was recognized as a necessity, it became a commodity, and the press as we know it started to sell the news from distant places. This dissemination of ideas by free men who did not depend upon, or seek, public office created the conditions for the liberal democratic spaces in which critique of public affairs became the norm (Figures 1 and 2).

In this chapter I will show how a kind of public sphere connected with national politics emerged during the twentieth century in the Orinoco Delta. Nevertheless, contrary to what Habermas describes, it did not produce a free space for the exchange of ideas or the criticism of public authorities. Instead, it created an unequal space in which the Warao were racialized and discriminated against. As Briggs (2008, 2016) has shown, the open space for criticism against the state and for hearing citizen's voices in the legal, medical, and political system of the Orinoco Delta is not open to forms of indigenous discourse. Indigenous voices are subjected to forms of linguistic and narrative inequalities (Hymes 1996; Briggs, 2016). Therefore, the public sphere in the Delta became a surrounding force that hijacked participation in public debates

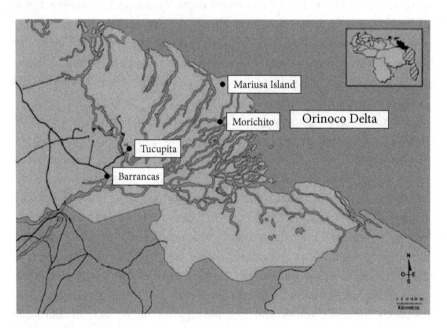

Figure 1 Map of the Orinoco Delta, Venezuela.
Original source: http://www.adventure-kayaking.com/Orinoco%20Delta%20Map .htm. Accessed February 25, 2011.

Figure 2 Town of Morichito, Lower Orinoco Delta (picture by Juan Luis Rodríguez).

favoring the criollo (nonindigenous) voice. Instead, the Warao became subjects of paternalistic policies that silenced their voice in political debates because they were not considered citizens but "Indians" (Briggs and Mantini-Briggs 2003). Since 1915, according to the Venezuelan *Ley de Misiones* (missionary law), the Warao, like many other indigenous groups in Venezuela, were under the patronage of Catholic missionaries who controlled their integration into the national society. The so-called Indians were a special case to be dealt with through a process of *reducción* (permanent settlement) and civilization. The Warao case is an example of how the emergence of the political public sphere outside of the so-called modern West creates a political economy of empowered and disempowered speakers based on their linguistic and cultural competence, as well as their interaction with the nation-state as peripheral subjects.

Fraser (1985, 1990) has argued that the Habermasian public sphere is a partial depiction that privileges the point of view of the hegemonic, powerful, and gendered classes, creating a false image of equality in the public sphere. But the public sphere always emerges in relation to counter-public spheres in which the subaltern can challenge the all-encompassing hegemonic forms of discourse (Warner 2002). Similarly, Coronil (1994) has proposed taking non-essentialist views of subalternity to avoid disregarding the subaltern voices. Graham (1993) has also shown that in the context of indigenous Amazonia, the

public sphere encounters itself in contact with contrasting linguistic ideologies. She demonstrates that contrary to the idea that the public sphere is created by individuals who compete in the discursive arena, the Xavante of Brazil constructs political discourse as a collective endeavor. Dell Hymes (1996) also argues that Habermas's ideas about communication privilege the idea that linguistic communities are homogeneous and monolingual, that linguistic competence is uniform for all the individuals involved, and that linguistic resources are equally available for all. Finally, Irvine (1989) has also shown that linguistic competence and resources are subject to forms of linguistic political economies in which inequalities are pervasive.

I take inspiration from these criticisms to argue that Habermas's image of the public sphere, composed of free individuals, underplays its role in the expansion of capitalism and the postcolonial state. Habermas underestimates the role of the colonial exchange, giving the false impression that the European bourgeois class developed almost spontaneously from inside Europe. Nevertheless, capitalism, as we know it, is the product of a more complex interaction between European centers of power and the peripheries of colonial empires (Anderson 1991; Apadurai 1996; Errington 2001; Mintz 1985; Sahlins 1994; Thomas 1991; Wolf 1982; Yang 2000). What makes possible the formation of an independent bourgeoisie is not the development of an internal free market but the colonial process. This also produced the idealized model of liberal democracy that has become the yardstick to measure proper forms of government in the so-called underdeveloped world. The construction of a modern civil society that keeps the state's actions under public scrutiny is considered indispensable for modern participatory democracy. Nevertheless, one can wonder about the limits of this idealized model of participation, and the consequences for marginalized populations within a system that depends on this form of governance.

Capitalism (and liberal democracy) seems to require constant market expansion in a dialectical relation between centers and peripheries. I propose, following Federici (2004), that we can see this process as part of the constant expansion of what Marx called primitive accumulation. Federici proposed widening this concept to understand how the expansion of capitalism in and out of the West provoked not only the accumulation of capital but also the formation of new social relations in order to organize and control the labor and bodies of new subordinate subjects (e.g., savages and women). I suggest that the expansion of capitalism and liberal democracy also entails the formation of new discursive relations in which certain ways of speaking (Sherzer 1983) surround, exclude, and marginalize others (Hymes 1996).

Venezuela's liberal democracy of the 1960s surrounded the Warao population with new forms of political communication and created the conditions for their inclusion not as speakers and agents but as hearers and receivers within the public sphere.[1] My goal is to show that the current form of political discourse linked to party politics is the product of a complex historical process in which the expansion of state institutions made it possible for the criollos (nonindigenous) to monopolize all forms of political language and forms of communication until very recently.[2] Lomnitz (1995, 2001) has shown how the public sphere in Mexico is fragmented and localized showing contradictory ways of handling rituals and communication. I will suggest that the Orinoco Delta is one area in Venezuela in which we can see this kind of fragmentation. This process is the product of a modernist language ideology that excluded indigenous individuals whose language and communicative practices were not deemed suitable for democracy and modernity (Rodriguez 2008). This trend has recently started to change, creating spaces for counter-public spheres (Fraser 1985, 1990; Warner 2002). But, in order for us to understand how the current political discursive strategies came to be, we need to understand the historical formation and expansion of the Venezuelan state.

Here I pay special attention to the process of state formation in Venezuela and the Delta. I will describe a genealogy of the development of the Delta's political sphere and show how it crystallized in the post-1958 democratic era. Democracy in Venezuela has depended, according to Coronil (1997), on the division of the country into two bodies: a social body (population) and a natural body (natural resources, especially oil). The creation of a Venezuelan public sphere has been determined by the struggle to access the state in order to gain control of the resources produced by the natural body. Different from the European bourgeoisie described by Habermas, Venezuela's bourgeois class is not independent from the state. In Venezuela's history there are virtually no private economic activities or classes of property owners who are completely independent from the state. Instead, business, industrial owners, and especially landowners, were in control of the state apparatus. Control of the state, and not the formation of an independent public sphere, has always been the objective of the Venezuelan bourgeoisie. This became all the more apparent during the years of Juan Vicente Gomez's presidency (1908–35). Gomez was the largest cattle and land owner in the country and controlled both the natural and the social body of the nation. Hill (1999a, 1999b, 2000 see also Whitehead 1992, 1996) showed that the development of land and capital accumulation after the Venezuelan war of independence also resulted in the displacement of indigenous peoples in South America to new internal colonial frontiers at the margins of the nascent states.

For most of the twentieth century, Venezuela had a hyper-controlled political sphere. The century started with the coming to power of long dictatorial regimes (Castro for eight years, and then Gomez for twenty-seven years). This prevented the development of any form of free stable public sphere until 1958 when the last dictator in the country (Marcos Pérez Jiménez) was overthrown. Furthermore, until the mid-twentieth century, the state apparatus was so underdeveloped in the southern part of the country that most of its indigenous population was out of reach. That was the case of the Orinoco Delta, whose participation in the national public sphere is as recent as the history of its municipal council.

The Delta's Political History

The history of the Orinoco Delta as an independent political unit is very recent. Throughout the colonial period and long after independence from Spain, the Delta was part of the Venezuelan Guayana region and was governed by the authorities of this territory. It was only in 1884 when President Joaquin Crespo created for the first time a political unit called *Territorio Federal Delta* (TFD). The first governor of this entity was Manuel Modesto Gallegos, appointed on August 19, 1884 (Marín 1981). Following this appointment, President Crespo created the first TFD's Organic Code and declared the town of Pedernales as its capital.

Before the creation of this political unit, there was virtually no criollo population around the Orinoco Delta, and the government had virtually no political influence in the area. The few criollo settlers who existed in the area were in control of agriculture and commerce. Most of these individuals were newcomers from the island of Margarita in the north coast of Venezuela who had no intention of interacting with the local Warao population. But all of this changed with the creation of the TFD and the new influx of population at the turn of the twentieth century. Government institutions and nonindigenous populations started spreading in the newly founded TFD. These institutions brought about the development of new forms of political interaction and participation around the Warao.

At the end of the nineteenth and the first decades of the twentieth centuries, people from Margarita Island moved into the newly created TFD to establish farms and commercial businesses. Most of these adventurers came to the Delta for the same reasons: lack of employment or arable land on the island and the promise of free unlimited access to land in the shores of the TFD (Marín 1981).

Most of these first settlers did not intend to stay. Instead, their intentions were to take advantage of free public land, to reap one or two harvests a year and go back to Margarita. The majority of these early immigrants came mainly from two towns on the island, El Valle de Pedro Gonzales and Tacarigua. And although their initial intention was not to stay in this territory, they ended up founding the first permanent criollo towns of the Orinoco Delta. They founded towns such as La Florida, San José de Cocuína, San José de Chaguaramal, Clavellina, and Ceiba Mocha between the towns of Tucupita and La Horqueta (Marín 1981: 165–6).

The arrival of *margariteños* (people from Margarita Island) was slow and depended on the ability of these newcomers to establish their agricultural activities. Very often this was a family enterprise that brought to the Delta groups of brothers who established crops on empty plots where they built *rancherias* (small settlements). With time, these *rancherias* grew and became towns where entire extended families settled permanently. This process started in the Cocuina River with about one hundred families in what is nowadays La Horqueta (Marín 1981: 163). Other towns were also founded along the rivers Macareo (e.g., Vuelta de los Indios, Tiriral, El Muerto), Manamo, Manamito, Macareito, Araguao, Araguaito (e.g., Casupal, Juncalito, and Playa Alta), Rio Grande (e.g., Los Remolinos, Consejo, Buena Vista, El Sausal, Jeina, and Sacupana), and Manamo (e.g., Macareo Santo Niño, Coporito, Agua Negra, Paloma, and San Salvador).

In addition to these first *margariteños* whose main economic activity was agriculture, there were those who established themselves as permanent retail sellers. With the opening of small grocery shops, the growing criollo population started having some access to products from outside the state such as processed food and liquors. Before small bodegas opened, the commerce of products from outside the state was carried out exclusively by *bongueros*, retail sellers who wandered around the rivers in boats with merchandise to sell to *margariteños* and the few Warao who had access to money. Both of these forms of commerce still exist in the Delta.

Besides the influx of *margariteños*, there were other immigrant populations that came to the Delta during this period. Some Afro-Caribbean populations came from Trinidad during the first decades of the twentieth century and founded, or helped found, the towns of Jeina (in the Rio Grande), Gorgojo (on the Macareo River), Coporito Arriba, and Coporito Abajo. The town of Curiapo (current capital of the Antonio Díaz municipality) was also founded at the end of the nineteenth century by refugees from Ciudad Bolivar, San Felix, Uracoa, Maturín, Caracas, Coro, and British Guyana, people who in most cases wanted

to avoid the contingencies of the constant civil wars occurring during this period (Marín 1981: 164). This town is one of the most linguistically diverse places in the Delta. Most of its population is fluent in Spanish, Warao, and English due to the proximity of British Guyana and Trinidad.

This increase of criollo population was also followed by an increase in the number of state institutions. In order to control commercial activities and public order in this territory, the governor of the TFD created the police force in 1887. At the beginning, the first police force in the area consisted of fourteen men. They patrolled the major rivers and the lower Delta by boat to stop the contraband of commercial goods from Trinidad. They were also in charge of the mail and communications between the capital and the isolated towns of the lower Delta (Marín 1981: 65). With the creation of a police force, although minimal and poorly equipped, the federal government started to show its presence. Parallel to the police force, Governor Froilan Caliman created the first public prison in 1888. The early presence of these two institutions was part of the expansion of the incipient justice system in Venezuela.

On November 14, 1887, the capital of the TFD was moved from Pedernales to Tucupita, which remains its current capital. This was an important change because this established Tucupita as the center of all bureaucratic activities in the Delta up to the present. Tucupita is located near the apex of the Orinoco Delta, which gives it easier access to bigger cities such as El Tigre and Maturín (the capital of the State of Monagas) to the north and Ciudad Bolivar (in the Bolivar state) upriver following the Orinoco. This town was the best location to keep fluid communications with the regional centers of administrative power. Moving the capital of the TFD from Pedernales to Tucupita guaranteed the connection with the rest of the country, and therefore the national political sphere could expand at least to the outskirts of the Delta.

Following the creation of the police force, the public prison, and the move of the Capital city, the first two federal schools of the TFD were established in 1889. These were federal school number 1623 and 1624 in Pedernales and Coporito respectively (Marín 1981: 65). This was followed by the establishment of two federal schools for girls in Pedernales and Tucupita (1891) and one for boys in Pedernales (1891). These five schools were the first attempt to bring the criollo population of the TFD under the umbrella of the national educational system. The expansion of the state and political life into the Delta required the creation of a local intelligentsia, but the lack of educational institutions impeded this development. The foundation of public schools aimed at correcting this situation by bringing the rudiments of basic education to the state.

This national expansion into the TFD continued under General Santiago Rodil, appointed as the colonizer of the Delta (Marín 1981: 66). Colonization at this time meant the establishment of a criollo and/or foreign (preferably European or American) population. It also entailed the attraction of foreign capital for agricultural and mining operations. As we already saw, the criollo population from Margarita and neighboring states were moving into this territory, but the appointment of General Rodil aimed at a different process. *Margariteños* and other criollo populations were not the most desirable colonizers in the view of the government because they moved into the Delta in a spontaneous and uncoordinated fashion. The goal of the state was to organize this migration with the help of American and European colonization companies such as the Manoa Company Limited, property of Cyrenius C. Fitzgerald. By the end of the nineteenth century the TFD was in the middle of an international dispute between competing American companies that claimed the rights to "develop and civilize" the entire territory (this dispute will be described in the next section).

The government's will to reach and incorporate the Delta into a coherent national project was also reflected in the foundation of the first postal office in the town of Coporito and the collection of information for the national census in 1891. The first census in the Delta was recorded by General Manuel Carias who was appointed for this task by the central government in Caracas. Regular postal mail reflected the need to create means of communication with the central administration in Caracas. The census also meant recognition of the Delta as part of the social body of the country. In 1810, for the first time since independence, the Orinoco Delta was counted in the census (excluding the indigenous population), and its population was incorporated into national plans. This also meant that the Delta was incorporated into the national budget as an administrative unit.

Nevertheless, the life of this first attempt to establish the Delta as an independent political unit was short. The TFD lasted only nine years. In October 21, 1893, the TFD was abolished by a decree signed by General Manuel Guzman Alvarez, president of the government's council who succeeded President Joaquin Crespo. From this point on the Delta became part of the Bolivar state and depended on the government of the city of Angosturas. Notwithstanding its short life, the TFD was the first attempt to create an independent political environment in the Delta and therefore set the groundwork for the future development of a regional form of public politics. This was an attempt to break the political isolation that prevented the criollo population in the TFD from participating in the form of deliberative politics that we associate with modern governance. The creation of the first five schools, the post office, the first census, the first police force, the

first organic code, and the change of the capital city from Pedernales to Tucupita (Marín 1981) were all part of the first effort to allow the Delta, and its criollo population, to participate in national politics. This meant the creation of a public internal forum in which the discussion of political issues would become a matter of public opinion. As is obvious, the Warao indigenous population was excluded from this process at this point. They were not the population that was expected to develop this area. The Venezuelan government was more interested in attracting international capital, and intended to leave the process of internal colonization in the hands of American corporations.

International Capital and the Colonization of the Delta

The creation and abolition of the TFD happened in the midst of a controversial colonization plan promoted by President Antonio Guzman Blanco at the end of the nineteenth century (Ugalde 1994). On September 22, 1883, a year before President Joaquin Crespo took office, Minister of Development Manuel Caraballo, acting on behalf of the Venezuelan government, signed a contract with Cyrenius C. Fitzgerald, for the colonization, development, and exploitation of natural resources of the Orinoco Delta. Fitzgerald almost immediately transferred all his rights and obligations to the Manoa Company Limited on June 14, 1884. Thus, this company was granted exclusive rights to the Delta's natural resources for ninety-nine years in exchange for the creation of a colony. Article II of the contract stated:

> The Government of the Republic grants to the contractor, his associates, assigns and successors, for the term expressed in the preceding article (99 years), the right of introduction of houses of iron or wood, with all their accessories, and of tools and other utensils, chemical ingredients and productions which the necessities of the Colony may require; the use of machinery, the cultivation of industries and the organization and development of those undertakings which may be formed, either by individuals or by companies which are accessory to or directly depending on the Contractor or Colonization Company; the exportation of all the products, natural and industrial, of the Colony; free navigation exempt from all national or local taxes, of rivers, streams, lakes and lagoons comprised in the concession, or which are naturally connected with it; moreover the right of navigating the Orinoco, its tributaries and streams, in sailing vessels or steamships, for the transportation of seeds to the Colony, for the purpose of agriculture, and cattle and other animals for the purpose of food and development of breeding; and, lastly, free traffic of Orinoco, its streams and

tributaries, for the vessels of the Colony entering it and proceeding from abroad, and for those vessels which, either in ballast or laden, may cruise from one point of the Colony to another. (Orinoco Company LTD 1899: 4)

In exchange for these concessions, Fitzgerald was bound to pay 50,000 bolivars for every 46,000 kilograms of Sarrapia (tonka bean or *Dipteryx odorata*) and *caucho* (rubber). But even more importantly for the political development of the area, the company was bound to establish a system of immigration commensurate with the growth of the economy and to civilize "the savage tribes which may wander within the territories conceded" (Orinoco Company LTD 1899: 4). Besides these attributions and obligations, the Manoa Company was also charged with funding the future police force, which was organized by the federal government. Likewise, for twenty years all citizens living within the "colony" would be exempted from military service and taxes (Ugalde 1994).

The contract with the Manoa Company shows explicitly the ideological division between the natural and political bodies of the country that would become an important aspect of the conformation of the magical state according to Coronil (1997). At the end of the nineteenth century, the state was incapable of positioning itself as a mediator between nature and society. Surrendering control to foreign investment was the only hope for placing the natural resources under what was considered civilized control, and to bring order to a social body that was beyond the reach of the state. Since the state was not able to place itself in a mediating position between the natural and political bodies of the nation, it was impossible to control the transformation of natural resources into political influence. In other words, the semiotic process of translation, transduction, and transformation required for the fetishization of the state as a magical entity simply did not exist. The magic of the state is a product of its positioning as an intermediary between nature and society which at this time did not exist.

This lack of capacity to mediate between the natural and political bodies of the nation was striking given that President Antonio Guzman Blanco was known as Venezuela's modernizer. Under his presidency the nation began its most ambitious transformation of public spaces. He built public theaters, plazas, public walkways, and trains, and promoted all forms of urban development. His fascination with European, and especially French, architecture and modernity was famous in the country. His modern ideas about law, order, and science put him at odds with the Catholic Church. But while his project of modernization for the north side of the country consisted of a total transformation of public spaces and infrastructure, his stance toward the less developed south consisted of a process of colonial expansion which, different from Spanish colonial times, entailed

granting these territories to private enterprises (Ugalde 1994). The most famous of these concessions encompassed the State of Bermudez (today's Anzoategui and Monagas) and was given to Horatio R. Hamilton, who transferred his rights to the New York & Bermudez Company. This company was the model for Fitzgerald's Manoa Company and was famous for its exploitation of asphalt which was mainly exported to New York to be used for road construction (Thurber 1907).

Both the Manoa Company and the New York & Bermudez Company were part of Guzman Blanco's plan to modernize Venezuela. Nevertheless, if we compare the conditions that the government imposed on both companies, we realize that the Manoa Company was expected to undertake a more comprehensive transformation of its concession. Fitzgerald was responsible for the "civilization of the savages" as well as organizing the immigration of new populations into the Delta within six months of signing the contract. The New York & Bermudez Company was never held responsible for this kind of policy. The Delta was conceived as a more backward, untamed, and uncivilized place that had to receive not only capital investments but also a new population to make this new capital grow. In other words, it not only had to develop the natural body but also had to build the political body itself. The activities of the Manoa Company were brief. Its operation started in August 1884 but was restricted only to exploration and exploitation of iron in the Imataca region in the southern Delta and lasted only a few years (Orinoco Company LTD 1899).[3]

In January 1886, General Antonio Guzman Blanco signed a second contract granting the Manoa Company's concession to George Turnbull, which started a complicated legal process in which he transferred the rights of exploitation of the Imataca iron mines to the Orinoco Company LTD from Wisconsin. Then, the Manoa Company sued Turnbull contested his rights to this concession. After this legal action, the Orinoco Company sold the Imataca mine to the Orinoco Iron Company, and in November 1895 George Turnbull reappeared in Venezuela with an English company named the Orinoco Iron Syndicate Co., to which he had transferred "all his rights." Finally, the Venezuelan government advised the American Orinoco Iron Company to purchase the concession again, this time from the Venezuelan government to avoid further legal problems, which the company did in 1898.

Territorio Federal Delta Amacuro 1901–91

In the course of the disputes over the private "colonization" of the Delta, Cipriano Castro and his compadre Juan Vicente Gomez took control of Venezuela and

started what is known as the pacification. During this period, Castro and Gomez developed the first organized modern national army to defend the central government from the constant uprisings of local political/military leaders, known locally as caudillos. As part of this general reorganization of the country, on April 26, 1901, Castro created the Territorio Federal Delta Amacuro (TFDA) (Marín 1981: 73).

The first capital of the newly created TFDA was San José de Amacuro but in 1905 it changed again to Tucupita. With the creation of this new political unit the Venezuelan state resumed the construction of the administrative and political infrastructure that was abandoned after dismantling the TFD. Nevertheless, the territory and its inhabitants in general were deemed incapable of self-government. From the central government's standpoint there was no need to articulate the discussion of public policies, the election of governors, or the development of new laws with the population of this territory.

The first governor of the TFDA was Pedro Alcantara Leal, appointed in 1901. According to the Organic Law of Federal Territories, the governors of these areas were appointed by the president and had executive power over the region. Also, among his responsibilities he had to

(1) protect the indigenous peoples in his jurisdiction and promote their culture and well-being by any means;
(2) make possible that the indigenous people acquire residential and working habits;
(3) prevent the exploitation of the ignorance of the indigenous people, the abuse of their ignorance in any form or making them vile through gambling, alcohol, and other degrading vices;
(4) enforce, as far as possible, labor laws and its regulations in favor of the Indians;
(5) make sure that the people in the camps or villages for whom an indigenous person works pay stipends, education, and fair wages;
(6) communicate notorious deficiencies and abuses to the mission's directors in the territory. If, in spite of this communication, no action is taken, he will notify the national executive;
(7) make sure that all commodities expressly introduced to the indigenous communities are sold at a fair price (Marín 1981: 86).

The TFDA was not conceived as a political unit meant to allow the flourishing of a regional public sphere. Not only were all local authorities appointed by the president but the indigenous majority in the territory was considered incapable

of participating in the national political process. Instead, they had to be protected from the influence of merchants and other sources of corruption. At the beginning of the twentieth century, the government also considered the coming of *margariteños* and other immigrants to the zone as a threat to the Warao, who instead of being included in the new forms of local politics had to be kept separate, supposedly for their own good. As a result, neither the *margariteños* nor the Warao participated as a public with a political voice in open discussions about policies, laws, regulations, and elections of regional authorities.

Nevertheless, the TFDA's regional government continued building the infrastructure and institutions that were considered necessary for modern political development. Schools were very important in this period. In 1911 the governor decreed the creation of four new schools: a first-grade coed school in Tucupita, a first-grade school for boys in Coporito, a first-grade school for girls in Curiapo, and a first-grade school for boys in Piacoa (Marín 1981: 94). These schools were criollo institutions that did not admit indigenous students. This first phase of the development of educational institutions was devoted mainly to promote the idea of the nation and the preparation of criollo individuals for work.

Between 1908 and 1935 the government of General Gomez discouraged all forms of political participation in the form of public, open political discussions in the whole country. The long dictatorial regime of Gomez prevented the participation of individuals in any form of political criticism of the central government. On the other hand, becoming a president or governor of a state, or territory, meant to form a political alliance with the central government. Yarrington (2003) has described how these alliances, based on the creation of cattle and liquor business, were the base of the newly achieved peace in the country. It was widely recognized in the country that the state and the figure of General Gomez were one and the same. Gomez was the state and the state was Gomez. Not for nothing was he called the *Benemerito* (the all deserving) by his accolades. This taking over the natural body of the nation, which at the time was conceived as Gomez making the country his own hacienda (ranch), started the process of positioning the state as a mediator between the two bodies. Nevertheless, Gomez's iron fist ruling impeded the development of any form of free public sphere.

The apparent (I emphasize the superficial character of this participation) "free" political participation in the Delta started in 1928 when General Gomez reorganized the administrative structure of the state allowing the development of municipal councils. The first members of this council were appointed by

the executive as a transition period for the elections of November 1929. In spite of this electoral facade, political participation in matters of the state or a democratic spirit of participation was still discouraged and no forms of political organization or forums for political discussion were allowed. The government maintained an official ideology of zero tolerance of dissident views. In addition, the majority of the population in the territory was excluded from voting because they were "Indians." During this period voting did not mean participating in the public sphere; there was no open exchange of ideas, and any form of dissent was punished by incarceration or death.

Although some forms of underground opposition to this regime had their base in the Delta, they did not take the form of public protest or public discursive exchange. Instead, much in the style of the nineteenth-century invasions from Colombia (of which Gomez's and Castro's in 1901 were the last to succeed), in 1934 Generals Bartolome Ferrer and Doroteo Flores tried to overthrow the government from the Delta, but were defeated by the newly organized national army and died on the shores of Pedernales. As a consequence of this uprising several military and political activists were sentenced to jail.

A year after this uprising, General Juan Vicente Gomez died leaving behind his legacy of forced pacification of the country and his reign of state terror. During his regime, the new political elite was formed in universities and *Liceos* in Caracas. From the Central University of Venezuela, the student organization called the Generation of the 1928, who were in exile or hiding, went on to form the political parties that would allow a new form of public political participation in the country. The future leaders of political parties such as AD, the Christian COPEI, Unión Republicana Democrática (URD), and the Partido Comunista (PCV) who were in jail, in exile, or in hiding resurfaced. The death of the dictator opened a space for them to participate in new forms of open political expression. Furthermore, the work of the dictator had firmly positioned the state as mediator between the natural resources of the nation and its political body—something that Gomez accomplished, not only by taking control of the agricultural sector but by turning Venezuela into an oil exporter.

Symptomatic of this new opening to public political discourse was the first recorded public demonstration in the Delta's capital. On June 3, 1936, demonstrators gathered in the city of Tucupita to demand that the municipal council resume its activities after it stopped working during the tumultuous transition between Juan Vicente Gomez's regime and President Elezar López Contreras (Marín 1981). The executive government also suffered rapid changes at the regional level. In 1936 the Delta had three governors: Luís Barberi, Enrique

Acosta, and Alejandro Matheus. In the midst of this political transition, the municipal council, composed mainly of *Gomecistas* (Gomez supporters), was shaken, but when Elezar López Contreras (minister during Gomez's regime) took power, the establishment of local *Gomecistas* in the Delta felt safe in a period that started moving only slowly toward democratic change, but with no abrupt overthrowing of the status quo in the country.

Slowly, the political landscapes of the Delta started allowing the display of new forms of political performances. Individuals, in this case the candidates to the municipal council, started to campaign trying to lure the public to vote for them for the first time. This was a new way of doing politics that did not depend on appointments from Caracas. This represented a deep transformation in the Delta's political life. After Gomez, the era of political parties started in the country. Also, the rising of PCV, AD, URD, and COPEI coincides with the opening of Venezuela as one of the largest oil exporters in the world. These two processes changed the way in which politics was conducted in the country.

The 1940s was the time when the Delta's political elite started organizing public political forums. During this time political talk in the form of discussions and exchange between the economic and political elite of the territory started having spaces that resembled something like the coffee houses, and social gatherings that Habermas describes. The Tucupita Club, created in 1940, was conceived as a cultural organization to bring together the learned and educated elite of the territory. Its members considered themselves the representatives of the intellectual and political establishment. As Cruz Jose Marín stated, "The Tucupita Club can be considered as the ultimate representation of Tucupita's aristocracy" (1977: 87–8 author's translation). After General Gomez's twenty-seven-year regime, the Tucupita Club became the first public organization in which some sort of open public political talk was articulated. Nonetheless, the political character of this organization led to its division in 1942.

That year the differences between those who supported the national and regional government and those who opposed it and considered themselves closer to the people or "masses" caused the club to split in two (Marín 1977: 87–8). On January 31, 1942, was founded the Centro Cultural Deltano in a meeting held at the federal school Petión. This cultural center was conceived as a counterbalance to the elitist Tucupita Club. Its first president, Ceferino Rojas Diaz, was a businessman and also the president of the municipal council. He saw the creation of this center and his participation in the municipal council as an opportunity to help the poor and dispossessed in the TFDA. As an act of generosity during the first session of the municipal council in 1939, he

donated his entire salary and representation budget to the Junta de Damas to help feed malnourished infants in the territory (Marín 1977: 99–100). Ceferinos Rojas's participation in the new political space of the Centro Cultural and his charitable acts represented the first public opinion strategy that included both the organization of a new space for political speech and the display of gift giving for public political reasons. This shows how the development of new forms of political communication in the twentieth century entailed the management of both gifts giving and the creation of new rhetorical forms and spaces for political talk. These strategies, that today seem to be a common tactic of populist politicians in Venezuela, had their origins in the opening up of "democratic" spaces in which politicians not only wanted to talk about politics but also wanted to gain the support of the masses by reaching them with state resources that helped create a public persona for themselves. The goal of the Centro Cultural Deltano was often translated into charity to the poor and the distribution of gifts with the aim at creating a name for itself and its members.

A parallel organization created after the Tucupita Club and the Centro Cultural Deltano was the Centro Casacoima. The Centro Casacoima was founded by students from the TFDA who were finishing their education in the capital of the country, Caracas. The main purpose of this organization was to help the cultural, social, and economic development of the TFDA (Marín 1977: 88). In a country in which communication with the capital and the connection with the public national sphere were difficult and unreliable, they aspired to be a link between the national public sphere and the Delta's political elite. The Centro Casacoima provided a connection with the national intellectual life, especially in universities and cultural circles.

During this time most people in the Delta traveled to Caracas by steamship from the Venezuelan Navigation Company (Marín 1977: 63). The mail and national press depended on these steamships and therefore organizations like the Centro Casacoima intended to bridge the gap between the local rural intelligentsia and the national public sphere. At the same time, communications within the TFDA were also difficult and the connection between the indigenous communities and the capital of the territory was weak. The use of outboard motors in the Delta was not common before the 1960s and access to this form of transportation was out of reach for most Warao until the 1970s and 1980s. Even today with the help of outboard motors and radios the Warao find it difficult to keep up with the news from Tucupita.

Another form of public political forum for the discussion of political issues was the press. After 1917 a number of newspapers were founded in the TFDA.

The first newspaper in this area was the *Delta Amacuro*, which was published for nineteen years. After the *Delta Amacuro* the following newspapers were founded: *Manamo, Timon, Ecos, Ideales, El Guarao, Oriente, El Deltano, Horizonte, Manare, Delta Dos, El Fiel, El Regional I*, and *Motivos*. Cesar Rodriguez, Ramon Zaragoza, Felipe Natera Wanderlinder, Miguel Sanchez Castros, Pastor Cedeño, and Francisco Lugo Bello were among the directors (owner/editors) of these newspapers (Marín 1977). These men were not only in the news business but also active participants in local politics. For example, Felipe Natera Wanderlinder was at the same time director of a newspaper, member of the Club Tucupita, member of the Centro Cultural Tucupita, and representative to the municipal council. The press in the Delta was never a profitable business but allowed their directors to be at the center of public attention.

The 1940s was also a decade when the country experienced some relapse into authoritarianism. This back and forth from authoritarian regimes to democratic politics during the 1940s and 1950s had consequences on the way in which the municipal council of the Delta was organized and the way in which its members were elected. The first major backlash that the council experienced was its complete dismissal in 1945. That year, General Isaias Medina Angarita was overthrown by a coalition of military commanders and the newly organized party AD. This new political party (founded in 1941) held the promise of real democratic change and brought to the government what Fernando Coronil (1997) has identified as one of the most important philosophical turns in Venezuelan politics—the idea that oil revenues can be the source of the country's material progress. We call this in Venezuela *sembrar el petróleo* (to sow the oil). But in spite of championing democratic ideas, the new AD government of President Romulo Betancourt dissolved all the municipal councils in the country. In its place Governor Ceferino Rojas Diaz appointed Dr. Delfín Rojas, Jesus Maria Bauza, Visitación Rojas, and José Velasquez as members of the temporary Municipal Junta in the Department of Tucupita. This junta lasted two years and was replaced in the general elections of December 14, 1947, through which all political offices in the country were elected.

In 1948 another coup d'état, this time to overthrow the democratically elected government of the novelist and AD activist Romulo Gallegos, shook the organization of public administration in the country. The municipal councils elected the year before were again dismantled and a new administrative junta was appointed. The new junta started activities on December 22, 1948, and was constituted by Isolina de Revollo, Oscar Mata Mata, Pedro Piñatel, Jose Antonio

Rodriguez, and Federico Nuñez Garcia (Marín 1981). In this junta for the first time a woman held public office in the TFDA. Even though Isolina de Revollo was not elected, and her appointment was clouded by being the product of the new dictatorial regimes of the 1950s, she was the first woman to hold office at the municipal level in the Delta. This of course was more the exception than the rule and women in general have been excluded from public office in this region until very recently. Between 1948 and 1958 the governor of the TFDA was in charge of appointing the members of the municipal council. The only exception was in 1953 when the constituent assembly in charge of drafting the new national constitution elected its members. This change reflected the coming to power of Marcos Pérez Jiménez.

Pérez Jiménez was the last Venezuelan dictator of the twentieth century. During the previous years of tumultuous political environment, the oil boom in Venezuela started to transform the relation between state representatives and their constituents. In order to develop the social body of the nation, it was necessary to take advantage of the natural resources. The putative father of this ideology was Venezuelan writer and intellectual Arturo Uslar Pietri. He popularized this vision of the nation in his famous 1936 article "*Sembrar el Petroleo*" published on July 14 in the newspaper *Ahora*. For Uslar Pietri, the wealth produced in the destructive extractive activities such as oil production must be reinvested in more stable and reproductive activities such as agriculture. Most generally, during this time it came to mean diversifying the economy taking advantage of the more ephemeral oil revenue.

This ideology permeated the political milieu of the post-Gomez era and transformed the conception of the economy and Venezuela's understanding of democracy. During the period between Gomez and Pérez Jiménez, democracy, political participation, and the idea of modernity took a particular shape. On the one hand, there was the idea that people were incapable of self-governance. Ideologues such as Laureano Vallenilla Lanz (minister during Pérez Jiménez's regime) considered the social body of the nation (*el pueblo*) as incapable of making decisions by itself. He argued that the elite should take care of the country in the name of all its citizens. Following his father, he adhered to the idea of what they called "democratic Caesarism": the idea that the nation required a strong leadership (especially its intellectual bourgeoisie and the military establishment) that would move the people toward development. Pérez Jiménez was a firm adherent to this idea. Furthermore, much in the style of nineteenth-century modernists like Antonio Guzman Blanco, he equated progress with building infrastructure and macroeconomic growth.

On the other hand, the newly founded political parties such as PCV, URD, and AD aspired to open the spectrum of political participation. For them, progress also meant the development of public political spaces for open participation. They wanted universal and fair elections for public offices. But as Coronil (1997) argues, since the Venezuelan political imagination was co-opted by the division between the natural and social bodies of the nation, to achieve democracy also came to mean giving the people access to the state and its control of the oil revenue. According to Pérez Jiménez, the people were not prepared to access this wealth; only elite individuals would know what to do with it. The right thing to do was to create infrastructure, literally to build the nation by making highways, bridges, and hotels. Pérez Jiménez never conceived the state as mediator between nature and the political body but as a guardian of some idealized political form.

During Pérez Jiménez's regime the public political sphere was restricted and the forms of political oratory and communication were heavily controlled by the state apparatus. Only in the interstices between the regimes of Gomez and Pérez Jiménez some form of public political sphere was formed in the Delta. During the dictatorship, the municipal council's offices were not open for election. Furthermore, the use of state resources from oil revenues to create political clientelism was unnecessary. There was no need for politicians to lure or create bonds with their constituents by distributing state resources of any kind. Their offices did not depend on the people's will. Only a few individuals participated in elections, all the indigenous population was excluded, and the government's control of the electoral system meant that there was no real need to invest material resources or to develop rhetorical strategies to convince people to vote for a candidate. This form of politics required the development of a democratic system based on party politics in which votes counted. This era coincided with the positioning of Venezuela as one of the most important oil exporters in the world, which made the redistribution of revenues a national problem.

Democracy After 1958

During the democratic era the two major political organizations in Venezuela were AD and COPEI. These two parties shared a de facto bipartisan government from 1958 to 1998 thanks to the Puntofijo Pact. The Puntofijo Pact was an agreement to ensure the recognition of electoral results and mandates by the parties (AD, PCV, COPEI) that reestablished democracy after the dictatorship of General Pérez Jiménez. Soon AD, COPEI, and URD excluded the Communist

Party due to international pressures and ideological reasons. With time URD was also displaced from the political scene, and only AD and COPEI were capable of having presidential candidates with real chances of winning elections.

The new political situation produced the need to expand the electoral base of the new political parties, and this included the indigenous and rural population. As Vidal (2002b: 9) argues, competition for the new indigenous voter resulted in the creation of two contradictory images: they were depicted first as naive and ignorant people that could be persuaded to vote with gifts such as food, gasoline, money, and so on; on the other hand, they have been depicted also as unreliable voters with no party discipline who change alliances seeking petty benefits that they could obtain from candidates and different political parties.

The newly created political parties found a country that was becoming increasingly dependent on oil exports and a rural population that was migrating en masse to cities in northern Venezuela. After 1958, Venezuela not only became one of the few Latin American democracies at that time but also became increasingly rich and dependent on a single source of money: oil. This allowed the government to engage in grandiose development projects that held the promise of rapid and sudden improvement of living conditions (Coronil 1997). The development of the nation's natural body seemed to make people forget about the need to diversify the economy (sowing the oil). In such conditions AD and COPEI did not need a coherent economic plan to govern the country since oil could make and was making the economy grow by itself. The political parties only needed to be the mediators. They only needed to promise to redistribute these revenues.

During the years between 1958 and 1998 an electoral ethos of high expenditure developed in the country. Venezuela developed the most expensive electoral apparatus in the hemisphere and one of the most expensive in the world. AD and COPEI had access to the budget of an oil-exporting country in a world that was becoming increasingly dependent on this energy source for its industrial development. Images of political candidates distributing all kinds of gifts during campaigns and for political propaganda started catching the attention of not only the urban population but most importantly for AD the rural population. AD was the first democratic party to extend its political campaigning into the countryside during the 1960s with the foundation of party houses all over the country. These houses served as local representatives of the party. They were the place where people came to pledge support and claim benefits after the election was over. In the 1960s, AD political supporters had for the first time a member of the party close to them who they could contact for political favors and with

whom they could negotiate the redistribution of state resources for political support. Soon COPEI started imitating this strategy, and it became the rule among political parties to have a house in each town to ensure direct contact with the constituents.

These party houses formed the tip of the spear of public opinion formation in rural Venezuela. Most political discussions circulated from Caracas to the countryside by being talked about in the premises of the party house. Also, the promises of material benefits followed this path. In the Orinoco Delta, this process started as early as the 1940s with the expansion of the PCV into the Delta. In 1940 the PCV founded its local branch. In 1945 AD also established a branch in Tucupita. URD would follow in 1946, and COPEI established its organization in 1958. In the 1960s and 1970s these branches became full party houses and spread throughout the territory (Figure 3).

With the new democratic system political campaigning became a necessity. The indigenous population of the state, so far excluded from political participation, became the target of the new rhetorical strategies. Unreachable by traditional media such as newspapers or radio, the political campaigns in the Delta were, and still are, carried out by boat. Caravans of boats circulate in the Delta with numerous people chanting, shouting slogans, and showing the

Figure 3 COPEI's Political Party House in the town of Curiapo (picture by Juan Luis Rodríguez).

party colors. During my fieldwork I saw these boats competing for space in the rivers. Passengers in boats of opposed political parties shouted their slogans at each other and tried to ridicule the opposing candidate. This form of political campaigning gave the Waraos the first face-to-face contact with the national public sphere.

This form of campaigning also included political gifts and promises. One of the first items to be popularized as a political gift was the outboard motor, which had been introduced in the Delta in the 1930s and 1940s but was always out reach for the Warao, who were relegated to secondary jobs or were completely left out of the national monetary economy. The outboard motor became a desirable object during this time because it made it easier to travel from the rivers to the coast and to towns to sell the fish, *ocumo*, and crafts, and buy cheaper commodities. The politicians in canoes with outboard motors could reach all parts of the Delta and start constructing alliances with local *kobenahoros* (governors), and other indigenous leaders.

Since the 1960s national political parties were able to make promises and deliver gifts because the politicians in power had access to unprecedented oil revenues which help them create public relations strategies based on this wealth. One way in which the resources and money of the state started to be channeled to indigenous communities was including the Warao on the public payroll. A position on the payroll of either the *Gobernación* or the *Alcaldía* became one of the most desirable gifts for political alliance. Both AD and COPEI started to promise paid positions, or *puestos*, in the *Alcaldía* or municipal council as a reward for votes during certain elections. These *puestos*, which in many cases do not entail actually working for the *Alcaldía*, gave certain local leaders access to money and influence in their communities.

At the same time, new forms of political oratory developed in the Delta. The Warao started to participate in political performances that were delivered in a new language (Spanish) and in new genres of speech (e.g., political speeches, meetings, and political gossip). In the 1960s the Warao started experiencing political speeches from candidates in the form in which we know them today: a candidate in front of a public audience delivering a speech about the social conditions of the community and the territory, linking these issues with national politics, and promising solutions for the people. The Warao listened to such speeches and judged them and gossiped about them among themselves but were not actually included as interlocutors. In this sense the post-1958 coming of political parties and the booming oil economy made possible the development of a joint semiotic strategy in which political oratory and political gift giving

became prominent. Public speeches and oratory converged with gifts to produce a new political scene in the Delta.

By the end of the 1960s the national public sphere had completely surrounded the Warao indigenous population. The Venezuelan political process had created the institutions of the state, the media, and the political party branches that would link the Warao with national politics. It had also established political gift giving as the principal strategy to gain political influence and had allowed the development of a new form of political oratory in the territory. But all these developments did not include the Warao as political actors/speakers. Democracy and the oil booming economy allowed them only to be hearers/receivers. This was also due to the lack of competence in the new genres of political speech as well as in Spanish in certain sectors of the population. Among the Waraos the traditional forms of oratory did not include the form of speech connected to the world of political parties and national politics. This form of speech required bilingual leaders who could mediate not only between languages but also between forms of performances and semiotic strategies.

Conclusions

With the expansion of the Venezuelan state into rural areas, thanks to the oil boom and the advent of democracy in 1958, the public sphere expanded into regions where indigenous peoples had retreated after colonial times (for an analysis of this retreat, see Hill 1999b). I linked this expansion with a more general process of original capitalist accumulation that requires the surveillance and control of subordinate subjects' labor and bodies (Federici 2004). I suggested that we also expand this process to understand the political economy of communicative and semiotic processes. The history of the Delta shows how the public sphere created a new political audience in the TFDA between 1958 and 1998. The expansion of party politics and the conspicuous use of political gifts created a new form of public political sphere that surrounded the Warao population, fencing off indigenous forms of discourse, and ways of speaking in the name of democracy and modernity.

Habermas associated the expansion of the public sphere with freedom, democracy, and modernity. Nevertheless, the expansion of the capitalist public sphere to non-European social spaces depends on a more general process of subordination of those who do not belong to the bourgeois educated class. The expansion of the public sphere is the expansion of a very particular language and

semiotic ideology (Keane 2006, 2007) that discriminates against the "other's" (non-bourgeois) ideas about communication (Graham 1993). Habermas's analysis does not account for inequalities produced by the public sphere because his analysis is based solely on the "positive effects" that it produced in Europe, forgetting about the interaction between centers of power and peripheral subjects. These interactions produced the expansion of an individualist language ideology into populations with little or no competence in the new forms of communication and genres of discourse. The result of this process is more often the forceful incorporation of these subjects into educational programs (boarding schools, missionary schools, etc.) to incorporate them into dominant forms of discourse or their complete isolation from the public sphere (Hill 1994b).

This is the case of the Warao of the Delta Amacuro who during the twentieth century witnessed the development of the Venezuelan public sphere around them. The peak of this process came with the democratic era in 1958 that changed the political landscape in the country. The rising of party politics is associated with high oil revenues producing a "magical state" (Coronil 1997) in which the connection between politicians and the social body (the people) required grandiose performances and giving wealth to the people in the form of infrastructure building and direct distribution of money. In this environment, the Warao became hearer/receivers of speeches and gifts. The required linguistic and semiotic competence to partake in the Delta's public sphere prevented the Waraos until very recently from fully participating in political issues. Nonetheless, this position has recently changed. After the 1999 constitutional reform the struggle of indigenous communities to gain a voice in local and national politics paid off. The rest of this book deals with the new forms of political speech and the old semiotic practices that pervade the political sphere of the Orinoco Delta in the new era of post-1999 constitutional reform.

From Spanish to Warao

The Translation of Poverty and the Poverty of Translation in the Orinoco Delta

Transforming the public sphere in the Orinoco Delta was more than a matter of internal colonialism and the spread of state institutions. The Warao were not only a population living out of the purview of the state but also a people with a different language. Becoming citizens of Venezuela implied, then, not only building the state's infrastructure around them but also transforming their culture and translating their language into Spanish. The main actors in this process of transformation and translation were Catholic missionaries who came back to the country during the 1920s after the efforts of private American companies of colonization failed. The regime of General Juan Vicente Gomez invited them back to be the main colonizing force in southern and eastern Venezuela. The main task of the missionaries was to civilize the indigenous population, to translate their languages, and to make the Warao into skilled workers. This implied a general linguistic shift from Warao to Spanish. It is therefore important to trace the practices of translation that these missionaries implemented in the Delta in order to understand the process by which the Warao came to be counted by politicians as members of a political public and ultimately to be under the influence of the magical state.

Translation of indigenous languages in the sixteenth- and seventeenth-century colonial expansion proved to be a fruitful instrument of colonial influence and control (Errington 2001; Rafael 1993). Walter Mignolo (1992) pioneered the study of what he called the "philosophy of language" behind the publication of dictionaries, grammars, and historical narratives during the colonization of the Americas. For him, a philosophy of language is the underlying set of ideas that supports the process of linguistic colonization. In linguistic anthropology we broadly refer to these philosophies as language ideologies (Kroskrity 2000; Schieffelin, Woolard, and Kroskrity 1998; Gal and Irvine 1995). In this chapter,

I analyze the ideas behind the production of language descriptions produced by missionaries and the Warao response to these linguistic practices. My intention is to show that the process of integrating indigenous peoples into a national economy and political system required transforming the public sphere linguistically in order to make the Warao recognizable as an imagined political public. In order to imagine an individual Warao as a voter, or as embracing a particular political position, it was necessary for the state to transform the way in which Warao can be addressed and interpellated. The indigenous person is thought of as needing to develop a political voice to live under a modern political system (Kunreuther 2014). In order to produce such a transformation, language must shift to a national, modern language, and forms of "cultural" expressions must be translated into the dominant language.

Here I intend to explore the nuances of the linguistic transformation of the surrounding public sphere described in Chapter 1. I will point out also how these language ideologies were dynamic, and what the process of linguistic interaction looks like when the Warao point of view is also considered. The main focus in this chapter is the Capuchin missionaries' attempts at linguistic description and translation, and the responses by Warao speakers who survived the colonial period by retreating into the swamps of the Orinoco Delta. This strategic retreat allowed the Warao to remain considerably more isolated than other indigenous groups of lowland South America until the 1920s, when new historical circumstances put them in the way of the expanding Venezuelan nation-state (see Heinen and Henley 1998–9, 1975; Heinen, Lizarralde, and Gomez 1994–6; Suarez 1968; Wilbert 1997, 1993).

While Mignolo's work provides a general panoramic perspective on the indigenous resistance to literacy practices across the Americas, I have set the more modest goal of trying to look at this process in a particular area. In the highly hierarchical societies of Mesoamerica and the Andes, the written work of the indigenous elites enabled the process of breaking with what Mignolo called the European classical tradition. But in lowland South America the process was not exactly one of resistance, at least in the sense of overt opposition. From the Warao standpoint, language differences had to be explained, and at the same time served as an explanation for new historical circumstances. In this chapter, I will show how the linguistic and cultural encounter made language the object of thinking; in other words, it sparked a metalinguistic analysis on all sides. Here, I show both how Warao language was an object of thinking for the missionaries and how lack of understanding of Spanish was an object of thinking for the Warao. These productions of linguistic rationalizations produced a rising

awareness of subordination among the Warao that was expressed in narratives of loss and linguistic misunderstanding.[1] In other words, at the moment when the missionaries started explaining Warao as a backward language, the Warao explained their situation as a product of mistranslation.

The Arrival of Missionaries

In 1912, Catholic and Protestant missionaries from Brazil and Guyana entered the national territory of Venezuela without President Juan Vicente Gomez's[2] permission (Fundación Polar 1995; Martin 1977). This arrival sparked alarm because it exposed the vulnerability of Venezuela's borders, a very inconvenient situation due to constant territorial disputes with neighboring countries. The answer to this threat was slow. It took three years for the Venezuelan Catholic Church to convince the government to pass a law giving the church political control over the region. On June 16, 1915, the Ley de Misiones (missionary law) was approved (Armellada 1954) based partially on the ability of the missionaries to convince the government that they would create a political presence at the borders of the nation. This law stated in its first article that it was created to give control of this area to the Venezuelan Catholic Church, giving them the task of populating the southern border and civilizing the indigenous population.

This was politically convenient for Gomez because this way he could avoid appointing civil authorities without business or family links with him to these positions (Yarrington 2003). At the same time, he avoided wasting troops in the "pacification" and surveillance of these territories. Missionaries were seen as the cheapest and most reliable way to deal with the untamed countryside. They began surveying the zone as early as 1917 in order to create mission posts, but the final arrival of missionaries was delayed a few years. Their real activities began with the signing of an agreement between the Ministerio de Relaciones Interiores (Ministry of Internal Affairs) and Fray Felix de Vegamian, director of the Franciscan Capuchins in Venezuela. The Convenio de la Misión del Caroni (Caroni Mission's Agreement) was signed in 1922 giving control of great swaths of Bolivar state and TFDA to the religious authorities.

The first zone where missionary posts were founded was the Orinoco Delta. The earliest missions were La Divina Pastora de Araguaimujo (1925), Barima (1925–7), San José de Amacuro (1927–40), Guayo (1942), Pedernales, Curiapo, and Imataca (Fundación Polar 1995). In these places, the missionaries created the first boarding schools with the idea of transforming Warao children into citizens.

The strategy was to separate the children as early as possible from the influence of their parents to teach them to be part of the new nation. They would then be returned to their communities to spread "civilization" among their peers. The so-called evolutionary process, as it was called at the time, entailed, of course, the appropriation of criollo values and sense of proper behavior. This was supposed to be a cultural, moral, and spiritual transformation. One of the main concerns was teaching the young Warao children basic skills to deal with the criollo world and become productive workers. This moral and spiritual transformation was meant to transform the visual and audible signs of these children's bodies through new dressing, speaking, and behaving. These outward signs of modernity were pushed by the missionaries as a way to not only transform the soul but, just as importantly, shift the political/affective dispositions of these Warao children toward the nation-state. At the same time, such transformations could be showcased to show the Venezuelan government their civilizatory effectiveness. Being at once agents of religious and political transformation, the missionaries needed to show the government that they were capable of transforming the Warao into effective workers and peaceful, obedient citizens.

Depicting Warao Mentality and Teaching Spanish

Teaching Spanish was a priority, and it was conceived as the replacement of a backward language that, according to Father Bonifacio Maria de Olea (1928), could not express "subtle" and "delicate" ideas. Language and thought seems to be one and the same as the Capuchin Fathers conceived it. Furthermore, the formal organization of the vocabulary and grammar of the Warao language was seen as a representation of the way in which the Warao people think and as the reason they are trapped in an incorrect form of reasoning. According to Father Olea, these are intrinsic, essential features of the Warao language:

> The dialect of these Indians is the guarauno, very deficient in its vocabulary and without flexibility whatsoever. So, it is not easy to express subtle and delicate ideas in this dialect, which has not progressed beyond the most rudimentary state. To explain many of the ideas about unknown things for the Indians, **we** have to resort to detours, for example, to call trains "steamships of the earth," and airplanes "steamships of the air or steamships from above."[3] A lot of words acquire a more or less different sense just by adding a syllable to the beginning or the end of the word. The numerical system is the primitive one; they count with their fingers and toes and when they get to twenty, it is a guarao; this operation

is repeated as many times as needed, resulting in one, two, three, four, etc., guararos. (Olea 1928: X–XI, translation by the author)

These opinions were published in Olea's *Ensayo Grammatical*, which constitutes the first attempt made by the missionaries to describe the Warao language in the twentieth century. The Warao's "inflexible" language, then, lacks the capacity to express the "subtleties" of modernity. According to the Father, it cannot express in single words concepts such as train, or airplane. These are interesting comments because they show a form of reverse logic by which the Warao are judged not by how they use their language but by how the missionaries use it. Notice in the quote that Olea starts by describing the Warao language as an object of analysis in the first two sentences of his evaluation—but then he switches to a description of the way in which "we," the missionaries, used it. When he says that in Warao there is the need to create a torturous detour to name airplanes as steamships of the air or from above, he is not describing a Warao person using his or her own language. Instead he is describing himself as limited by the use of the Warao language. So, it is Olea who feels that the Warao vocabulary is inflexible, not any actual Warao speaker. This is a reversal that passes almost unnoticed in his comment and that we can use to untangle how this modernist linguistic ideology operates. The missionary first produces an evaluative comment about the language, and then he provides an example of how he is constrained by using the language. Finally, he attributes this constraining to not only how he feels about the Warao language but also how he imagines Warao speakers must feel. This logic is masked by the way it is presented in the paragraph. It is interesting to notice that seventy years later Father Basilio Barral's Warao-Spanish dictionary lists the following two words as translation for airplane: *jejukubaka kuaya* and *aviona*. The first one has the same literal sense attributed by Olea as "steamship from above." The second word, *aviona*, is an obvious lexical borrowing from Spanish and is to my knowledge the most commonly used form. Olea's assertion that *jejukubaka kuaya* is more cumbersome than the word "airplane" seems to be more a description of his own difficulties in understandings and learning Warao than an accurate description of the Warao incapacity for describing modern technology. *Jejukubaka kuaya* is not a clumsy Warao way of saying "airplane," but rather an expression invented in conjunction with the missionaries in this language contact situation. The expression has then been elevated to a lexical item by virtue of being repeated in text after text, thus reproducing the linguistic products of a foundational language ideology. The Warao themselves never had any problem thinking or speaking about airplanes since they are perfectly happy with borrowing a word such as *aviona* or using *jejukubaka kuaya* as the missionaries wanted.

Because of linguistic misunderstandings of this kind, the missionaries conceived the Warao language as a barrier that prevented them from fully comprehending the modern and moral ideas that they were bringing to the Delta. Airplanes and trains were by 1920s at the forefront of modernity in Venezuela and the world. Under Gomez, these two means of transportation were deemed to be the future of the connection among the country's regions (Fundación Polar 1995). But from the missionaries' standpoint, Warao seemed utterly inadequate to teach science and conceptualize this new civilization. The Warao's language was therefore imagined as doomed to disappear as soon as modern teaching started to spread through the rivers of the Delta.

In the missionary's opinion, one of the main obstacles for modern thinking was the Warao numerical system. Olea depicted this system by saying that it is the "primitive one." The primitive quality here refers to the use of the body as a ground for representing numeric operations. It relies on the use of the fingers and toes, and once one counts to twenty, the reference is to one person (*isaka Warao*). The use of the body to ground the act of counting is supposed to be a less-abstract form of thinking, but again this idea seems to be a projection of the missionaries' use of Warao language in the hope of showing the primitiveness of Warao cognitive capacities. The use of the body for counting is then ideologically associated with a lack of development.

If we link this comment with the previous one on the lack of "flexibility" and feasible concepts for technological advances, we can infer that Olea saw Warao as lacking the capacity for expressing abstraction and scientific thought. He is concerned with a sort of Cartesian division between body and mind in which abstract knowledge is considered superior to any sensory experience. The use of the body for counting is then interpreted as a signal of a childish approach to knowledge. These ideas would remain in the background of missionary thought in the Delta throughout the twentieth century, and we will see how the "misuse of numbers" and supposed lack of abstract thought is a pervasive theme when the missionaries addressed "Warao mentality."

Olea, and most of the missionaries that came directly after him, implied that their work was to help the Warao to transit the evolutionary path that goes from the concrete use of the body as a device for knowledge to a system in which mathematics and scientific thought are the ultimate goal. Notice that this is also grounds for denying the Warao any form of political voice within a political system based on rational speech as the basis for participation. It was not only the numeral system—in general the Fathers considered the Warao as trapped by a primitive code—which prevented them from conceptualizing civilization,

so their language needed to be replaced. The only reason for the missionaries to study and translate Warao was to use it for religious conversion and teaching. In this sense, Olea's *Ensayo Gramatical* is an impressive example of the importance of language during these first steps of the conformation of a public sphere in the Orinoco Delta. The book was published in 1928, just three years after the inauguration of the first missionary post in the Delta. It is evident that there was a tremendous interest in the topic in order for the book to be the first published work from any missionary in the Delta during the twentieth century. Even the book's title is a perfect example of what Olea had in mind, since he called the Warao language a "dialect." By using this term, he was asking the readers to think of Warao as a less-complicated verbal code than a "language." By dialect, he does not mean a geographical linguistic variety bound by isoglosses. What he means instead is that Warao does not deserve the same consideration as Spanish. Olea's final remark in the preface of his book is in the tone of a farewell to a language that was supposed to be replaced by national, uniform, and more abstract Spanish. According to Olea (1928: XII), his book is a

> humble work, that at least will help preserving the memory, in the future, of one of the most important tribes of Guyana; at the same time, this is a gift of gratitude to Venezuela, its government and the hierarchy of the church, and to all of those who have helped and sympathized with the Missions.

By recording the Warao language he intended to create a manual for the missionaries to teach Spanish and to record a disappearing primitive knowledge for future scientific use. Olea's work has to be understood in academic terms as an attempt to preserve this language as a museum piece and to advocate for its replacement in the name of civilization. Understanding this ideological stance is fundamental because it explains the marginalized position that the Warao occupied for most of the twentieth century in the expansion of state formation and Venezuelan public sphere. In the examples that follow we will see more of this direct and indirect influence from anthropology, linguistic, and psychology.

Idioma Warao

Another interesting textual example of this linguistic ideological process of description is Antonio Vaquero's *Idioma Warao* published in 1963. As we can judge by the title, Warao had gained the status of language by this time. This marked a somewhat different attitude to its study. Vaquero shared with Olea the

vision that Warao language is a representation of something deeply different in the Warao mind. Nevertheless, he explained in the introduction to his book that this difference is not biological but merely cultural. Then, he goes on to assert the influence of Edward Sapir's ideas in his own work, writing: "Well, culture in general, and language in particular, shape the lenses with which man observe the world in which he is immersed. Language and our ways of thinking—wrote Edward Sapir—are intimately related and are, in a way, the same thing" (Vaquero 1965: 11). Vaquero advocated a somewhat extreme linguistic relativism and deemed translation of concepts between Warao and Spanish impossible. As an example of this linguistic incompatibility, he used the following mathematical problem:

> What is easier for a Spanish speaker than to understand that one plus one equals two? Said in this way—and in plain Spanish, of course—with difficulty the Warao Indian would realize the meaning of this proposition. We conceive additions as horizontal, in linear addition. In contrast, the Warao conceives it in vertical formation, by juxtaposition, in the form of a tower. We would have to say to them—making violence to Spanish: "one on top of one equal two," the equivalent to: "Isaka aria isaka manamo." (Vaquero 1965: 12)

Vaquero challenged Warao's numerical abilities by arguing that mathematical operations are constrained by the way in which Warao organize the propositions. Unlike Olea, he does not categorize Warao as primitive but as completely different. For him, the way in which numerals are spatially arranged (as a tower, one upon the other) for arithmetical operations affects the translation of mathematical knowledge, but he does not go further into explaining why. It is also unclear how he got to the conclusion that the Warao organize arithmetical operations in vertical formation. Likewise, it is curious that he represented the spatial organization of these operations as if the Warao would be thinking of them in a written form. The only way of imagining this operation in the form of a tower is by writing it.

By the 1960s the influence of these linguistic and anthropological ideas, especially the idea of cultural and linguistic relativism, began to be adopted and reconfigured by the Capuchins. These ideas, although not shared equally by all of the missionaries, strongly influenced their explanations about language. Yet, this relativism had nothing to do with putting cultures on an equal footing. Acknowledging coevalness was not the plan. Spanish speakers were still thought of as more civilized, and the missionaries had the obligation to bridge the gap and translate modernity to the "Indians." According to Vaquero, we cannot

expect the Warao to translate the terms of modernity into their language by themselves; this is the task of missionaries, anthropologists, and other more-civilized criollos.

As we have seen previously, the 1960s is the beginning of the democratic period in Venezuela. This is the moment in which the liberal public sphere started to open up, and when modern political parties, such as AD and COPEI, started to develop a public connection with their electorate. This form of the Venezuelan public political sphere expanded to the rural parts of the country, luring in sectors of the population that never participated before in any form of elections. Nevertheless, the Warao could not fully participate in this process. In order to belong in the modern, democratic nation, the Warao needed to be transformed; and to be transformed, their language and their culture had to be intelligible for Spanish speakers but not the other way around. Their relationship with that new democratic state was tenuous, and it was mostly mediated through the infrastructure provided by the missionaries. The missionaries, then, became the first mediators between the modern, democratic form of the Venezuelan state and the Warao. Their translation practices were, in effect, the linguistic realization of a broader process of mediation between the political body of the nation and this new imagined public. This process eventually resulted in a general dynamic process of transforming not only the Warao into Spanish speakers but also the oil-producing Venezuelan state into the source of livelihood for many of the missionized Warao. But this process depended on a unidirectional process of translation and transformation from Warao into Spanish.

Narratives and Discursive Practices

Through their translation efforts, the missionaries challenged not only the lexical and numeric understanding of the Warao language but also their traditional genres of discourse. The missionaries collected traditional narratives, or myths, to reveal the "Warao soul." Traditional narratives were conceived as windows into the essence of Warao mentality and cognitive capacities. Most of the narratives selected for book collections were about the world prior to the encounter with "civilized, white men." Narratives that made sense of current political relations were excluded as not original or "pristine." This was also an attempt to show that certain forms of discourse are expressions of a time when the Warao lived in harmony with nature, apart from the destructive forces of the modern world. A good example of these translation efforts is Argimiro

García's *Cuentos y Tradiciones de los Indios Guaraunos* (Tales and traditions of the Guarauno Indians) in which he tells us in its introduction:

> Finally, we can say that these stories, together with their numerous beautiful chants, form the only history and the only literature that is known about this tribe. Some ancient European people and some American tribes, such as those from Mexico, had at least their temples, their idols, their organized towns, and sometimes, a rudimentary form of hieroglyphic writing and painting. But none of this can be found among the guaraúnos Indians, which proves their backwardness, and as their "world" is limited, limited are their topics. The jungle where they live, the forest where they hunt, the rivers where they fish, the animals surrounding them, the planets that shed light on them, the houses where they sleep, some extravagant and fanciful ideas about the supernatural world, and some scenes of family life, all these considered in a superficial and superstitious manner, this is all their ideology, and those are all the themes in these "Tales and Traditions." (García 1971: 16)

By writing that "as their world is limited, limited are their topics," García is asking the reader to contrast the Warao with the classical Mesoamerican and Andean societies, and of course, Europe. The simplicity of narrative content is supposed to match the simplicity of Warao architecture, and both, at some level, are iconic of each other and indexical of a lower stage of evolution, even in comparison with the other so-called Indians. These narratives supposedly show that the content of Warao discourses and ways of speaking render them unable to grasp more "advanced" social, aesthetic, and by extension, moral concepts. Narrating their immediate world was a sign of their disregard, lack of interest on, or even awareness of the vastness of world history.

But it was not only among missionaries in the Delta that these ideas prevailed; this attitude reflected the way in which history was taught in Venezuela. For Venezuelan children who learned about world history in a Venezuelan school, "universal history," as the course was titled at school, meant European history. Official history books described Greek and Roman history, the Ottoman Empire, the Middle Ages, the Renaissance, and of course the French and Industrial Revolutions. It was evident that Latin American colonial enclaves had no place within those books. As Europeans, García and other missionaries were educated at the center of these historical narratives, and thought of it as the "real history."

By the 1980s and 1990s, the interest of some missionaries became more psychological. For instance, works like Julio Lavandero's (1991, 1992) *Ajotejana I and II* were aimed at understanding the Warao's rational capacities. In his introduction to the second volume, Lavandero recommended further

psychoanalytic research regarding the Warao propensity to disbelieve scientific facts and their bias toward irrational explanations. He argued that the Warao have the tendency to believe the fantastic, which compels them to live in a series of "paranoid fantasies":

> The Waraos manifest a permanent credulity to the fantastic and incredible, and to unruly and unfounded rumors, while offering a firm mental resistance to the evident and clear. Therefore, news coming from the Warao, or circulated by them, are undependable, to the point of coining the derogatory phrases: "guarao Radio: do not believe it." And the other one: "Guarao Tales" (intrigues), who understands them? And the resistance to guarao accusations by experienced policemen and judges, because most of the time they come from conjectures without any support, from dreams or shamanic sessions. (Lavandero 1992: 11; translation by the author)

For Lavandero, Warao's discursive practices are the product of a childish mentality. Warao tend to believe in rumors, and what they say is to be filtered by rational authorities. They are not prepared to be citizens or take care of themselves in the modern world. The sources of this undependability are their "shamanic sessions." Therefore, any form of accusation or complain would be observed as the product of their "imagination." Any Warao using non-Western ways of speaking will be singled out as irrational, and racialized as a backward Indian. These are the linguistic ideologies that pervaded the transformation of the surrounding public sphere in the Delta. Under these circumstances, the public political sphere, represented by state authorities such as the police and judges but also anyone with any form of political authority, constituted a surrounding force put in place to care for the Waraos without actually listening to them. Literally, they were not supposed to be heard or listened. As we saw in Chapter 1, during the twentieth century a tremendous amount of infrastructure was put in place to develop the Delta as part of a national political unit, and ultimately as part of a modern democracy. But, this particular political formation grew in the back of a form of linguistic ideology that denied Warao coevalness with other Venezuelans.

In the first volume of his work, Lavandero also presents some methodological considerations for his collections of narratives aimed at understanding the Warao psychology. He divided his work into two different sets of narratives. *Ajotejana I* is devoted to mythological narratives. The second volume, *Ajotejana II*, is a collection of narratives about everyday life. In both cases the explicit goal is "1) to revalorize the Warao culture; 2) to reinforce the indigenous image and self-esteem; 3) to infuse them with self-confidence; 4) *to rescue them from*

unreal neurotic tendencies (emphasis added)" (Lavandero 1991: 11; translation by the author). Very interestingly, it was Lavandero's practice of translation and transcription that was supposed to achieve this goal. Translating Warao into Spanish acquired, then, the dual power of exposing the shortcomings of the Warao mentality by making available the content of Warao ways of speaking, and of subjecting the material written form of these unruly speeches to a modern, recognizable form for psychological analysis.

Lavandero collected this corpus of narratives during a long period that expanded from the late 1960s to the 1990s. According to Lavandero, he admitted all themes, all kinds of narrators, and all kinds of contexts. He claimed to have devoted more time to accurate transcription than to translation and annotations, implying a shift from previous missionaries who concentrated almost exclusively on the referential content of these narratives. His intention was to develop a system of transcription that reflected the linguistic contact with Spanish. He deemed international systems of transcription as misleading with regard to the "actual" situation of contact with Spanish. He preferred to use what he called *literaturismo*, namely, the free rearrangement of the sentences to fit into "flawless" (literature-like) Spanish. In so doing, he intended to avoid the technicalities of formal linguistics. He gives the following example of this transcription and translation process, illustrating the changes in his transcription techniques and what he called *traducción literalísima*, *traducción literal*, and *traducción literaria*.

> Utterance transcribed following what Lavandero called "academic orthodoxy":
> *Mauka ahanokoeku ubajakotaiwitu, wete akohokowitu aranitumasi iabannae.*
> (Lavandero 1991: 14)

> Same utterance following Lavandero's preferred transcription practices:
> *Mauka ajanokeku ubaiakotaiuitu,* **uete** *akookoitu aranitumase iabanae.*
> (Lavandero 1991: 14)

Example 1

The differences between these two transcriptions are basically spelling choices. Some of the most notorious changes are the choices of representing the glottal fricative *h* which Lavandero represents as *j*; the substitution of some symbols representing clustered vowel sound such as *oe* for *e*, or *we* for *ue*, or *wi* for *oi*; the substitution of final *i* for *e*, and the reduplication of the alveolar, nasal sound *n* for *nn*. The purpose of these substitutions is not just a matter of personal preference for Lavandero. What he wants to accomplish with these

transformations in the written form of the word is to influence the way in which the aural form is also perceived. He is adamant that Warao is a language transformed by contact with Spanish, and that the new reality in which the Warao live is determined by their interaction with Spanish-speaking people. This historical reality must have, in his view, an impact not only in the content of Warao but also in its very material aural form. He prefers to represent Warao phonology as gradually approximating the target language that the Warao should be shifting to, namely Spanish. This is at once an imagined description and a forceful prescription about the linguistic reality of language contact in the Delta. There is certainly no denying the influence of Spanish in Warao, but here Lavandero is not concerned with the actual problem of language contact. He is not concerned with the fact that Warao has also had a tremendous amount of influence on the lower Delta's form of Spanish. Instead, what he wants to show is that the transition of Warao to modern life in Venezuela must be understood as an ontological transformation of Warao representational forms, not only at the level of their content but also as a function of the materiality of their linguistic forms.

The written form here is supposed to have the power to make us perceive a Hispanized Warao. But who is this public who is supposed to perceive Warao sounds through Spanish spelling? Lavandero's intended public seems to be both young Warao people studying under the guide of religious and secular teachers, and the missionaries and criollo public that he is able to reach with his book. But these are either bilingual individuals who never really model their speech after a standard form. The effect is that Lavandero's spelling imposed an imagined sounding that is confortable not for the Warao themselves but for the also imagined, and however small, criollo public who will be able to approximate Warao speech to their own.

Lavandero's preoccupation with linguistic form is not restricted to prescribing Warao phonology and graphic representation. He is also concerned with the form that this language would take after it is translated into Spanish. It is not enough to get the content of Warao speech right, as its translation also has to sound appropriate for Spanish-speaking ears. In order to accomplish this, he distinguishes between three possible forms that a Warao utterance can take after its content is translated to Spanish.

First, we have what he would call a *traducción literalísima* (very literal translation). What he means here is a one-to-one correspondence between the lexical units and the syntactic arrangement of the source and target utterances. Following with his analysis of the utterance given before he proposes the following example:

traducción literalísima:

Warao:

Mauka ajanokeku ubaiakotaiuitu, uete akookoitu aranitumase iabanae (Lavandero 1991: 14)

Spanish:

mi-hijo su-casa-en duerme-que-el-solo, mismo su-oreja-solo su-mamá-ellas-propia abandonó (Lavandero 1991: 14)

English:

My-son his-house-in sleep-that-he-alone, own his-ear-only his-mother-they-own abandoned (translation by the author)

Example 2

The second kind of translation that he describes is the *traducción literal* (literal translation), which is a translation that adjusts the order and form of lexical items to resemble Spanish a little more but is still close to the original Warao source.

traducción literal:

Warao:

Mauka ajanokeku ubaiakotaiuitu, uete akookoitu aranitumase iabanae (Lavandero 1991: 14)

Spanish:

Mi hijo que duerme sólo en su casa, solamente por su misma oreja, abandono a sus propias madres (Lavandero 1991: 14)

English:

My son that sleeps alone in his house, he only by his own ear, abandoned his own mothers (translation by the author)

Example 3

Finally, he proposes the adoption of *traducción literaria* (literary translation). Literary translation is the transformation of a Warao utterance into an aesthetically pleasant Spanish expression. The production of this last form of translation becomes then a matter of taste.

traducción literaria:

Warao:

Mauka ajanokeku ubaiakotaiuitu, uete akookoitu aranitumase iabanae (Lavandero 1991: 14)

Spanish:

Mi hijo que sólo vive en su casa abandono a su propia familia solamente por sospechas infundadas (Lavandero 1991: 14)

English:

My son, who sleeps alone in his house, abandoned his own family only because of unfounded suspicion (translation by the author)

Example 4

Literary translation is for Lavandero a necessary step in the process of representing a language that due to contact with Spanish is becoming more "Venezolanized" (1991: 13). Thus, both form and content have to be adjusted to this transitional process. Literary translations are supposed to be a better form to achieve the transition of texts from Warao to Spanish, and the integration of the Warao as Venezuelan citizens. Adding the creative voice of the translator becomes then an intervention on a text in a political context in which the movement of meaningful elements between the Warao and Spanish must be controlled. For Lavandero, a deep psychological understanding of what a Warao is saying requires more than mere literal understanding. It is necessary to delve behind the superficial referential meaning of their sentences, and this can only be done as process of scholarly interpretation similar to psychoanalysis in which the form is taken as the surface representation of a deeper truth. In the same way in which a psychoanalyst looks for the clues of deeper processes on the surface of what is said or dreamt, he recommended listening to the Warao and look beyond those words; this is the only way to understand their illogical behavior.

As other missionaries before him, Lavanadero also resorted to arithmetic to explain the hidden mental logics of the Warao. In the introduction to *Ajotejana II*, he describes a conversation with a former worker at the mission post. Lavandero described the worker as dependable and "rational." The former worker was always on time and was very active. A short time after he finished one of his piecemeal jobs at the mission post he came back to Lavandero to complain about his payment. The Father describes the conversation that took place between them from memory. In order to render the text clearer I changed its original presentation in paragraphs to the style of a conversational transcript based on conversational turns[4] (A stands for the Warao man, B stands for Father Lavandero):

1. A: Well sir, you completely paid me all worked days, but not the extra hours.
2. B: What hours?
3. A: The two extra hours I worked every day.

4. B: You did that?

5. A: Yes.

6. A: Look, I worked from eight to twelve every day in the morning, and from two to six in the afternoon. That is ten hours, but the working day is eight.

7. B: But man! From eight to twelve are four. And from two to six are four. And four plus four is eight everywhere in the world!

8. A: No sir, from eight to twelve is five. And from two to six are five. And isn't five plus five ten?

9. B: No man!

10. A: Yes sir!

11. A: Look, (and he counted each one of his fingers in the Warao way) 8,9,10,11,12: they are five, one hand, *mohabasi*. (Then counted with his other hand) Now look 2,3,4,5,6; they are five, clearly. Five plus five, isn't it ten? What do you teach in the school? Two hands are ten, *mojoreko.*

12. B: Well, if you think that is the case go and explain it to the *Jefe Civil* of Curiapo. But afterwards come here and tell me how he made fun of you. (Lavandero 1992: 18)

Example 5

Lack of mathematical knowledge is regarded here as evidence that the Warao's conflicts with criollos is the product of their inadequate, illogical framing of the world. Like Olea, Lavandero presented the Warao counting with their fingers and hands as evidence of their lack of abstract knowledge. This reproduced the same tenet that numerical knowledge linked to the body is inferior. It is a rather childish way of counting. Lavandero considers this form of framing as "Documents from a people that have not reached the wisdom of the Stone Age, but that already, by contagion, is dissolving itself in our technocratic and consumer culture" (Lavandero 1991: 17). In other words, the Warao are not ready to be part of the modern world, let alone be part of a rational public political sphere, or of a rational market economy. They are also not rational speaking subjects of a Habermasian capable of participating in a liberal democracy.

This last conversation with the Warao worker sums up some fifty years of language ideologies. For the missionary, it is enough to know that the police are not going to believe the Warao complaint because of the way in which it is framed, as an "improper" arithmetical operation. The missionary does not even bother about it and challenges the Warao man to tell his story and to face the

mockery of the authorities. The Father is certain that the way in which the man frames his complaint will be regarded as a "Warao fantasy" and will prevent his account from becoming a legal or political issue at all.

Although the conversation could also be read as the Warao man's attempt at translating his own sense of poverty and inequality into a different linguistic code, Father Lavandero is not willing to consider this dimension of the interaction. We can interpret this complaint as a failed translation of the worker's own sense of marginality. It is an example of the difficulty to convey, in a different semiotic and linguistic system, the feeling of not being treated fairly. The worker, probably poorly trained at school, resorted to dealing with these frustrations by using the means taught by the missionaries themselves. After all, it was the missionaries themselves who taught him how to count with his fingers. But by framing the dispute in terms put in place by the missionaries, the Father can easily dismiss the claim challenging the competency of the Warao speaker. It is arguable that this kind of everyday challenge, in which desperate feelings of poverty and marginality are dismissed because they do not fit into proper discursive frames, is part of what makes poverty so difficult to translate in the Delta. These are also the linguistic basis for understanding how in the mid- and late twentieth century the Warao were excluded from the developing of a democratic political public sphere that was mostly the product of the transformation of the country into a petro-state. At the time in which Venezuela was becoming the magical state described by Coronil (1997), the Warao were not supposed to understand what this development meant. Instead, they became an object of interpretation, and of unidirectional translation, and exclusion.

Creating Marginality

By the 1920s Venezuela became an oil-producing country, which meant a transition from a country dependent on rural agricultural production to a very centralized state dependent on the rent produced by oil concessions (Tinker Salas 2009; Coronil 1997). This produced a huge population movement from rural areas to oil-producing areas and to the capital, Caracas.

The Warao were excluded from this transformation. They were "Indians" who needed to be transformed into citizens. In order to achieve this, the missionaries resorted to schooling, religion, and the teaching of Spanish. The teaching of history, geography, mathematics, and Spanish were intended to create in Venezuela's capital an unattainable heterotopic[5] center of national power. The

children were taught their belonging to a broader polity by teaching them their peripheral status. During this process, the students had to memorize historical dates, names, places, and, most importantly, learn to speak Spanish in order to change their mentality and allow the internalization of the concepts of nation and modernity.

But this was not a frictionless process. Transforming the very sense of self of the Warao required a traumatic process that started with separation between parents and children. For the missionaries this was a key issue. Older Warao people were considered set in their ways, and other than saving their souls through Christian conversion, there was not much more than missionaries felt they could do to transform them into modern subjects. The children, on the other hand, were in a formative stage, and missionaries were ready to prevent their parents from influencing their mental and spiritual upbringing. Boarding schools became the center of the missionaries' battle for the hearts, minds, and souls of these children. The idea, as in many other parts of the world, was to separate the children and give them a proper modern and Christian education.

As we could expect, separating children from their parents was not an easy thing to sell. Many people in the Delta hid their children from the missionaries in the forest as soon as they saw their canoes approaching the communities. Anthropologists working in the area during the 1950s also noted that Warao mothers used to scare their children by saying that if they do not go to sleep early, the missionaries would come in the morning (e.g., Lizarralde 1956). This anecdote can give us an idea of the difficulties that the missionaries faced when they began enrolling children in their boarding schools. The missionaries had first to develop a system of economic and political dependency to recruit individuals who then would go back to their communities and convince the parents to let their children go to the boarding school. The missionaries first contacted some families in the area and engaged them in economic relations. They then named the head of extended families *kobenahoro*, a borrowed term from Spanish that is the equivalent to governor, and sent them to convince the parents to send their children to school (Lizarralde 1956). The children were selected, then enrolled, under the auspice of state and religious institutions invested in the development of new economic and political relations with the missionaries.

The missionaries wanted to create a new political structure. For this purpose, they instituted the offices of *Gobernador*, *Capitán*, *Fiscal*, and *Policía*. The Warao soon borrowed these Spanish names and made them fit into Warao phonology as *kobenahoro*, *kabitana*, *bisikari*, and *borisia*. These new political figures had privileged access to rare commodities, but their position put them also in conflict

with their own communities. Although the missionaries usually depicted the Warao as docile and easy to enculturate, we can glimpse the conflicted situation they were in through the lens of their expressive discursive forms and verbal art. In some of these expressive forms, we find powerful examples of the moral and emotional struggles that letting go of their own children implied for Warao mothers, and of the deep understanding they had about the transformation that their children were about to undergo. A good example of these discursive forms is the following *hoa* song recorded by the late anthropologist Dieter Heinen:

> Yae ye ye yee.
> Ye ye ye.
> The father, the father, the father,
> That he should not covet the children,
> The poor children,
> The poor children,
> (…)
> The children,
> They do not want to abandon our food.
> They are used to moriche grub,
> They are used to moriche grub,
> They are eaters of meat of wild pigs.
> Eh eh eh
> The fathers,
> The father who wants our children,
> The children do not know your food,
> Therefore, your desires,
> The desires that you have,
> They should take you back to your land again.
> Ye ye ye. (Heinen 1985: 40–1)[6]

Example 6

This song shows the reluctance of Warao parents to be separated from their children. It also shows how conscious they were about the level at which the missionaries' strategy worked. It is at the most intimate level of the body, and its dispositions, that these parents felt their children would be transformed. This was a way to make the Warao body docile and disciplined (Foucault 1977). The song focused on habitual behavior: the changes in everyday activities, the children's diet. These are things the children are not used to, and their parents know the missionaries will change inevitably. They are also aware that these changes in their children's dispositions will result in changes in their desires and

the things they will want in the future. These are changes that troubled Warao parents because it produced an abrupt generational gap between the things these parents want and know to exist in the Delta and things they can imagine these missionaries will make their children want. They know this gap will make their children into a different kind of subject, even if they do not exactly know what the end result will be.

What we view in songs like this one is an ideological struggle fought in Caracas as a process of nation building that is instantiated on the ground, in the Delta, as a battle over the separation of children and parents, and changes in food, clothes, education, and language. The surrounding public political sphere that will develop in the 1960s around the Warao will depend on these transformed individuals who will develop the dispositions of modern political subjects thanks to the efforts of the missionaries. By translating Warao texts into Spanish and transforming the Warao children's bodies through acquiring modern habits, the missionaries made possible the acquisition of a taste not only for new kinds of food but also for other forms of political performances and linguistic strategies that we will explore in other chapters.

Through discourse practices such as *hoa* sorcery, the Warao began also to express a consciousness of their marginality in which they started to see themselves as the object of oppressive practices by a larger polity. These songs are part of the process of knowing their place within the nation (Keane 1997). This rising awareness about new historical circumstances was expressed in their own terms and narrative genre, but was also mediated by anthropologists such as Dieter Heinen who recorded the experience of some of the first children enrolled in the boarding school. These stories give us an idea of the shock that being enrolled at a boarding school produced in these children. For example, Idamo Kabuka, an elder from the Winikina River, told the following story about his enrollment in a boarding school:

> We arrived at the mission. The house was covered with *temiche* palm leaves and was in bad condition. There was Father Santo, Father Samuel, a Father by the name of Brother Rogelio. There was a *baretida* [nuns] by the name of Michaela, and Sister Inocencia, and Sister Gloria. There was a chief and two workers, three sisters in all.
>
> …I arrived there, at the house of the father, like proper Warao. Right then the father said: 'Quick, sister, bring pants for these boys.' Quickly a bundle of pants appeared. Since I did not know how to get into pants I put both feet into one leg. The father saw me: 'Not like that! Take them out again, take your leg out! One leg into one hole, the other leg into the other. Now it is all right.'

I took off my loincloth and the moriche fiber string and threw them away. At this very moment, there were pants and shirt. I am still crying. I want to return to my father. The next boy is also weeping, we are all crying. (Heinen 1985: 42)

Example 7

Idamo Kabuka gives us a powerful image of the shock of arriving at a mission. Everything changed in a moment. Suddenly he was away from his parents and suffered the stresses of not being dressed properly, not knowing how to behave properly, and not knowing how to express his ideas in a different language. Throwing away his loincloth and wearing pants and shirts is the point that separates his life as a "proper Warao" from the new process of transformation into a citizen of a country. By exchanging a loincloth for pants, he is forced into a new process of subjectification linked to the formation of the nation-state in the Delta.

The use of uniforms was one of the strategies adopted to transform the Warao children into pupils. A national school in Venezuela requires uniforms to identify children in the category of students. The loincloth is an external symbol that is incompatible with the modern knowledge taught at school. At the same time, the uniform was intended to produce a visual display of the new social category to which these children belong. It was intended to show your peers that you were a student, not a random child from the forest.

Control over the body was also carried out through physical training. For the missionaries, a sound mind required a sound body. The students were supposed to acquire control over their bodies, making them docile, by repetitive gymnastic training and learning how to fit within structures like lines while singing the national anthem (more about the national anthem will be discussed in Chapter 3). The Warao children were required to perform their activities like those of the other criollo students. The process of being-made in the mission was undertaken through covering and giving order to their naked bodies.

Waraos' Interpretation of the Encounter

In the long run, the Warao internalized the discourse of nationalism, but the process of imagining themselves as citizens of a nation-state did not remain in control of the state alone. The Warao also learned about the nation and reinterpreted their place within it. The discourses of the nation began to be the subject of Warao discourse as well. In various forms of verbal art, the Warao

produced interpretations of their own marginal position. In the Delta there are two narrative genres that allow the performer to recount historical events, *Dehe Nobo* (stories of the ancestors) and *Dehe Kaimotane* or *Dehe Hido* (stories of recent times) (Briggs 2000). Through Dehe Hido the Warao *hoaratus* (curers) can also explain the nation and its construction.[7] For instance, in a passage of a narrative about the origin of the *jotarao* (criollos) and their commodities the late Santiago Rivera from Mariusa Island narrated:

> After traveling that far,
> they ended up in front of a town,
> (…)
> There are horses,
> there are cows,
> there are goats,
> there are cats,
> there is everything.
> And when the people spoke,
> the Warao couldn't understand them,
> because they couldn't understand Spanish,
> they couldn't understand English.
> (…)
> They couldn't understand their language.
> Now these Warao had a pet parrot
> who was good with languages,
> a parrot who was good with languages.
> (…)
> The one who could talk,
> the parrot,
> was already speaking Spanish.
> The macaw spoke English,
> he did the same with English,
> he was already speaking English.
> When they spoke English,
> the macaw understood.
> And the parrot understood Spanish.
> (…)
> "that fellow is saying this:
> all these goods,
> they're going to give them to you,
> it's said,

they're going to give you motor boats,
enormous motor boats."
The Warao replied.
"We're not going to take them."
They gave them the horse,
they didn't take it
They gave them the cow,
they didn't take it.
They gave them the horse,
they didn't take it.
they didn't take any of the goods.
With all the things that they gave us,
if we had taken all the things they gave us,
we would be just like the criollos.
Because we didn't take them,
we became Warao,
Just like we are today...
But we didn't understand all this,
because the parrot didn't tell us what they had said,
he only told us what they said about the tree that was felled over here,
over here toward the setting sun. (Briggs 2000: 190–1)

Example 8

This passage is the story of the arrival at a criollo town. After traveling very far, a group of Warao arrived at a town where nobody spoke anything but Spanish and English. These languages were unintelligible, and the Warao needed the help of a parrot and a macaw. It is very difficult to determine what exactly the parrot and the macaw represented. Nevertheless, if we link this narrative with the process of language ideology exposed in missionaries' work, we can see that the Warao were also constructing their own ideological explanations about the colonial languages that were surrounding their world, for example, Spanish and English. These ideological explanations did not deem the Warao language as a better mean of communication, or as a structure worse in quality to criollo mentality. Instead, as the Warao became more and more involved in the national political system, they began to conceive of themselves as part of a dispossessed periphery.

The marginality of the Warao is due to mistranslation, or rather lack thereof, which we can also understand as misunderstanding between two cultural worlds. Neither the parrot nor the macaw translated properly, so the Warao did not know

the terms of the arrangement with the criollos. This metaphorical interpretation of the situation appears to be more sophisticated than the missionaries. While the missionaries focused on imposing one language over the other, justifying this action by depicting Warao as primitive, the Warao focused on explaining the situation as a product of a foundational semiotic incommensurability. For the Warao it is not a matter of whose language is more appropriate to deal with the other, but the issue is to understand their social position as a product of a lack of communication.

Conclusion

Since the 1920s Warao language has been an object of thinking for missionaries and government institutions. It has become a kind of fetishized object of description and representation of Warao essence and identity. Translating Warao into Spanish became a necessary step in the process of bringing the Warao into the nation and its magic. The translation of their language was supposed to help us understand their minds, and at the same time it was supposed to help the Waraos understand their new political and economic reality. This was a linguistic movement that was supposed to move the Warao away from their traditional fantasies and into civilized rationality. Linguistic translation was not only a linguistic commensuration of texts. This was also an overall semiotic procedure by which a nation-state—which was coming together in a particular historical shape as magical state by the new discovery of immense oil reserves— was moving its citizens into a single unified political system. The national unity produced by the discovery of oil during the Gomez regime compelled the dictator to bring the missionaries back into the country as a civilizational force. This move translated the new economic position of the nation into a set of institutional forces that surrounded the Warao. But at that time the forces that governed the transformation of the Warao into Spanish speakers did not make them into a political public. Translation during the first half of the century operated in the Delta as a force for transforming Warao language and culture into Spanish, not to translate Spanish and Venezuelan culture into Warao. This is a move that we will explore in Chapter 3.

The representation of Warao mentality through their language became one of the main tropes used by the missionaries to discuss and popularize their "mission" in the Delta. This produced a variety of interpretations that show the dynamics of linguistic ideological stances during a century in which the

Venezuelan state struggled to consolidate its presence in the peripheries of its territory. In this process the missionaries developed a policy of replacement intended to eliminate the irrationality of Warao language and minds.

On the other hand, the Warao showed an ability to develop a profound understanding of this process. At the same time that the missionaries imposed citizenship on them, they developed a consciousness of their marginal position within the nation. That helped them to develop expressive discursive forms to deal with the emotional burden imposed on them. The production of narratives, *hoa* songs, and other forms of poetic expressions helped the Warao to reformulate their struggle in a process that they conceived as a collision with a semiotic system that was at once surrounding them and excluding them. Warao narratives show that Spanish or English is not a better or a worse code for understanding life. They are just the reason why understanding between the two cultures and Warao has been delayed for so long. This disposition to understand their own marginal position is probably one of the reasons why, in spite of the prediction made by missionaries, and the existence of a good deal of bilingual Warao, there still exist more than 35,000 native Warao speakers in the Delta, and their population is growing.

From Warao to Spanish

Translating the National Anthem in Warao

In the last chapter, I traced how the development of state institutions that surrounded the Warao during the twentieth century also produced translation practices meant to transform Warao speech and texts into Spanish and to transform the Warao into Venezuelan citizens. After Venezuela became a democratic country in the 1960s, those practices of translation created the possibility for the development of a public political sphere around the Warao. This non-inclusive public sphere demanded the Warao comply with rational, modern ways of speaking, but did not allow the Warao to become political subjects representing themselves. That linguistic and semiotic move from Warao to Spanish made also possible the development of the magical state around the Warao by opening the possibility of new forms of interaction between politicians and this new constituted public. The Warao were ready to listen to the politicians and to participate in magical performances of development as hearers, spectators, and receivers of political gifts. Liberal democracy since 1958 depended on translating everything from Warao to Spanish, but not the other way around, because the government's intent was to phase out Warao's culture and replace it with Venezuela's oil-based modernity. It would take a new revolutionary regime to change this early version of the magical state into a new form of revolutionary magic (Coronil 2000). Coronil (2008) suggested that with the election of Chávez in 1998 a new kind of magical state, that put the people back center stage in the public sphere, was inaugurated. This new magical state has three features that differentiate its new revolutionary magic from previous Venezuelan regimes. First, the goals of the state shifted from national development to idealized welfare. Second, the illusion of unity was substituted with the ideal of justice. Finally, political devotion gave way to devotion as politics, and I will add the ideal of loyalty to the figure of Chávez. But for as much as these ideals changed the state remained equally fetishized, grounded in the transformation of oil revenue into

state magic. The revolutionary instantiation of the magical state proceeds then through the same infrastructural means but redirects the terms of the translation process among the Warao, producing the need of moving texts from Warao to Spanish in order to create a more inclusive public sphere. Indigenous peoples under the magical revolution started by Hugo Chávez are no longer spectators. They have become subjects of a new form of participatory democracy. This is reflected not only in official rhetoric but also in the translation practices put in place by the new revolutionary institutions.

In order to exemplify this process, this chapter analyzes the translation of the Venezuelan national anthem from Spanish to Warao. It focuses on publicly available videos and written versions of the lyrics to understand the material dimensions of this translation. The chapter argues that the transformation of the linguistic materiality of the anthem resulted in a parallel break between types and tokens in the oral and written versions. This break gave the anthem new semiotic affordances, making possible seemingly contradictory ways of using it. The anthem in its translated form affords indigenous peoples a strong political stance. At the same time, it also affords nonindigenous peoples the production of stereotypical depictions of indigenous languages and cultures. This openness is part of a changing ideological landscape in which overt political exclusion has been replaced with open-ended and contradictory inclusion of Venezuelan indigenous peoples into an imagined socialist society.

Spanish was the only language in which the Venezuelan national anthem could be found in written or oral form during the twentieth century,[1] but in the early 2000s the anthem was translated into a number of indigenous languages as a matter of state policy. As a result, indigenous and nonindigenous teachers, event organizers, and local political leaders can now choose to perform the anthem in an indigenous language at any public event. These performances are always serious business meant to display one's patriotism. But besides paying respect to the power of the state, these translated texts also afford both indigenous and nonindigenous publics[2] contradictory ways of using the anthem. For example, Indigenous leaders can use the new Warao anthem to pledge alliance to national authorities while also indexing their indigenous identity. At the same time, nonindigenous Spanish speakers now use the anthem to created stereotypical depictions of indigenous peoples. I argue that these different uses are made possible by the manipulation and recontextualization of this translated text. I explore how these new translations are used in publicly recorded performances and focus on the new performative affordances of this

text-artifact. This chapter is ultimately about how translation changes the possible semiotic uses of a text.

Although texts have always been of interest for linguistic anthropologists, their study became the focus of particular attention in the 1990s and early 2000s (e.g., Briggs and Bauman 1992; Hanks 1999; Urban and Silverstein 1996). In a separate but related development, A. L. Becker (2000) was calling for a new philology understood as the study of text production in ethnographic context. A number of ideas coming out of this literature became widespread in linguistic anthropology. First and foremost, the idea that particular stretches of discourse can become entextualized, or lifted out of context, and made into text-artifacts that can be recontextualized in relation to other texts became fundamental. This implies that a particular stretch of discourse can become a semiotic, material object. Second, the features and qualities of these entextualized stretches of discourse are manipulated and surveilled in the processes of reproduction and circulation. This implies the existence of gaps between types and tokens of these texts. Finally, in these publicly available texts we find meta-discursive and meta-cultural processes at play. These ideas paved the way to approaches to texts as semiotic artifacts with multiple layers of signification beyond its semantico-referential meaning.

In this chapter, I move this discussion to more current preoccupations in linguistic anthropology with the semiotic properties of texts as enregistered linguistic materiality (Agha 2007; Cavanaugh and Shankar 2017). Text-artifacts, like any other material object, are bundles of features and qualities, the more prominent of which is the linguistic code in which they are composed. When a stretch of discourse becomes a text-artifact, these features and qualities become stabilized so its reproduction is possible and its semiotic properties understood. Translation is an intervention on these stable features that change the semiotic affordances of texts. In what follows I want to provide an example of how the changing features of text-artifacts affect the semiotic ground on which they become meaningful. By semiotic ground I refer to the specific respect in which a sign is related to an object (Pierce 1955). In Pierce's semiotics the ground is a specific form of acquaintance that the interpreting mind must have with an object so that it recognizes a sign as standing for it. In other words, signs stand in our minds for objects familiar to our perception. I argue that translation forces us to get reacquainted with transformed text-artifacts so that our interpretation of these new texts must be semiotically re-grounded. The new linguistic properties of translated texts are then open for uptake by different publics that make use of these text-artifacts in new meaningful ways.

Learning the National Anthem in Spanish

Warao indigenous children in eastern Venezuela were first forced to learn the national anthem in Spanish during the twentieth century in Catholic missions and public schools. Learning the anthem was part of their education as citizens and conversion to Christianity (Allard 2010; Heinen 1988; Heinen, Lizarralde, and Gomez 1994–6; Rodríguez 2011; Suarez 1968; Turrado Moreno 1945; Wilbert 1972). This practice was first established among the Warao in the 1930s coinciding with the beginning of oil extraction and the political and military unification of the country.

The Spanish version of the anthem, known as *Gloria Al Bravo Pueblo*, was a piece of discourse that could be reproduced and deployed in missions and schoolyards across the country. It circulated from Caracas, where President Antonio Guzman Blanco declared it the national anthem in 1881, to the peripheries of the country. More importantly, the Spanish version of the anthem was a text used to transform the supposedly uncivilized contexts of indigenous communities in which it was deployed. For example, it was used to start the day in boarding schools, to be sung by indigenous children in front of the national flag, to greet local authorities when they visited the mission posts and during special community events. Catholic missionaries were completely dependent on funding from the state according to Venezuela's mission law of 1915. Making the children sing the national anthem was a performative effort that indexed loyalty and respect for these authorities. The anthem was also part of a whole repertoire of semiotic means by which the space of the boarding school itself was meant to have a transformative, modernizing effect on Warao lives. In the boarding school Warao children learned how to work as modern subjects, how to form a proper family, and how to be proper citizens of Venezuela. Learning how to sing the national anthem was a symbolic part of this process that followed many Warao for their entire life. Even after they left the boarding school, the anthem remained part of daily life for many people who married and ended up building their houses in the proximities of the mission post. There they would hear the anthem every morning, sometimes sung by their own children.

The geographical spread of the anthem from Caracas to indigenous communities was part of a modern and Catholic semiotic ideology (Keane 2007) meant to transform the Venezuelan public sphere (Habermas 1989), which contrasted, for example, with Protestant religious logics in other parts of the world. Protestant texts, like the Bible, have circulated all over the world to indigenous peripheries mainly in the form of translations into indigenous

languages. This strategy is also transformative—but these religious texts are not supposed to change, just the public context in which they are deployed, as much as the hearts and souls of the heathens (Handman 2014; Robbins, Schieffelin, and Vilaça 2014). Protestant religious texts are meant to reach the innermost heart of the convert through their own language (Keane 2007; Handman 2007). On the contrary, what we have in the spread to indigenous communities of modern texts like the Spanish Venezuelan anthem is an attempt to create and transform the public visible/audible political context, making it uniform and monolingual.

This process has changed as of recently with the translation of the national anthem into Warao and other indigenous languages. The text in itself is still a symbol of the nation-state, but its translation to Warao gives it a new linguistic quality. In its Warao form the anthem has acquired new features that allow it to represent new meanings associated with indigenous authenticity, and to be used in new kinds of performances produced by indigenous leaders and the Spanish-speaking public. I take this translated text to be a public semiotic sign open for uptake. I explore the uses of this public semiotic sign to argue that changes in the linguistic features of the text produced changes in the semiotic ground (Pierce 1955) on which it is taken as a sign. C. S. Pierce (1955) proposed that the process of semiotic mediation requires a vector of determination running from object to sign to interpretant. A sign can only represent an object if it has a recognized relationship with it. This recognized relationship is the ground. The qualities of the object compel and constrain the sign, which then determines and constrains the interpretants or thoughts[3] that are formed in the mind. The translation of the anthem is a change in the linguistic qualities of this text that has repercussions on the semiotic ground linking the new anthem and the new socialist state in Venezuela. The Spanish-language anthem allows Venezuelans to perform and reproduce the nation-state, but its translation changes its performative and representational capacity. This is a change with consequences for the indexical relations that the translated text can formulate. Instead of just representing the nation-state as its object, the new anthem can now also stand for indigenous authenticity and identity to different publics (indigenous and Spanish-speaking). This process implies that the translated text not only represents the nation-state but also has the potential to help us reimagine the nation-state as a semiotic object.

Inoue's (2002, 2006) work on Japanese women's language and Webster's (2014) work on semiotic calquing are good examples of this kind of process. Inoue's ethnography shows how turn-of-the-twentieth-century schoolgirl talk in Japan turned into stereotypical Japanese women's language later on. This

language indexes a form of femininity that is often thought as preexisting this fairly new register, but as Inoue tells us, "Often, language does not wait until the category it refers to or indexes is 'out there'" (Inoue 2002: 412). In other words, schoolgirl talk was instrumental in building the kind of femininity that it was supposed to just index by providing examples of feminine ways of speaking to a specific public.

Webster's (2014) analysis of Navajo linguistic landscaping in Ft. Defiance draws a similar conclusion. He shows how street signs are deployed in a process of calquing a non-Navajo logic onto the Navajo rural landscape. Some of the streets in Ft. Defiance have been rearranged and organized following a suburban logic. This is a process of iconic re/production of American suburbia onto an indigenous physical space. This suburban logic did not exist in the Navajo Nation before the use of new street signs started. The physical landscape of the reservation is therefore not so much represented as it is intervened upon so it can then be labeled and linguistically engaged. This landscape had to be crafted at the same time as the new Navajo spelling for street names. This semiotic calquing is also based on an assumption that Navajos can read Navajo (when most of them are only literate in English). But as Webster insightfully explains in his conclusion, "The signs in Navajo are written for an audience—a legitimate imagined linguistic community—that does not yet exist" (Webster 2014: 405). These signs are then part of a semiotic intervention aimed at building a new public that can read in Navajo, and who live in a transformed landscape. We can imagine a future in which this process will be forgotten and the signs will be taken as naturally standing for a timeless suburban logic.

Birth (2008) has noted a similar transformation in Trinidad and Tobago addressing directly the use of the national anthems after independence in 1962. He describes how the new postcolonial government of Trinidad needed to create the very symbols that would represent the new nation. But the lyrics of the new anthem failed, at least at the start of independence, to evoke the expected sentiments toward the multicultural background of the ex-colony. These sentiments needed to flourish over time. I would call this a case of semiotic re-grounding in which the new nation had to become a recognized meaningful object capable of producing those sentiments in its citizens. Birth calls our attention to the fact that we should not take these sentiments for granted.

These examples compel my argument that the translation of the Venezuelan national anthem is an attempt by the Venezuelan government at crafting a new semiotic dimension into the country's political landscape. We can see this attempt at two levels: (1) in the transformation of the anthem into a multilingual

inclusive text linked to socialist revolutionary changes in Venezuela; and (2) in changes in the relationship between types and tokens of the new text resulting in linguistic appropriations by nonindigenous peoples.

When the Venezuelan anthem was translated into Warao, it became more than an index/icon of the new socialist political landscape in Venezuela. It became a semiotic and performative instrument used to build that very political landscape. It came to stand for Venezuelans for the political inclusion that indigenous organizations earned through their struggles since the 1970s. The anthem became a new kind of text with overlapping but different semiotic possibilities from the Spanish version. It is no longer a text supposed to civilize and reproduce the nation, but one linked with the inclusion of indigenous cultures into Venezuela's political system. Indigenous linguistic/cultural expressions are now embraced by the state instead of rejected as they were in the early twentieth century (Hill 1994a). Through translation the anthem was therefore transformed into an instrument/sign of imagined political inclusion.

This also changed the anthem's affordances understood as "features or properties of the object, the environment, or the context that are perceived as possibilities for action. An affordance is neither an objective property nor a subjective property; or it is both if you like . . . it is equally a fact of the environment and a fact of behavior" (Gibson 1986: 129). In this sense, any entextualized linguistic unit can be perceived by different subjects as affording or enabling different kinds of action in a variety of contexts. And yet, it needs to be stressed that taking a quality of an object as an affordance requires our previous acquaintance with it (Keane 2013). An object's material characteristics, our physical and cognitive limitations, and our cultural/political stance toward a feature or quality all influence if and how it is taken as a particular sign or as having particular potentialities for action. In other words, qualities must become qualia before being object of interpretation and use (Chumley 2013; Harkens 2014).

In its Spanish form the affordances of the anthem, the ways in which it could be used politically and otherwise, were restricted by a strong nationalist and civilizational ideology. As such, every performance of the anthem had to be in Spanish. Translation into indigenous languages broke the type-token relationship of the Spanish version. Tokens of the anthem can now be found in indigenous languages, and more importantly, the indigenous-language versions of the anthem also vary in both written and oral forms. These are new qualities that allow for a new ground, for a new acquaintance with the anthem, that help us understand its use in new contexts for new purposes. But this process is not

without its irony since the translation allows simultaneously for Warao speakers to express their Venezuelaness in their own language and for nonindigenous Spanish speakers to perform an essentialist cultural appropriation of Waraoness.

To explore this process, I focus on public videos and circulating written versions of the national anthem in Warao. I take essentially a discourse-centered approach to these texts analyzing their public use and circulation as naturally occurring instances of language use (Sherzer 1987; Urban 1991). These are texts and performances with online and offline lives. They have been recorded both in and out of the Orinoco Delta by government institutions, Warao leaders, and nonindigenous performers who then post them online. The public constructed through these texts and videos is composed mostly of people who have found them on the internet or learned about them from someone else. I will use these publicly available instances of discourse to shed light on the processes of semiotic change in political life in Venezuela.

Dokotu Ka Jobaji Aisia: A New Type of Anthem

The Division for Learning Resources of the Venezuelan Ministry of Education released the most-viewed online video of the Warao version of the national anthem. The video was uploaded to YouTube on August 17, 2010.[4] It features the government-recognized version of anthem translated by Father Julio Lavandero, a Catholic missionary who has lived among the Warao for many decades. He provided the text in 2010 to be adopted as the official translation. Other Warao language versions of the anthem exist, including some by Warao teachers from the Orinoco Delta. But these other translations do not have the backing of the government. Lavandero's version is circulated for a national public while other versions of the anthem reach only a very restricted local public in the Delta.

The video from the Ministry of Education starts with an open view of the Orinoco River and the lone voice of a girl singing. The girl's voice is the focus of the video. Our attention is being directed to the aural qualities of the song. For a moment, all the Spanish-speaking listener gets to experience is the voice of the girl in a language that they don't understand. These are unrecognizable words imposed on a familiar melody, that of the *Gloria Al Bravo Pueblo* song. At this moment the anthem establishes itself as having a new set of linguistic qualities. The melody calls our attention to the fact that the unrecognizable linguistic material is matching the musical structure of the national anthem.

Then a headline appears announcing in Spanish the *Himno de la República Bolivariana de Venezuela en Warao* (Anthem of the Bolivarian Republic of Venezuela in Warao) followed by the title of the national anthem both in Spanish *Gloria Al Bravo Pueblo* (Glory to the Brave People) and Warao *Dokotu Ka Jobaji Aisia* (which literally translates as "song for our people"). This is a meta-discursive moment that tells us explicitly that this is a translation of the national anthem into a new linguistic code, and that this new code is Warao. This is also a moment in which the Spanish-speaking viewer who is listening to the anthem for the first time acquires a first impression and a first form of acquaintance with the new anthem.

The video continues, showing the Warao girl who sings the anthem with other Warao children in the background. It then takes the perspective of a boat rider traveling along the Orinoco River on a simulated journey into Warao territory. It proceeds to move away from the natural environment back to a close-up of the singer's face, which is immediately followed by a series of paintings. The first painting shows the face of a Warao woman. The second painting shows a bare-chested woman surrounded by animals and a man rowing in a traditional canoe. The third image shows a Warao woman covered with the national flag. Finally, the fourth painting shows a Warao family in front of a traditional house. In the final painting the father is wearing shirt and pants, the mother is wearing a dress, and their only child is naked. These paintings suggest a transition to national/civilized subjectivity. The woman becomes a citizen embracing the national flag and then becomes a mother with a family. The father, who appears in a traditional boat in the second painting, appears to undergo a similar transformation. The naked child is an un-socialized being. His nakedness seems to indicate that he or she still needs to be transformed into a Venezuelan citizen like the parents. After showing the paintings, the video goes back to the boat traveling through the Delta to finish the journey, with the credits running over the image of the Orinoco River. This is the only professionally produced video of the Warao national anthem circulating on the internet.

There are several possible interpretations that the non-Warao-Spanish speakers can be expected to draw from this video: (1) that there is, at least minimally, some space for indigenous cultures in the nation-state; (2) that indigenous languages are valuable forms of communication recognized by Venezuela's revolutionary government; (3) that nationhood can now be expressed through familiar textual devices infused with indigenous linguistic and cultural features. What remains to be seen is what this text is good for. An important dimension of this dynamic is that the new Warao anthem, unlike the Spanish version, inhabits an ideological space in which the relationship between types and tokens of the text is relatively disconnected. This break is due to a de facto

lack of control in the reproduction and circulation of the new Warao anthem. Neither national authorities nor teachers monitor the reproductions of written samples or performances of the new Warao anthem (Figure 4).

As mentioned already, Julio Lavandero translated the Warao version of the anthem used in this video. He is fluent in Warao and has produced a variety of linguistic and ethnographic studies. He is no doubt an individual with a great deal of knowledge of Warao language, and his version of the anthem is accepted by a number of Warao leaders and school teachers who use this version of the anthem without hesitation. It is a version that fits beautifully in the musical frame of the anthem syllable by syllable. It is also a "purist" version, by which I mean that it has no borrowings from Spanish, in contrast to local versions discussed later. This purism seems to go unchallenged by Warao leaders and teachers who use the anthem with no problems.

The anthem performed in this video is then a version composed by a non-native speaker of Warao who, deliberately or not, excluded any form of language mixing from the final text. This text allows the Ministry of Education to provide an entextualized piece of discourse aimed at a public that will find it out of context in the YouTube page. This public is unable to question the linguistic form of the anthem and reproduces the written form of the text with variations

Figure 4 Warao girl singing the national anthem.

From "Himno de la República Bolivariana de Venezuela en Warao," RPAAlter YouTube channel: https://www.youtube.com/watch?v=7l5ylT7bTrE&list=PLGSOK WvPJPy3-5NzkrCtmf4vr2oRgM40M&index=1.

that break any kind of type-token relationship. More importantly the new public would develop an acquaintance with this purified version of the anthem as an expression of Warao nationalism.

Reimagined Lyrics

One of the most popular reasons to look for this video on the internet, as indicated by viewer's comments, seems to be that learning the lyrics is a popular homework assignment in elementary schools outside indigenous areas. Spanish-speaking students and parents from all over the country go online looking for the lyrics of the anthem in Warao. They are sometimes in a rush to meet a deadline for a school performance or for a final class report. Occasionally, parents who are helping their kids with their homework leave messages in the comments sections of these videos asking for help finding the written lyrics. A common answer to these requests on YouTube is that the anthem in Warao is "written as it sounds" which suggests that the oral form of the anthem can be perfectly represented with the Roman alphabet used by Spanish speakers. They seem to believe that they can write down the Warao lyrics with no problems after listening to it a few times. They also seem convinced that writing the lyrics this way will help them reproduce the Warao lyrics orally in school performances after a few hours of memorization.

The Warao language does not have a writing system of its own. Missionaries, government agencies, and particular individuals have written down and translated Warao texts using the Roman alphabet since the 1920s. More importantly no missionary, expert linguist, or government agency has been able to impose a standard written form for the anthem. There exists a written version of the anthem posted online by the government-owned Tourism Corporation of the State of Delta Amacuro (CORTUDELA). This version follows Father Lavandero's written example, but is not by any means an example followed by parents and students. Most Spanish-speaking parents who I have encountered online struggle to learn the anthem from videos like the one described earlier. They then write down the anthem by themselves or copy one of the most commonly posted versions of it (see Table 1). In practice, this has resulted in inconsistencies in spelling and grammatical choices and in a number of token versions of the lyrics circulating online with no connection to any standard type. Furthermore, since the people trying to come up with written versions are mostly monolingual Spanish speakers, they write down the anthem as it sounds to them, producing in effect a phonological and grammatical reimagination of the anthem.

Table 1 Written Versions of the Venezuelan National Anthem in Warao

	Version 1[1]	Version 2[2]	Version 3[3]	Version 4[4]
			(CORTUDELA's Version)	
Chorus	(Missing heading)	Dokotu a kua	(Missing heading)	(Missing heading)
	1. Uarao tuma iori	1. Warao tuma yori	1. Warao tu mayory	1. Warao tu mayory
	2. Kuare asaia	2. Kuare asaya	2. kuare asa ayá	2. kuare asa ayá
	3. Aidamo a ribu	3. Aidamo a ribu	3. aydamo aribu	3. aydamo aribu
	4. Nome nokobuae (bis)	4. Nome kokobuabuae.	4. nome noko buabae (bis)	4. nome noko buabae (bis)
	5. Mojojutanaka (bis)	5. ¡Mojojutanaka!	5. Mojo jutanaka (bis),	5. Mojo jutanaka (bis),
	6. Dokojotubuae (bis)	6. Dokojotubuae:	6. dokojotu buae(bis).	6. dokojotu buae (bis).
	7. A koejobona	7. A koejobona	7. Akoejobona	7. Akoejobona
	8. Nomo ebubuae	8. Nome ebubuae:	8. nome ebubuae,	8. nome ebubuae,
	9. Tane nokokore (bis)	9. Tane nokokore	9. tanenoko	9. tanenoko
I	10. A isanamo tuma	10. A isanamo tuma	10. koreays a namotuma	10. koreays a namotuma
	11. Detabune uitu (bis)	11. Detabune witu	11. de tabune güitu	11. de tabune güitu
	12. Nome jakanae.	12. nome jakanae	12. nome jakanae.	12. nome jakanae.
	(Missing text)	Dokotu a kua	Tanenoko kore(bis), aysa namotuma	Tanenoko kore(bis), aysa namotuma
			(detabune güitu nome jakanae bis).	(detabune güitu nome jakanae bis).
			Warao tu mayory kuare asa ayá aydamo	Warao tu mayory kuare asa ayá aydamo
			aribu nome noko buabae (bis)	aribu nome noko buabae(bis)

	13. Kuana oko **ua**raki	13. Kuana oko **ua**raki:	13. Kuana oko **güa**raki(bis).	13. Kuana oko **güa**raki (bis).
	14. Narukunara**hi** (bis)	14. !Narukunara!	14. Narukunar**á** (bis).	14. Narukunar**á**(bis).
	15. Ma **wa**rao tuma	15. Ma **wa**raotuma,	15. Ma**güa**rao tuma	15. Ma**güa**rao tuma
	16. Kuar**i**kate oko	16. Kuar**u**kate oko;	16. kuar**eu**kate oko,	16. kuar**eu**kate oko,
	17. **Ka** tejo **h**isaka (bis)	17. **Ke** tejo **j**isaka	17. ketejojisaka	17. ketejojisaka
	18. Tane oko abakore	18. (Missing line)	18. (Missing line)	18. (Missing line)
II	19. Ka idamo tuma (bis)	19. Ka idamo tuma,	19. kaidamo tuma	19. kaidamo tuma
	20. Atae ka**r**amate.	20. Atae ka**n**amate	20. ataeka**n**amate	20. ataeka**n**amate
	(Missing text)	Dokotu a kua	dokotuakua. Ketejojisaka (bis). Kaidamo tuma (ataekanamate dokotuakua, bis).	dokotuakua. Ketejojisaka (bis). Kaidamo tuma (ataekanamate dokotuakua,bis). Warao tu mayory kuare asa ayá aydamo aribu nome nokobuabae(bis)
	21. Ka **nobo** obojona (bis)	21. Ka **oko a** obojona	21. Ka**oko** abojana,	
	22. Ka nonatu **tahi** (bis)	22. Ka nonatu **tai**	22. kanonatu**tay**,	
	23. (Missing line)	23. (Missing line)	23. kanonatu**tay**,	
	24. Am**a**rika a rao	24. Am**é**rika a rao	24. Am**e**rika arao	
	25. **H**isaka tane.	25. **J**isaka tane;	25. ysakatane	
III	26. Ka **i**sanamo tuma (bis)	26. Ka **i**sanamotuma	26. kaysanamotuma	**Missing paragraph**
	27. Atae na**o**kore.	27. Atae na**o**kore,	27. ataenakore	
	28. Karaka mo**n**ika (bis)	28. Karaka mo**k**ika	28. Karaka mo**k**ika	
	29. Oko ejobate.	29. Oko ejobate.	29. oko ejobate	
	(Missing text)	Dokotu a kua	Warao tu mayory kuare asa ayá aydamo aribu nome noko buabae(bis)	

[1]https://cortudelta.wordpress.com/2013/05/13/himno-nacional-en-warao/.
[2]http://www.geocities.ws/isla_cangrejo_language/Himno_Venezuela_1.htm.
[3]https://es.answers.yahoo.com/question/index?qid=20110505064744AAsJOKI.
[4]http://www.scribd.com/doc/60916702/Himno-Nacional-de-La-Republica-Bolivariana-de-Venezuela-en-Warao.

In Table 1, I provide a comparison of some of these lyrics as found on different webpages on the internet. Usually the authors of these transcriptions are anonymous. I have selected these versions because they are the most commonly found versions on the internet. Comparing these versions, it is clear that Cortudela's (version 1) and version 2 stand apart from versions 3 and 4 for what is included and excluded in the text. Differences between versions 1 and 2 consist mostly of discrepancies in punctuation. The only noticeable textual addition here is the phrase *dokotu a kua* in version 2, which appears at the beginning of the chorus and at the end of each paragraph. This phrase can be translated as "song's head" or "chorus." In this version of the anthem, it is not clear whether the transcriber meant to include this phrase as part of the lyrics out of confusion or if it was a cue to sing the chorus again. In versions 3 and 4 the confusion with this phrase is even more noticeable since *dokotu a kua* does not appear to be a heading but part of the text itself, as if it were part of the lyrics. We can see the confusion in the added text in paragraph II of versions 3 and 4. Finally, line 18 in paragraph II appears only in version 1, and line 23, which is a repetition of line 22, only appears in version 2, paragraph III. Paragraph III is completely deleted in version 4.

Differences between versions are more pronounced when it comes to spelling and grammatical choices. Versions 3 and 4 resemble each other more closely than versions 1 and 2. Almost all lines show some spelling or grammatical variation. Table 1 shows spelling differences in bold letters. Morphological reanalysis and grammatical differences are underlined. The pervasive linguistic differences and inconsistencies between all these versions demonstrate the lack of a clear type-token relationship. This lack of fixed types only results in "written as it sounds" tokens and in "sounding as it is written" school performances. As it could be expected these oral performances have then various degrees of accuracy with respect to the original Warao version translated by Lavandero.

Solidarity with Syria

Regardless of the accuracy of these transcriptions, Warao leaders find the new translated text to be a useful tool for public political performances in support of revolutionary politics in Venezuela. This is the case with political support for causes like the current war in Syria. The government of Venezuela took a stance in support of President Bashar al-Assad, in opposition to American support for the rebel side. The Venezuelan National Assembly approved a leave of absence

for a congressman of Syrian-Venezuelan dual citizenship who wanted to join the Syrian army. In response many local political organizations linked to the government sought to show their solidarity with this congressman by addressing local Syrian organizations and the Syrian diaspora in the country. One of these organizations was the Environmental Network of Warao, Chaima and Kariña Indigenous Women of Venezuela, which organized an act of solidarity with the Syrian Union of Delta Amacuro. As part of this show of solidarity, they posted an online video of Warao children singing the national anthem in Warao during a meeting with representatives of the Syrian Union. This is a short video[5] showing only a small performance within a larger event. The video starts at a random point during the meeting showing a Warao man announcing the performance. He finalizes his introduction saying, "nobotomo himno nacional dokotu warakitane" (the children will sing the national anthem).

Then some of the organizers set the stage by placing in front of the audience Warao musical instruments used during the *nahanamu* and *habi sanuka* rituals, a small ornament holding two small flags (one Syrian and one Venezuelan) and pictures of Presidents Hugo Chávez and Bashar al-Assad shaking hands. They also raised a Syrian flag in the background. Then Dalia Herminia Yanez, the Venezuelan indigenous representative in the Latin American Parliament, took over the introduction announcing the following in Spanish:

Spanish	**English**
Van a cantar en este momento	They are going to sing now
Como apoyo a los niños,	in support of the children
lo que es la vida de los pueblos Warao	about the life of the Warao people
El himno nacional en Warao	the national anthem in Warao
Para que vean los Sirianos [sic]	so the Syrians can see
que los niños y los indígenas	that the children and the Warao Indians
les estamos mandando un mensaje cantado	are sending them a sung message
en solidaridad a los niños Sirianos [sic]	in solidarity with the Syrian children

Example 9

Following the introduction, a group of Warao children dressed in traditional attire was prompted to sing the national anthem. As they sang, Yanez moved behind them to pose for a photo opportunity. The camera panned out to the left showing the rest of the audience and the video finished with Yanez and other politicians chanting in Spanish *Viva Syria! Viva Venezuela! Viva los Warao!*

What is remarkable here is that this particular performance of the national anthem in Warao is being used as a semiotic resource to construct a political

point of view. Yanez frames (Goffman 1974) the singing of the anthem as an expression of support for Syria's government coming from the entire Warao people. Nevertheless, it seems more appropriate to conclude that what she is doing is a performative act (Austin 1962) meant to produce rather than describe this public opinion. She is calling the anthem an expression of Warao political solidarity making it stand for the political opinions of an entire indigenous population. This Warao opinion is then supported by the new translated anthem, which helps to construct a sense of cultural and political authenticity during the performance. These kinds of semiotic uses of the anthem fly below the radar of concern for most Warao people. These performative manipulations are peripheral to the comings and goings of everyday life in the Delta, which allows these kinds of semiotic interventions to go unchallenged. The new translated text-artifact then helps some Warao politicians to authenticate the idea of a uniform Warao public. This is something that the Spanish version of the anthem does not allow them to do because the anthem in Spanish is a text with different linguistic/semiotic qualities, and therefore a text with very different semiotic affordances. While the Spanish version allows performers to show their belonging to the nation-state, it does not allow for an association with indigenous political voices. The translated text to Warao allows for such association, and therefore for the creation of a newly imagined Warao uniform political opinion (Figures 5–7).

Figure 5 Singing the national anthem for the Syrian children.
From "Frente de Red Ambiental de Mujeres Indigenas Waraos, chaimas y kariñas de Venezuela," UnionSirio Venezolano YouTube channel: https://www.youtube.com/watch?v=7dxYjDnM3dQ&list=PLGSOKWvPJPy3-5NzkrCtmf4vr2oRgM40M&index=3.

Figure 6 Dalia Herminia Yanez introducing the children.

From "Frente de Red Ambiental de Mujeres Indigenas Waraos, chaimas y kariñas de Venezuela," UnionSirio Venezolano YouTube channel: https://www.youtube.com/watch?v=7dxYjDnM3dQ&list=PLGSOKWvPJPy3-5NzkrCtmf4vr2oRgM40M&index=3.

Figure 7 Ornament celebrating Presidents Chávez and Assad.

From "Frente de Red Ambiental de Mujeres Indigenas Waraos, chaimas y kariñas de Venezuela," UnionSirio Venezolano YouTube channel: https://www.youtube.com/watch?v=7dxYjDnM3dQ&list=PLGSOKWvPJPy3-5NzkrCtmf4vr2oRgM40M&index=3.

New Tokens, New Affordances

Shifting now to school performances outside of the Orinoco Delta, where the national anthem in Warao is sung by Spanish-speaking students, the anthem has opened new performative possibilities as well. Children from all over the country

are asked by their teachers to memorize the anthem in an indigenous language and sing it as part of end-of-school-year performances, or in celebrations of indigenous resistance day (formerly known in Venezuela as Columbus Day). Parents and teachers record videos of these events and are proud to upload them to YouTube to show their children's linguistic feats. This is the only contact that most of these children will ever have with an indigenous language. They memorize or read the lyrics for their performances but are not required to develop any further knowledge of these languages. In other words, these children are encouraged to become familiar and develop an acquaintance with the oral and written form of a text that will then stand in their performances for the entire Warao language and culture. These children are becoming acquainted with the qualities of an entextualized piece of discourse producing a semiotic ground on which to interpret the anthem as a text, but they are not learning Warao. They approach the anthem only as a sample of Warao language and culture. The translation has worked for them as a semiotic re-grounding of the relationship between the features of the anthem as a text-artifact and what it stands for—which is now not just the nation-state but Warao culture and language as well.

The performances that these children produce are often recorded in video and sometimes uploaded to online pages like YouTube. These videos are usually recorded in front of a live audience using a single handheld camera or smartphone by one of their parents or teachers. Here, I analyze one such video. I have chosen this video because it is relatively longer than others, and because it shows the details of a public school performance better. These school performances take different forms, but they all have in common the use of the indigenous-language anthem as a form of token knowledge about indigenous people in Venezuela.

Daniel Alvarez

Daniel Alvarez's performance of the national anthem in Warao was uploaded to YouTube on May 9, 2013. Daniel is a nonindigenous child of about nine or ten years of age whose first language is Spanish. His performance takes place in a schoolyard in front of an audience of students, parents, and teachers.[6] The performance starts when one of his teachers calls him on stage to appear in faux indigenous regalia. The camera shows Daniel presenting himself with these words: "Good morning. My name is Daniel Alvarez, son of our land, of the Indians. I will sing for you the national anthem of the Bolivarian Republic of Venezuela in Warao language."

Daniel then proceeds to sing the anthem in Warao following Julio Lavandero's translation. He is dressed in what is called in Venezuela a *guayuco*, a generic loincloth that stereotypically imitates nonspecific indigenous attire. He wears a headband adorned with a few feathers, which are held together with a small ribbon with the colors of the national flag. He also has an armband held together with a similar piece of ribbon. In his left hand he holds a pointy stick that is supposed to represent a spear and wears a small shell necklace. The total effect of his self-presentation (Goffman 1959) is a stereotypical Indian image. Daniel's rendition of the national anthem in Warao has, of course, linguistic shortcomings, but this is not important in this context since no one in the audience can judge his linguistic abilities. What is important is that his performance takes on an oral form that resembles Warao. The written lyrics that Daniel has memorized allow him to perform without any further knowledge of Warao.

Daniel finishes his performance by giving the audience some facts about what he characterizes as "**our**" indigenous peoples. The use of the possessive pronoun here is not random. It is a typical paternalistic way of referring to indigenous peoples that almost every Venezuelan has learned at school. He tells the audience in Spanish:

<u>Spanish</u>	<u>English</u>
En Venezuela existen cuarenta y cuatro pueblos indígenas	In Venezuela there are forty-four indigenous groups
Sus costumbres, tradiciones e idiomas se diferencian entre una comunidad y la otra	Their customs, traditions, and languages are different from one community to another
Están distribuidos en los Estados Amazonas, Anzoategui, Apure, Bolivar, Delta Amacuro, Monagas, Sucre y Zulia	They are distributed in the states of Amazonas, Anzoategui, Apure, Bolivar, Delta Amacuro, Monagas, Sucre and Zulia
Estos Pueblos son los Hiwi, Yanomami, los Piaroa, los Kariña, los Añu *entre otros*	These peoples are the Hiwi, Yanomami, Piaroa, Kariña, Añu among others
Mis compañeros y yo les vamos a presentar un baile sobre **nuestros** *indígenas, gracias.*	My peers and I will present you with a dance about **our** indigenous peoples, thank you.

Example 10

For the final dance he is joined by a group of girls dressed also in stereotypical Indian costumes. They carry wooden sticks mimicking the dancing sticks used by some indigenous groups in eastern and southern Venezuela and Guiana. They stand next to each other in a line dance that bears a slight resemblance

Figure 8 Daniel Alvarez performing the national anthem in Warao.
From "Frente de Red Ambiental de Mujeres Indigenas Waraos, chaimas y kariñas de Venezuela," UnionSirio Venezolano YouTube channel: https://www.youtube.com/watch? v=7dxYjDnM3dQ&list=PLGSOKWvPJPy3-5NzkrCtmf4vr2oRgM40M&index=3.

to Warao, Pemon, and Kariña traditional dances. During the performance the children remain silent but produce twice what can only be described as a stereotypical Native North American "war cry" flapping their hands against their mouths as seen in any mid-twentieth-century Western film. This final gesture sums up a process of cultural exoticization, which draws on globalized images of Indians and cowboys in American movies. The new national anthem becomes, then, in these kinds of school performances a text-artifact that can be used in a process of cultural essentialization, which is a semiotic possibility afforded only by the act of translation and the free circulation of the resulting text over the internet.

Erasing Mixed Linguistic Materiality

There is at least one translation of the anthem done by Warao speakers and performed in schools in the Orinoco Delta. This translation is different from Julio Lavandero's. To my knowledge, there is no written version of this particular translation on the internet, and it does not correspond with any of the written versions shown in Table 1. I found this version by chance in a short video posted

by Fred, [7] a YouTube user who claims to have recorded it in the town of San José de Buja, a Warao community in the State of Monagas in eastern Venezuela. This video shows only the chorus and first paragraph of the anthem. The main difference with Lavandero's translation is that this version contains a few lexical items in Spanish (Figure 8).

This video has a more restricted circulation than the video from the Ministry of Education. As of August 6, 2016, the San José de Buja video has been viewed 22,898 times, while the Ministry of Education's video has been viewed 94,375 times. Only eight people have written comments on the page of the San José de Buja's video, while the Ministry of Education has over fifty comments on its YouTube page. Although I have no further knowledge of how this version of the anthem was produced, the one thing that is obvious is that this translation reflects better the close language contact situation between Warao and Spanish. This version, produced by native Warao speakers, contains at least one clear lexical borrowing from Spanish, the word *cadenas* (chains), in the chorus of the anthem. The lyrics and translation per se are also different although there is no written version available.

This video exposes the paradox that the translation done by a Spanish-speaking missionary seems to rule out any traces of Spanish while Warao native speakers allow the language mixing even if it is with a single lexical item. Lavandero may or may not have intended his translation to keep Warao and Spanish separate, but the popularity and recognition of his translation add to the illusion of Warao as an indigenous untouched language.

By omitting any Spanish-language influence, Julio Lavandero produced a veiled semiotic intervention. The anthem can now be used to create imaginary performances of Warao identity in part because it is written only in Warao. The potential Spanish-language material that is excluded from Lavandero's translation can only be made visible in contrast with other texts like Fred's videos. Without such comparison the complete separation between Spanish and Warao language would go unnoticed. Just like Warao leaders use the Warao version of the anthem to create an imagined unanimous Warao public opinion, Lavandero has also supported the illusion of Warao as a completely separate language from Spanish and of Waraos as completely monolingual individuals. The re-grounding of the anthem as a semiotic sign is greatly influenced by Lavandero's linguistic purism. It is only this purism that allows his Warao-only version to create stereotypical performances like Daniel's. Essentialism requires purism, and in turn, purist versions of texts help produce semiotic grounds for essentialist interpretations.

Conclusion: Translation and Changing Semiotic Grounds

C. S. Pierce's semiosis (1955, 1998) can be thought of as a kind of translation in which a sign represents an object and produces an idea or interpretant in our minds. The sign is then in a mediated position between the object and the interpretant. The object in Pierce's theory determines the sign, and the sign is what the mind perceives in order to interpret. The vector of mediation runs from object to sign to interpretant. At the same time, an object is not represented by a sign in all respects but only given certain qualities with which one is already acquainted. This acquaintance is what Pierce called the ground. Thus, a sign represents objects that we have experienced and recognize by their qualities. These grounds for recognition and acquaintance must preexist the process of interpretation because signs "cannot furnish acquaintance with or recognition of the object" (Pierce 1955: 100). This is another way of saying that we cannot produce interpretations of things that we are not familiar with or have not experienced in some respect. A sign works just as long as we know what we are looking for.

What, then, if we change the qualities of the objects that we are familiar with? In such cases we need to be reacquainted with the object's features to find new grounds for its interpretation. This is what I mean by semiotic re-grounding. The recognition and acquaintance with signs and objects are never done once and for all because objects can change, and signs can come to represent those objects pointing to different qualities and features. This is precisely what I argue occurs with familiar texts translated into a different language. As Venezuela has changed over the last seventeen years into a socialist nation, the Venezuelan revolutionary government has developed the need to change the signs that represent the nation. New translated texts such as the national anthem come now to stand to us for a transformed nation-state (as semiotic object) demanding its citizens to be reacquainted with the new relation (the new semiotic ground) between the socialist nation-state and its signs. The translated text of the national anthem is just one of such transformed signs. Translation in this case can be taken as an intervention on the sign-object relation prompting a reacquaintance with the qualia of the object. The text-artifacts produced in translation are then more than equivalences of semantico-referential meaning between two linguistic codes (Handman 2010; Keane 2013; Hanks 2014; Leavitt 2014; Silverstein 2003a). Once a text is translated, its meaning and material qualities are changed, as are its semiotic and performative affordances. A translation taken in this fashion is always a

double transformation. On the one hand, it is an attempt to find semantic correspondences of referential meaning, but at a different level, the change in linguistic materiality produces the recognition of new sets of potential features that in turn afford different potential forms of social action.

The Warao translation of the Venezuelan national anthem offers a glimpse into how this changing semiotic ground affects what texts allow different publics (Warao leaders and Venezuelan Spanish speakers) to do. In translating the national anthem into indigenous languages, the Venezuelan government is in fact intervening in the political symbolic landscape of the country. The root of this intervention is a change in the relationship between the state and indigenous peoples shifting from total rejection of indigenous expressive forms to its embrace. In this shifting ideological environment, the challenge has been the also shifting meaning of indigenous forms of expression. This has resulted in the discovery by both Warao leaders and Spanish-speaking students of new possibilities for performative action.

The paradoxes created by this translation are an example of the power of linguistic form in allowing new forms of representation and semiotic interpretation. In wishing to create a new socialist and inclusive society, the Venezuelan government has resorted to changing the interpretative ground set between the nation-state and the signs that represent it. But the Venezuelan government cannot control the social life of these transformed and translated signs. The translation into indigenous languages has given indigenous peoples a text that they can use in political performances. At the same time, it has also taken the reproduction of tokens of indigenous languages away from the hands of indigenous speakers. This combined effect has made it possible for Spanish speakers to appropriate the linguistic resources that are supposed to be at the heart of indigenous inclusion. Once committed to a text-artifact that Spanish speakers feel some familiarity with, samples of indigenous languages can also become curiosities that Venezuelan children memorize so their parents record videos to post on the internet.

4

Greetings and Promises

The last two chapters have shown a redirection in translating and political practices. Texts are no longer translated from Warao to Spanish but in the opposite direction, for example, from Spanish to Warao. This transformation has been instrumental in making Venezuela a revolutionary state where a new indigenous public is supposed to partake in a new model of participatory democracy. Mass participation in the revolutionary process, not just political representation, is one of the main promises of the socialist revolution of the late president Hugo Chávez. This implies a change in the politics of inclusion of indigenous peoples as full participants in the political public sphere. This also implies changes in the model of distribution of power and state resources to indigenous populations and other previously excluded classes. The magical state, the state that produces magical acts of development for the Venezuelan electorate, is now supposed to break down the barriers between constituents and state representatives. Venezuelan revolutionary politicians are supposed to be ones with the people, not some dancing Jacobin as Rafael Sanchez (2016) has proposed. But in order to accomplish that, a different kind of dance has to be performed, a new magical revolutionary dance in which the politician creates a link with his or her constituent, not as a representative but as a member of a collective revolutionary force. Paradoxically, the only way to do that is by resorting to the same state resources that created the representative and democratic magical state while convincing the public that something has changed. Since Venezuela's new revolutionary state has not changed the basis of its economic infrastructure, all the revolutionary leaders can do to produce participatory democracy is to invite new political representatives to partake in what ultimately becomes the same performative magic of the state, but framed differently. In other words, they promise revolution but resort to the same performative tricks that only an overblown, centralized oil economy like Venezuela can produce.

In this chapter I address this paradox by paying attention to details of political performances. I concentrate on the use of greetings and promises in political speeches performed by Warao and non-Warao indigenous politicians to show that a lack of promises can jeopardize the rhetorical effectiveness of their performances regardless of their use of other discursive framings. Just as the previous two chapters should be read as the two historical sides of a single process regarding translation, this chapter and the next one is meant to complement each other. In this chapter I concentrate on how promises are important for the Warao because they link political speech with other meaningful events, especially political gift distribution. This is crucial for the new, inclusive, revolutionary magic of the state to happen. Promises create semiotic links indexing the possibility of a continuous relationship with political representatives. In Chapter 5 I will turn to the delivery of those gifts and to the challenges that politicians face around making good on the promises of the revolutionary state.

Promising and Giving

In the Delta one frequently hears discussions about politics among the Warao. Promises made by government representatives are always a favorite topic in these conversations. It is not that people just talk about promises in the abstract but that in the course of normal social life—while sitting on a bench in the Plaza Bolivar of Tucupita or in the *malecón* in Barrancas del Orinoco, or in the frequent visits to friends and family—someone will always talk about some government representative or agency that they have business with. Very frequently someone will report that so-and-so politician promised this or that to them or to their town. These conversations feel sometimes like inconsequential political chitchat and, in many ways, they are. Like everybody else, the Warao like gossiping about politics just for the sake of it. But while I felt familiarity with this kind of talk during my fieldwork, I also got the sense that there was more behind it than meets the eye. This became clearer as I wrote and learned more about the history of the public sphere in the Delta. What caught my attention about this familiarity is that the Warao did not participate in local elections until 1992. While they have been able to vote in presidential elections at least since the 1960s, it was not until the 1990s when the TFDA became a state. It was in the 1990s when local politicians really needed to engage in building up the magical state at a local level. No longer were the Warao, and other inhabitants in the state, just voting for a central government that is often times just an abstraction, but they now have the

right to vote for the branches of government that they have more direct access to. This access also meant more direct access to the resources of the state. Before the 1990s there was no incentive for local politicians to campaign and promise anything to the Warao since governors were appointed. But after 1992 these politicians have engaged in the reproduction of the national electoral theater at the local level. Promises and gift giving from state representatives have come to have an importance that is hidden behind the apparently inconsequential political chitchat that the Warao engage in. I realized that it is only now that this kind of familiar talk can be done in reference to the governor of the state and in reference to local Warao politicians. This is a novelty that is only perceived if we start thinking of the magic of the state as something also new that has become revolutionary over the last seventeen years.

Some of the things that local politicians now promise as the product of this revolutionary magic are government jobs, free motorboats, housing programs, medical assistance, and inclusion in the new *Misiones* (special government programs inaugurated by President Hugo Chávez for education and community development). While listening to the Waraos talking about these potential gifts, one also realizes that the new indigenous leaders[1] connected with the Venezuelan government are expected to make promises just like any other politician. Ideally, these politicians deliver what they promise, and this creates a sense of good faith between them and their indigenous electorate. This cycle of promise and delivery of state resources fits the stereotype of populist democracies in which politicians "deceive" the naive Indian with superfluous gifts (Lauer 2006; Vidal 2002). Contrary to this stereotype, the Warao engage in complex semiotic interpretations of these political gifts. Any successful political speech in the Delta needs to precede political gifts and must make clear the possibility of a committed engagement with the community through the specific speech act of promising (Austin 1962).

But before these promises become the object of everyday talk, they are made in performances addressing the Warao and Spanish-speaking publics of the Delta. By publics I refer here to Warner's (2002) idea of groups organically organized around particular texts. The public performances in which these promises are made are always framed with some kind of introduction. Greetings in Warao or Spanish always precede the events of promising. The greetings are also an opportunity for the politician to index to the kind of event they are trying to preside over and the kind of individual public image that they want to project. I take greetings then as a multifunctional part of the larger speech that frames the event and helps create the public standing of politicians, giving legitimacy

as well to the rest of their speeches where promises are much more important. Interestingly, Warao-speaking politicians use Spanish and Warao language differently during greetings and promises. While speaking in Warao or any other indigenous language effectively indexes authenticity during greetings regardless of semantico-referential content, the rest of any political speech in the Delta must refer to promises of political gifts regardless of the language in which it is performed. Not promising in any language means losing the interest of potential audiences and voters.

In this chapter I show how offering greetings and making promises of political gifts function as a first step in a co-referential semiotic process shared between speech events and acts of gift giving. Further, I show that this process is subject to semiotic hazards (Keane 1997, 2007) and failure. These hazards are a consequence of semiotic gaps similar to what Briggs and Bauman (1992) have called the intertextual gap. This gap is the distance between a genre or idealized textual form and its realization in performance. Correspondingly, the semiotic gap between speech acts and political gifts is a lapse between two corresponding semiotic modalities. The first event is not necessarily an idealized generic form, but it produces expectations of future performances (e.g., promises set expectations of proper gift giving and vice versa). While Briggs and Bauman's (1992) idea of intertextuality refers to all aspects of the spatiotemporal relations between texts, the semiotic gap that I explore here refers to the relationship between semiotic events that are different in kind. As with the intertextual gap, the gap between two semiotic events produces slippages of meaning and impedes complete continuity between them. Therefore, this gap is the source of much contention for legitimacy, power, and sincere connections between politicians and their constituents (Albro 2001).

In the next section of this chapter I follow Charles Briggs's work to describe and situate various genres of political speech in the Orinoco Delta. Then I show the importance of the semiotic gap with examples of greetings, promises, and failures to make promises by three indigenous politicians addressing Warao audiences. The first example is from a speech delivered by a *Ye'kuana*-speaking politician in which her performance of an unintelligible greeting in a different indigenous language (*Ye'kuana*) framed very effectively the promises of political gift giving made in Spanish. This made her speech a successful intertextual event. The other two examples are from speeches delivered by Warao-speaking politicians who greeted their audiences in Warao but did not make promises and failed to fulfill the audience's expectations. The lack of promises in the last two examples was so salient that it jeopardized the otherwise effective discursive

framings (Goffman 1974) in the Warao language. Greetings in indigenous languages are known to index legitimacy, authenticity, and solidarity in public political performances (Ahler 2006; Graham 2002; Silverstein 2005b; Webster 2009). But in the Orinoco Delta, if these framings are not followed by promises, political speeches do not circulate among a wider public and cannot be linked to future events of political gift giving.[2] Greetings in Warao can be accepted as indexes of authenticity and solidarity but not as indexes of a commitment to a sustained relationship between politicians and the Warao. Instead, promises, whether they are made in Warao or in Spanish, are far better indexes of a politician's sustained commitment.

Political Performance and Mediation in the Delta

In South American indigenous languages, ceremonial dialogues and greetings are at the center of political mediation,[3] and the Warao are no different in this regard. Discursive mediation takes a predominant role during conflict resolution in Warao everyday life. For example, Charles Briggs (1996b) has shown the importance of the *monikata nome anaka* ceremony in which internal conflicts within the community are resolved. During these ceremonies the parties in conflict tell their version of what is going on to the *aidamo-tuma* (elders or leaders). Then, the leaders in charge of solving the dispute evaluate what is being said and

> the official must make sure that good and bad words about the conflict emerge in the meeting in ways that enable him to control their production and contain their effects. His success or failure will ultimately depend upon his ability to regulate conflictual discourse that is produced and received beyond the confines of the *monikata nome anaka*. (Briggs 1996c: 234)

Thus, discursive mediation takes the form of a complex process in which multiple versions of an event are taken into consideration in the public space of a meeting.[4] The role of a leader is to evaluate the dialogic process and try to impose ideological order in the dispute. This is not to say that the *monikata nome anaka* has the function of reestablishing social order in itself, but the parties in conflict reconsider their differences by talking things through. Briggs also shows that conflicting language ideologies commonly defeat mediation. This process relies heavily on the deployment of multiple indexical orders, which impact the allocation of intentionality and responsibility.

Other genres of discourse that mediate gender and power relations among the Warao are ritual wailing and gossiping. Briggs (1992, 1993, 1998, 2008) shows how gender inequalities are discursively mediated during critical events such as death. For Warao women, mourning a dead relative is a moment during which intense feelings can be let out. Women are expected to be around the corpse of their relatives remembering and chanting about them. During these periods they publicly speak their minds about their conflicts with other people and about wider community problems. Furthermore, during their wailings Warao women create intertextual links with the words and public performances of men. During these events they not only recirculate men's public speeches but also criticize them and are able to position their own voice in relation to masculine discursive practices. In my own fieldwork I have seen Warao women performing a similar grief about their relatives while drunk. Intoxicated with the cheap alcohol that is sold by the boat vendors that roam the Delta, men and women sing sad songs about their relatives. They accuse others of sorcery or complain publicly about those they have argued with in the past. These complaints are not necessarily performed in the presence of those with whom they are arguing. Instead, they produce these public displays as if they were addressing everybody and no one at the same time. A woman would stand on the bridge in front of her house facing the river and complain in the direction of the nearest town to express her disgust or her anger. It is as if women wanted to project their voices at a distance and reach those who have caused them pain. But as important as this projection of the voice might be, it is the people in their immediate vicinity who would hear them complain and would empathize with these feelings of *sana* (sadness). Allard (2013) has suggested that these showings of sadness are not just representations of internal emotional states, but these are performative events in which grief is produced as much as it is represented.

We can see, then, that in the processes of conflict resolution and expression of public opinions certain discursive practices based on gender and linguistic ideologies mediate political life in the Orinoco Delta. Public encounters with politicians and government officials are not different in this respect. A public display of political speech requires the individual to conform to specific ideas about what a politician must accomplish with their speech. Rhetorical devices such as greetings and promises make political encounters fit certain performative expectations in the same way in which women's political complaints fit specific genres of speech.

In the following example, I present a case that places greetings and promises within broader dialogical interactions between political leaders and indigenous

publics in the Delta. In what follows I analyze performances intended to create empathy between national political representatives and indigenous constituents in the Delta. Like the ceremonial dialogues, the discourse of mediation and the women's ritual wailing described previously, these exchanges put participants in risky social situations. The first example that I present here illustrates a successful use of greetings and promises and will serve as a contrast for the following two examples.

Nicia Maldonado's Greeting

In February 2007, Nicia Maldonado, the Venezuelan minister of indigenous peoples, addressed a Warao audience in the center of Tucupita (the capital of the Delta Amacuro State). Maldonado is a Ye'kuana woman from the middle Orinoco region, upriver and to the west of the Orinoco Delta. Ye'kuana politicians are among the most influential indigenous leaders in Venezuela but are geographically isolated from the lower Orinoco where the Warao live. Maldonado was appointed Minister by President Hugo Chávez in early 2006 and was given the task of promoting the government's *Misiones* or special programs in indigenous communities all over the country. In her speech, she wanted to introduce what President Chávez called the "fifth revolutionary engine," also known as the "explosion of popular power" which is implemented through communal councils.[5] These communal councils are a new form of grassroots political organization intended to replace old and corrupt forms of government with new, smaller, and more democratic organizations created from the bottom up.

That afternoon Maldonado addressed local authorities and members of the newly formed United Socialist Party of Venezuela (PSUV). Most people in the audience were Warao speakers aspiring to become founders and organizers of communal councils. Other local political figures such as National Guard officers were also present. Maldonado's first rhetorical strategy during her speech was to use her greetings to create a connection with the audience based on the recognition of their common indigenous origins. For this purpose, she used Ye'kuana (her first language) to greet the Warao audience despite the fact that they could not understand her. Ye'kuana is one of the Carib languages of southern Venezuela, while Warao is an isolated language with no clear association with any South American linguistic family. Following the work of Graham (2002), I call this strategy maximally indexical because the performance had no referential

meaning that any member of the audience could understand. She performed her greeting in Ye'kuana mainly to index her condition and legitimacy as an indigenous woman and political leader.

Other indigenous people in lowland South America are known to use this semiotic strategy. Perhaps the most famous of these examples are the Kayapo, Yanomami, and Xavante leaders who perform for national and international audiences (e.g., Graham 2002, 2005; Turner 1991a, 1991b, 1992, 1995, 2002). Generally, ethnographic accounts of these events describe the display of indexical signs of authenticity in front of nonindigenous audiences (Ramos 1998; Oakdale 2004; Graham 2002, 2005), but Maldonado's case is different. She is speaking to indigenous people who do not judge her authenticity by the same standards used by government officials, NGOs, and nonindigenous political allies. She is not trying to convince a national or international community of the importance of the rainforest Indians (Conklin 1995, 1997; Conklin and Graham 1995). Rather, she is trying to empathize with the indigenous audience. This display of identity emblems (Ahlers 2006; Silverstein 2003c, 2005a, 2005b) is aimed at creating a consubstantial link with the new Warao leaders. She wants the Warao to feel that they are listening to a fellow Indian, someone like themselves. This is a semiotic process in which Maldonado uses her minimal knowledge of Warao and her command of Ye'kuana and Spanish.

In this sense Maldonado's greeting, like many South American ceremonial dialogues, can be conceptualized as a form of mediation between indigenous groups that are socially distant (e.g., Riviere 1971; Urban 1986). Her greeting, like traditional ceremonial dialogues, occurs between members of different indigenous communities (Ye'kuana and Warao) at the beginning of a political encounter. Yet, unlike traditional greetings, her greeting has a second indexical link connecting Maldonado to the Venezuelan state and with the Bolivarian revolution. Her greeting is not only an emblem of her Ye'kuana identity and a strategy to deal with ethnic difference but also an index of her condition as a leader sent directly by President Chávez.

At the speech event level this greeting showed Maldonado's effort to construct solidarity through coauthorship (Duranti 2003) since it was meant as an interactive event. But she had to deal with the fact that her greeting was performed in Ye'kuana and therefore no Warao or Spanish speaker could understand it. The only Warao word that she used during this greeting was *warao-tuma* "warao-pl" to open her speech. This first word is recognizably Warao, and she used the plural morpheme *-tuma* to refer to the whole audience and get their attention. Arguably, she uses this word to index respect and recognition for Warao as a

new official language under the 1999 constitution. However, not being a Warao speaker, she code-switched back to Ye'kuana. This code-switch allowed her to move to familiar ground without resorting to Spanish.

Spanish is the national language that has been imposed by missionaries and educators in the Orinoco Delta (Rodríguez 2008). As such, government officials are expected to use it in public events. In the course of her greeting, Maldonado used Spanish only to mention place names such as *Alto Orinoco* or *Los Llanos*. She also used Spanish to say *recibí instrucción* (I received instructions) to describe her relationship with President Chávez and her appointment as Minister.

This minimal use of Spanish and Warao complicates the audience's participation in the greeting and mutual understanding. This becomes more evident after a long pause just before ending her greeting. This pause made clear that the audience needed some help understanding what they should do to complete the greeting. Then Maldonado prompted the audience by saying in Spanish, "Tienen que decir eeeh" (You have to say eeeh) and the audience responded, their voices overlapping with Maldonado's as they say, "eeeeh." Maldonado then acknowledges the response in the next line, saying, "*Bien, bien*" (Good, good). She ends this interaction explaining in Spanish that her greeting was performed in Ye'kuana.

Promises in Spanish

After her greeting, Minister Maldonado switched completely to Spanish, changing not only languages but also rhetorical strategies. She'd moved from an indexical display to a referential use of language. This change allowed her to describe the benefits that the "fifth revolutionary engine" will bring to Warao communities in the Delta. She starts by summarizing other programs or *Misiones*, and explains how they fit within President Hugo Chávez's holistic vision of advancing both the building of infrastructure and the construction of new political power relations. In this stage of her speech, she attempts again to empathize with the audience by emphasizing their co-construction of the speech. For example, she repeatedly prompts the audience to answer questions. She enumerates all five revolutionary engines and asks the audience to repeat their names with her. This strategy is similar to the one she used at the end of her greeting when she asks the audience to respond to her Ye'kuana greeting by saying "eeeh." Yet, since she has switched to Spanish, the audience responds more rapidly, avoiding delay and the need for an explanation.

Then, taking advantage of the common semantic ground provided by the mutual understanding of Spanish, she starts making promises. She explains that the fifth revolutionary engine will bring state resources directly to the communities and to the hands of the members of the communal councils. She also describes the benefits of this new grassroots organization as a new step into what President Chávez has called the new "geometry of power" in which underserved populations will participate to a larger degree in community development and local politics. She calls the new geometry of power a gift from the president, and since they worked on the plan during the month of December, she even goes so far as to call it a "Christmas gift" for the indigenous people.

She also promised the creation of communal banks to channel money directly to the communal councils. Explaining this process in Warao was impossible for Minister Maldonado. She had to explain it in Spanish and rely on the rapport created by her greeting in Ye'kuana. She gains legitimacy with her greeting, but with her switch to Spanish she can explain the benefits of having communal councils and communal banks. In Ye'kuana, she can present herself as a fellow indigenous person, but in Spanish, she can make promises of money and development.

Months after the meeting, most of the Waraos of my acquaintance continued to comment on Maldonado's speech. Her speech had a positive effect on the audience. It satisfied the expectations of the Warao public. Even though the greeting strategy was convoluted, the framing of the discourse was appropriate and, more importantly, it was followed by a promise. The focus of further commentaries was not on the display of ethnic identity attempted during the greeting but on the promises made in Spanish. Her display of fluency in Ye'kuana language was well regarded and helped to create an intersubjective common ground but as with any good greeting, it was forgotten while the promises were remembered. As Firth (1972) has argued, greetings are the kinds of cultural devices to which people do not pay attention unless they are absent.

With her promises of communal banks and government assistance, Minister Maldonado opened up the possibility of a semiotic connection between her speech and a future delivery of economic benefits. In other words, beyond her display of identity emblems, she created a referential connection between her discourse and a future act of economic development. This made her speech a success in the eyes of those future communal leaders present that day in Tucupita. It was also the reason why her speech was talked about in subsequent conversations.

In her greeting in Ye'kuana and her promising in Spanish, Nicia Maldonado is therefore reproducing the magical state with a new revolutionary, inclusive

twist. Indigenous peoples that are now included in a new model of participatory democracy are invited to these new kinds of political events to become a new kind of revolutionary public. The magical state in which oil rent is used to produce magical acts of developments is now promised as a direct funneling of money from the central government in Caracas directly into indigenous communities. But this promise is not made as an act of political bribery. The new revolutionary magic of the state is mediated by the performance of common Indigeneity.

Maldonado's is the kind of performance that is usually criticized by most political analysts as populist because it creates political solidarity based on patron-client relations between a high level of the government and an indigenous people. A typical critique would argue that the display of identity emblems and the use of promises are rhetorical strategies designed to convince and somehow deceive the "Indians." But this kind of criticism neglects, among other things, the fact that this is only one part of a more complex semiotic process, and that the future event in which the political gifts are delivered need also to be interpreted in the context of this promise. Therefore, the delivery of the promised economic resources will confirm the legitimacy and sincerity of Nicia Maldonado's promises. On the other hand, Maldonado is not just following her own "deceptive agenda." She is also constrained by her position as minister, which creates expectations in the Warao audience. She is expected to not follow the pattern of coming to the Delta and then forget about the Indians. In order to create a sustained commitment with the Warao, she is expected to promise meaningful things that they can believe will be delivered.

In the same way in which past texts set the standards for future texts in intertextual relations, the Warao regard the promises made by politicians as the standard of legitimacy set for the delivery of future political gifts. Yet, the relation between what Maldonado has promised and what she will deliver is subject to hazardous gaps because time and political circumstances mediate between the moment of promising and delivering the gift. Maldonado's promise made her speech interesting for the Warao audience, but it is the future delivery of the gift that will complete the semiotic relation between speech and political gift giving.

The Circulation of Promises

Maldonado's promise to create communal councils and communal banks took place in the city of Tucupita. However, some of the Warao leaders present in that meeting live in the middle and lower Delta. Some of them had traveled up

to six hours by motorboat to attend this event and return immediately to their communities. Some others consider themselves as being from the lower Delta but live in towns near Tucupita such as Barrancas del Orinoco, Volcan, and La Horqueta. The diverse origin of these leaders was then a guarantee for the broad circulation of information about the new communal councils.

In the Delta, news like the announcement of communal councils and other government promises circulate in a variety of forms. News can be broadcasted over local radio, printed in the *Notidiario* (the only local newspaper), or it can reach the lower Delta by word of mouth. The constant flow of information between Tucupita and the lower Delta is due to the Waraos' need to know when they will receive their salaries from the government (payments from the government are unpredictable in this part of Venezuela) and receive news from relatives and friends. The flow of information also follows the movement of people seeking medical attention, temporary jobs, or those who constantly travel between the Delta and cities in eastern and southern Venezuela to spend periods of time as beggars in bigger cities. The Warao very frequently use the public services provided by local radio stations to send messages to the lower Delta. Though not everyone owns a radio in the Delta, important messages are recirculated by word of mouth until they reach their intended recipients. Finally, the Warao traveling and visiting back and forth from the city carry with them old copies of *Notidiario* in which other people find information about the political life of the state.

My friend Tirso Rivero took Minister Maldonado's promise to the lower Delta during one of his visits to the town of Morichito in the Winikina River. Soon after our arrival to Morichito, Tirso's nearest neighbors and the members of his extended family paid us the customary visits to greet us. They all wanted to know about us but also wanted to hear news about Tucupita, the government payroll and some family members who were living in Barrancas. Tirso then proceeded to talk about the promise of communal councils for which he quoted the words of Minister Maldonado promising the creation of communal councils and communal banks. He framed the quoted speech with the phrase *así dijo Nicia*[6] (Nicia said so) at the end of his account which established the origin of the information as coming directly from the minister. Quoted speech is a very common form for the circulation of political discourse in the Orinoco Delta. The use of quoted speech guarantees that the information comes directly from someone with authority like Minister Maldonado or President Chávez, who are very likely to follow through on their promises. Quoted speech is also a general Amazonian strategy used to qualify information (Basso 1985; Graham 2011) and to index the distribution of responsibility in discourse (Hill and Irvine 1993).

Another interesting aspect of this circulation is that people passing and receiving this information usually finished their interactions with some variation on the Spanish phrase, *Bueno, vamos a ver* (Well, we will see), meaning that the promise, though uncertain, had opened the possibility of a future engagement with the government. The people of Winikina did not simply believe Maldonado. Her promise merely referred to the possibility of a future engagement with them. It only indexed the creation of a link between the past speech act and the possible future delivery of the gift. This cautious reception was based on the Warao's interpretation of the likelihood that since Maldonado is a minister she was likely to deliver what she promised. Yet, it was not an automatic response to a deception, as depicted in theories of populism (Hawkins 2009, 2010). Rather, her rhetorical strategy had been successful in the limited sense of having made the Waraos of Winikina cautiously open to the possibility of a future relation with the Ye'kuana Minister.

Minister Maldonado's promises were fulfilled the following year. In 2008 President Chávez sanctioned the creation of the country's first communal councils and a Fundacomunal[7] office was opened in Tucupita. Through this office the communal councils of the Delta began receiving funds for a number of development projects. In Winikina, the creation of communal councils was interpreted as a confirmation of Maldonado's promises. The delivery of this "gift" closed the cycle and enabled the relationship between Minister Maldonado and the new leaders of the communal councils to stand on firmer ground.

Local politicians in the Delta do not always have Minister Maldonado's leverage and cannot promise as she did. Not every politician has President Chávez's direct support. I turn now to discourses in which the same kind of promises cannot be made to illustrate how it affects political communication in the Delta. I show that a speech lacking promises produces discontinuity between the discursive event and any other future meaningful interaction. In other words, the following two sections present examples of violations of the expected semiotic connection in public political speech.

Failure to Make Promises

Greetings in Warao are far more common than greetings in other indigenous languages in political events in the Delta. In February 2008, I had the opportunity to record a number of these greetings during a meeting called by the Regional Office for Indigenous Aid (IRIDA). That day IRIDA announced on the radio

that a meeting would take place in the *Auriwakanoko*[8] auditorium in Tucupita. The meeting concerned navigation licenses and permits to cut wood and buy gasoline. The call for the meeting was statewide and was intended to bring to town community leaders from every municipality in the Delta. My friend Tirso and I were in a *por puesto* car going from Barrancas del Orinoco to Tucupita when we heard the announcement. The meeting sparked my curiosity and I asked Tirso to come with me after all he was at the time president of Morichito's communal council in the lower Delta. Tirso was rather skeptical about the meeting but he agreed to come anyway. I was a little perplexed by his skepticism since the meeting was supposed to be attended by national authorities and military officers from the local National Guard's *Comando Regional* (regional command). We decided to stop by the auditorium anyway and I got ready to record the meeting. When we arrived, technicians were still preparing the stage and the sound system. They had the Eagles' "Hotel California" playing as background music waiting for people to arrive. Once we settled down in our seats and I had all my recording equipment set up, we joked about the music selection and Tirso was starting to feel that his suspicions about the attendance to the meeting were right. In spite of the statewide radio call, there were actually fewer people than I was expecting. We both started speculating about the low attendance, and Tirso attributed that to the potential result of the meeting. As I mentioned, the meeting was about permits and licenses, but Tirso actually saw this topic as irrelevant. These permits, after all, were meaningless papers and unenforceable rules. Tirso asked me with irony, "Once we get back to Morichito, is the National Guard coming to ask you for a permit to cut a tree?" The meeting was obviously much more important for the politicians who were about to perform on stage than for the Warao leaders that they called to town. Yet, this meeting lasted for over four hours and included some interesting performances that could help us understand the relationship between greetings and promises in political speech in the Delta (Figures 9–10).

One of the first speakers of the day was Fátima Salazar, director of IRIDA and the person responsible for organizing the meeting and bringing people from the lower Delta. She started her speech with the following greeting:

1. *Bahukaya-ra ma-warao-tuma?*
(How are you, my fellow Waraos?)
2. *Nome ama tamatika oko-ha*
(We are really here today)
3. *Ka-monikata isia dibubu-kitane*
(To speak about our conflicts/problems)

4. *Takore oko mia-kotai*
(But now we can see)
5. *Warao-tuma ekida*
(There are not [many] Waraos)

Example 11

Unlike Nicia Maldonado, Fátima Salazar is a native Warao speaker who is at home using her native language in public performances. In her greeting, and actually throughout the first half of her speech, Salazar addresses her audience exclusively in Warao even though it was not a Warao-only meeting. We need to remember that there were government representatives and military authorities that did not speak Warao. She starts by using the common Warao salutation *bahukaya*, which can be used by itself or in combination with the interrogative morpheme *–ra*. Pragmatically, this morpheme compels the hearer to respond to the greeting and to cooperate in the discourse. However, Salazar does not allow time for a response from the audience and jumps to explain the purpose of the meeting. She introduces the speech event to the audience by calling it

Figure 9 Auriwakanoko auditorium (picture by Juan Luis Rodríguez).

Figure 10 Regional and national politicians greeting the Warao audience (picture by Juan Luis Rodríguez).

a *monikata isia dibubu-kitane* (meeting to talk or to solve problems). Briggs (1996c), as mentioned earlier, describes the *monikata nome anaka* as a speech event in which intra-community problems get resolved and power relations are negotiated. Salazar frames the political event as a variation of these intra-communal *monikata nome anaka*. This framing allows the event to fit within a particular genre, giving the audience a sense of what is going to happen and how things are going to proceed. This rhetorical strategy indicates a relationship with traditional discursive genres and establishes a basis for monitoring the intertextual gap between the actual performance and the *monikata nome anaka* as an idealized type (Briggs and Bauman 1992).

In a *monikata nome anaka* people are expected to give their version of the problem, and their speeches are evaluated by the *aidamo-tuma* (elders/leaders). In these meetings people involved in disputes take turns explaining the motivations behind their actions. These are events in which personal problems are resolved with the help of a third party who holds some social prestige and who can convince the parties in a dispute to reach a reasonable solution. Sometimes there are also mediators who hold such social prestige that they can also punish one of the parties in the dispute. So, Salazar's framing of the Tucupita meeting brings to mind this kind of meeting and mediation even though we all knew that the meeting would not result in resolving anything at all. This was an

informative meeting to tell the communities about new government rules and procedures.

Nevertheless, there is a second function of the *monikata* meeting that is closer to what was accomplished that day. These meetings also have the effect of reproducing a particular community or political unit—and that is precisely what these politicians wanted to accomplish. Fred Myers has shown that certain speech events in small-scale societies constitute what he calls a "polity of feelings" in which "the meeting is a vehicle of communion, not so much representing a social grouping as constituting it" (1986: 444). I think that it is fair to think about the *monikata isia dibubukitane* performed that day as at least partially constituting a political unit. Now this political unit is not a Warao community but a particular instantiation of the nation-state. The meeting then was not so much about mediating anything with the Warao leaders but about representing the state for them.

But the moment that this was clear, the meeting became a boring event for all the leaders around us. Tirso whispered to me that the meeting was pointless and I couldn't figure out exactly why. Very soon though it was clear that framing the meeting as a *monikata isia dibubukitane* meant that no promises would be made and that maybe the purpose of the meeting was only to establish the positions of Warao leaders and to allow them to hear and recognize their constituents. Salazar's greeting, although intelligible to the Warao audience, did not transition into promises beyond those of permits that mean nothing in the lower Delta. The framing of the event was uninteresting for those members in the audience who didn't feel that they had anything to resolve with the National Guard. Some people, however, did use this opportunity as a chance to complain about abuses of power in the lower Delta.

After finishing her greeting, Salazar continues her speech in Warao. She explained the reasons for calling the meeting and described the lack of money and transportation for the communal council representatives. In contrast to Nicia Maldonado in example 1, Salazar does not switch between Spanish and Warao during her greeting. Her greeting is an emblem of identity and is at the same time referentially understood by the audience. Furthermore, she manages to achieve mutual acknowledgment by compelling the audience to respond in the course of her speech. This is apparent when she uses the interrogative in *bahukaya-ra* but also later when she prompts the audience to respond to her statements. Contrary to Nicia Maldonado, whose greeting failed to be co-constructed in her first attempt and needed to be repaired, Salazar maintains a referential connection with her Warao audience at all times.

Salazar also uses *ma-warao-tuma* (my-warao-pl.) after saying *bahukaya-ra* (greetings-int.). She uses the first-person genitive *ma-* to refer to the audience. Pragmatically, the use of this morpheme does not indicate possession but a consubstantial link between hearer and speaker. In English this is the equivalent to an expression such as "my fellow Americans." It creates a sense of unity and sameness. Therefore, Salazar achieves solidarity with her audience not only because she is recognized through indexical emblems of identity but also because she can tell the Warao audience that she is one of them.

Salazar is also aware that not all members of her audience speak Warao. Military personnel and representatives from the Ministry of Energy Petroleum with no knowledge of Warao also attended the meeting. Therefore, after she finishes explaining the issues in Warao, she switches completely to Spanish. But this switch is not like Maldonado's because it is aimed at the nonindigenous authorities and not the Warao audience. More importantly, it is not used to make promises. After switching to Spanish, she performs the following greeting:

1. buenos días
(good day)
2. al
(to)
3. a las autoridades presentes
(to the present authorities)
4. y a mis hermanos Waraos,
(and to my Warao brothers)
5. nosotros
(we)
6. le estaba diciendo a mis hermanos indígenas
(I was saying to my indigenous brothers)
7. que me
(that I)
8. que me apena mucho con ellos
(that I am ashamed) [**for the absence of Warao representatives**]
9. y con ustedes
(and with you all)
10. los que están presentes,
(those who are present)
11. porque es una problemática
(because this is a problem)

12. *que nosotros hemos arrastrado*

(that we have dragged)

13. *desde hace muchos años*

(for many years)

14. *y que hoy*

(and that today)

15. *que*

(that)

16. *que tenemos los derechos,*

(that we have the rights)

17. *establecidos en la Constitución*

(established in the Constitution)

18. *cuando se trata de hábitat y*

(when it comes to habitat and)

19. *comunidades indígenas*

(indigenous communities)

20. *también nosotros tenemos una ley*

(we also have a law)

21. *que nos ampara y es por eso que estamos aquí.*

(that protects us and that is why we are here.)

Example 12

Salazar switches from Warao to Spanish only for the benefit of the nonindigenous political authorities. She understands that in order to achieve agreement between the authorities and the Warao, she needs to act as mediator and translator. Different from Maldonado, whose aim is to bring a message from the president and to be recognized as a political leader, Salazar is trying to address both the criollo politicians and the Warao leaders. Therefore, she uses both languages so as to be understood by all the participants.

As Salazar introduced the topics of the day and the public authorities to the Warao audience, my friend Tirso had the urge to leave. He wanted to go to Fundacomunal where the money for the communal councils is allocated. He was more concerned with the transfer of funds to his communal council than attending a meeting in which no promises would be made. In both of her greetings (Warao and Spanish) Salazar had implied that the absence of community leaders was due to the Waraos' indifference and lack of organization. From Tirso's point of view the low attendance was because, like

him, other Warao leaders knew that no meaningful promises would be made in this improvised *monikata*. He told me that had the meeting been about giving gasoline to the communities or improving houses and walkways, or about donating outboard motors, the audience would have been much larger. Many of the participants blamed the small audience on the short notice, but Tirso and others challenged these opinions, saying that "gossip" alone would have brought the leaders to town. Salazar had failed to appeal to her Warao constituents in spite of framing the event as a familiar genre of speech and being bilingual and able to mediate between the two audiences (Warao and Spanish speakers). Her speech lacked the potential semiotic relation with political gifts created through promises. Without promises her words were placed within the confines of the meeting but had no connection with any future engagement. Later, it will be impossible to trace any distribution of resources back to this particular event.

A consequence of this performance's lack of promises was that it was never talked about in the lower Delta after the meeting. Unlike Maldonado's speech, this performance never circulated through the local media, was never talked about in visits, and news of it never got to the communities of the lower Delta. Tirso, who is always willing to bring news of these kinds to Morichito, never mentioned it when we visited the town shortly after the event. This lack of circulation and retelling of the story is just as important as the low attendance at the meeting. The lack of interest in meetings of this kind shows that for as much as the Warao are willing to attend political performances meant to reproduce the presence of the state in their communities or the personal image of particular politicians, these are not the aspects of political speech that interest them. Instead, public performances whether produced in Warao or Spanish must transition into an expected promise. That is what a politician is supposed to do if they want their events to have any chance to be reproduced and circulated in the communities in the lower Delta. Promising is not just something the politician does in the Delta to deceive a naive Warao audience, but something the Warao public also demand from a politician as a sign of a serious engagement with their communities. This is a particular semiotic ideology connecting the performance of public political discourse with the distribution of state resources. Ultimately these performances show that the magical state is not just an imposition made by politicians from Caracas, or by dancing Jacobins as Sanchez (2016) puts it, but these are also a demand of indigenous populations included in the new form of participatory democracy.

Addressing Indigenous Publics

A third rhetorical strategy used by many Warao-speaking politicians in the Delta is to deliver speeches in Warao without translating or switching to Spanish. This is a strategy preferred by Higinia Hernández, the regional representative of the Ministry of Popular Power for Indigenous Peoples. As a regional representative, she is in charge of advising Minister Maldonado on public policies affecting the Warao. She is a Warao speaker who grew up in the Delta being an indigenous activist for most of her life. As a Warao leader she tries to reach out to other local Warao leaders during her public appearances. Yet, as a lower-ranking official she is not in the same position as Minister Maldonado to make promises or to speak on behalf of the president. The following is her greeting during the meeting called by IRIDA that I described in the previous section:

1. A: *yatu yakera-ra ma-warao-tuma?*
   (My fellow Warao, are you all right?)
2. B: *yakera*
   (good)
3. A: *yakera hoko-nae?*
   (did you wake up all right?)
4. B: *yakera hoko-nae*
   (woke up all right)
5. A: *ama-witu*
   (today)
6. A: *oko tamatika*
   (we are here)
7. A: *sanuka dibu-bu-kitane nau-ae*
   (came to talk a little)
8. A: *noko-ae*
   (I heard)
9. A: *diana*
   (already)
10. A: *ama-witu irida-ha*
    (today IRIDA is here)
11. A: *aidamo dibuya-ha*
    (we have speeches from authorities)
12. A: (unrecognized line)

13. A: *oko yorikuare nakae*
       (we agreed to have a meeting)
14. A: *awahabara*
       (first)
15. A: *warao-tuma*
       (waraos)
16. A: *aidamo-tuma-witu yorikuare nakae*
       (the true leaders agreed to have a meeting)

Example 13

Hernández starts her greeting by asking the audience *yatu yakera-ra* (are you all right?) or rather (how are you?). Like Fátima Salazar in example 2 she also uses the interrogative morpheme *–ra* to prompt the audience to respond and interact with her audience. Yet, unlike Salazar, Hernández allows the audience to respond. Moreover, she follows the first question with a second one, *yakera hokon-ae* (woke up all right?) to which the audience also responds. This established a different mood between Hernández and the audience. It is probably just a subjective judgment on my part but the audience seemed more engaged with Hernández. By speaking in Warao she was able to distinguish herself from out-of-town indigenous politicians like Maldonado, and even from other Warao politicians like Salazar who switches almost immediately to Spanish to address national authorities instead of the Warao audience. Hernández was committed to talk to the Warao leaders in Warao about issues that she thought were important for them leaving out the Spanish-speaking minority in the room. This was not meant to snob out the Spanish speakers but to engage more intimately with the Warao speakers. She started her performance with the kind of question and voice that she would use if she were visiting a friend at their house. This was in a sense a way of using Warao as an intimate grammar (Webster 2015), a kind of public intimacy and felt attachment to linguistic code that is made evident by its display in a potentially uncomfortable situation. It is as if she is telling the Warao public that even in front of all these military officers and national politicians they can share a moment of privacy and of carrying business as Warao. This seems trivial in itself but it is not. There is a long history of language discrimination in the Orinoco where the Warao have been excluded from speaking in the national political public sphere (see Chapter 1). Against this backdrop of discrimination, a state representative talking exclusively in Warao in front of other Spanish-speaking politicians and military personnel sends a powerful message and creates

an atmosphere of public intimacy between Hernández and the Warao audience. This creates also a contrast with minister Maldonado who uses Ye'kuana—an indigenous language that nobody understands in the event—and Salazar who switches between Spanish and Warao. Hernández never intended to address the Spanish-speaking authorities, making her speech at once a display of linguistic intimacy with the Warao audience and an index of the new role of Warao in the new Bolivarian government.

After the series of questions and answers, Hernández starts explaining the reasons for the meeting. She depicts the meeting as an agreement with the *aidamo-tuma-witu* (real leaders). The morpheme *-witu* means "real" or "truly," and Hernández uses it to lend legitimacy to the nonindigenous state representatives. This grammatical choice adds a layer to how she is depicting these state representatives since it implies a sense of proper and legitimate qualities. This is a linguistically specific way of conveying importance through grammatical choice that is not available in Spanish. This choice in turn allows the speaker to suggest a specific serious tone and mood for the event and the character of the politicians. Hernández's grammatical choice is then a poetic device that sneaks into her speech to also create a distance between the authorities and the audience. By adding the morpheme *-witu* she is implying that whatever is said in front of these politicians carries a heavy load of seriousness, but she is talking in Warao and everybody knows that other politicians do not understand. In this way she is telling the audience indirectly that these are serious people who will talk about serious business, but she does it in a space of intimacy created by the isolation afforded by their intimate use of Warao.

Nevertheless, at the same time that she was engaging in this display of linguistic intimacy, it was also obvious that Hernández was failing to produce a completely satisfactory speech. Tirso and others in the audience had engaged enthusiastically in her greetings in Warao, but after that it was obvious that she would transition into promising anything to the Warao leaders. She, like Salazar, framed the discourse as a *monikata isia dibubukitane* (a meeting to talk). This characterization had tremendous consequences for the audience's expectations because it also meant that no significant promise would be made. There will be no outboard motors, no credit for the communal councils, no new houses or boats. The implication was that the state representatives were a moral presence but they were there to talk and nothing else. As soon as this was clear, the audience diverted its attention to denouncing the abuses of the National Guard and stating the necessities of specific communities, also a moral move suggested by the grammatical and rhetorical encoding of the event. It was a *monikata* after all and people were there to be heard.

In view of this change, the National Guard officials seemed somewhat offended and probably began to deem the meeting boring and pointless, or at least that is how I interpreted their facial expressions and general demeanor.

Although the National Guard was accused of abuses of authority and a solution to these issues was sought within the limits of the meeting, there were no signs that this meeting would have any impact upon the future relationship between the National Guard and the Warao. Hernández, like Salazar, was in no position to make promises and therefore no political gift or state resources could be expected in the future. The intimacy created by speaking Warao in front of other politicians didn't result in a memorable performance, either. Hernández's words stayed in the confines of this meeting; her performance was not spoken about in the lower Delta. In spite of her use of Warao, she never did what politicians are expected to do in the Delta. She never promised anything. After Salazar's introduction made it clear that no promises would be made, Tirso left the meeting in a hurry before it ended. He wanted to get to the offices of Fundacomunal to inquire about the communal council's money. He was a little annoyed at me for wasting his time with a meeting that would result in nothing but talk. This meeting was not further discussed after our return to Barrancas. No one was interested in spreading the conclusions at which the authorities had arrived. Hernández's speech, in spite of being intimately Warao, lacked the semiotic importance of the speech by Maldonado, who is a Ye'kuana speaker with no command of Warao. Promises are not just something that politicians make in the Delta to dupe naive Waraos—they are also something the Warao themselves have come to expect as a proper political speech. Promises are also the linguistic and performative device central to the creation and reproduction of the magical revolutionary state that these new Warao politicians represent.

Conclusion

In this chapter I have shown that the rhetorical effectiveness of political speeches in the Orinoco can be undermined by lack of promises. In the Orinoco Delta promises are not a deceiving rhetorical device as much as an expected part of any proper political speech. The Warao expect political performances to open the possibility of sustained relationships with politicians by linking political speeches with meaningful future events and texts. This is achieved by the use of strategic greetings and promises, which serves as links between events. By paying attention to these semiotic links, we can get a better understanding of

the relationship between the here and the now of political speech and a broader social and political context in which we find them.

The examples presented here show that in the Orinoco Delta intertextual relations set the standard for evaluating political speech. Those speeches in which politicians make no promises do not circulate in the same way as political speeches from legitimate authorities who make promises. The absence of promises creates meaningful gaps between the speech and any future interaction. This is the case illustrated by the examples of Salazar and Hernández during the Tucupita meeting in January 2008. By contrast, Minister Nicia Maldonado makes promises in a way that fulfills her audience's expectations, making them look forward to future a relationship that they expect will continue through the distribution of political gifts. This is not to say that promises made by high-ranking politicians are believed and produce automatic support. Promises are only signs of a possible durable connection with high-ranking politicians. They are only suggestive of this process, and by no means a behavioral stimulus. They have to be followed by the distribution of political gifts and interpreted as being part of this relationship in order to close the semiotic gap between political talk and gift.

These three examples also show that the display of fluency in Warao as an emblem of identity is insufficient to make political speeches create a durable relationship with Warao audiences. As the first example in this chapter shows, even a greeting in a completely unknown language (Ye'kuana in this case) is welcome if the politicians make a transition to meaningful promises in their speech. By contrast, Salazar and Hernández, two Warao-speaking politicians, failed to make this transition and therefore failed to link their speeches with any future involvement with their audiences. They could frame their discourse within familiar Warao genres of speech (e.g., *monikata isia dibubukitane*) and set the mood of the event with artful grammatical choices, but their performances offered no hope of future engagement with the Warao of the lower Delta. These examples demonstrate that the Warao's involvement with new indigenous leaders is mediated by the ideological demand of continuous engagement. This semiotic ideology pervades the interpretation of performances and semiotic events in the politics of the Orinoco Delta. Finally, the examples analyzed in this chapter call our attention to the centrality of promises in the creation and reproduction of the magical state in Venezuela. It is the promises that are expected from politicians that allow political publics in Venezuela to experience the benevolence of politicians as part of their magical persona. Politicians make promises and they become magicians regardless of the language they speak. I will turn in Chapter 5 to show how this magic is finally realized by giving away political gifts.

5

Frames and Revolutionary Magic

Public agonistic gift giving is well known in anthropology. Individuals and/or groups engage in public displays of wealth, giving away not only things but also a part of their own selves in the process (Mauss 1990). This creates a competitive milieu in which the parties try to outperform each other with displays of generosity in order to create their social persona (Beidelman 1989). These displays create acts of recognition in which individuals and groups construct their public images. The agonistic character of this form of material exchange is based on specific semiotic ideologies that provoke multiple interpretations of these acts of signification. A sign displayed as a public gift is also subject to political economies of discursive practices (Bourdieu 1991, 1977; Friedrich 1986; Hymes 1996; Irvine 1989; Gal 1989). This produces inequalities not only between those who give and those who receive but also between those who can and cannot talk about a gift.

This situation has been recognized for political performances and so-called populist politics (Albro 2001). Venezuelan politicians are constantly using state resources to gain political advantage (see Albro 2000; Britto Garcia 1989; Calello 1973; Celis 1986; Dix 1978, 1985; Hellinger 1984; Malavé 1987; Pineda 2000, 1992). The use of gifts in electoral campaigning and to maintain popularity in office is pervasive in Venezuela, and this includes indigenous and rural populations recently incorporated into the national public sphere. These "populations" are often imagined as the most "vulnerable" to the luring tactics of politicians who use petty gifts to win their support (Vidal 2002). This has prompted a gamut of public interpretations about the "real" boundary between state welfare and the distribution of state resources as gifts to foster personal political careers. Yang (1989) has argued that exchange between state agents and their constituent/clients can take multiple nuanced forms ranging from state redistributive economies to gift economies. Yet, the questions are: When does a state agent stop redistributing the state's resources for the benefit of the people

and start using it to support his personal political career? Can we differentiate economic redistribution from populist political gift giving? This is a similar question to asking the difference between gifts and commodities (Gregory 1980, 1982; Appadurai 1986, 1996, see also 1997). Is there a sharp distinction between gifts and commodities? Is there a difference between redistribution and political clientelism based on gift giving? This is, of course, a moral/ethical question, as well, in the sense that deciding when something is a gift or not is to speak at the same time about the ethical standing of those involved in a relationship. A political gift requires the recognition of the gift as such. The very performative effect of the gift requires, therefore, linguistic framing and interpretation.

In this chapter I analyze state resources that must be distributed among people who occasionally take them as gifts and sometimes deny resources their gift quality. Furthermore, the moral difference produced by different linguistic and semiotic frames is central to understanding the difference between the magical state as described by Coronil (1997) and the revolutionary magic of the Chávez era. I argue that the development of the magical state of the Venezuelan democratic era after 1958 is a process of state formation in which the political and social bodies of the nation are kept politically and ideologically separate from each other. The government and the people were conceived of as two separate entities, and the flow of state resources was always conceived as gifts to the people. Especially in areas like the Delta, where these gifts arrived from the center of power and came through unelected officials, the separation between the political and social body of the magical state implied a receiver's lack of control in the framing mechanisms for the gift. By contrast, the revolutionary magic of the Chavista socialist revolution is based on using the magical power of the state to create participation and inclusions without necessarily changing the economic and semiotic basis of the relationship between the populist state and its constituents. The Warao are now their own representatives and participate in the framing of the gifts they receive. Political revolutionary inclusion has changed the very mechanisms by which the gifts from the political body are framed, and this implies quite a bit of linguistic reworking.

Political gifts used as revolutionary magical instruments are intended to create the obligation to reciprocate with moral support among indigenous peoples in a way that the prerevolutionary gifts did not because before the revolution most politicians in the Delta did not need to be popularly elected. Under Chávez's socialist revolutionary magic, Warao politicians have come to feel the moral binding of the political gift, which I believe explains the loyalty that the Delta has shown to the revolutionary government even after Chávez died

and the disastrous first years of the Maduro administration. I have theorized the Venezuelan political gift earlier in this book as a semiotic transduction of oil wealth into a bundle of distributed state resources, which becomes revolutionary only under conditions of rhetorical inclusion and opportunities for political participation. Of course, this is not an easy and straightforward thing to do. The obligation to reciprocate depends on shaky ideological ground because the translation of state resources as gifts depends on unstable interpretations and non-hegemonic semiotic ideologies.

As I already mentioned, the revolutionary magic of the state needs framing. Why is that so? Because the giver (the politician) is not distributing something that belongs to them, that he built with his labor or bought with his money. They have to convince their constituents that what they are giving away is coming out of their generosity, their moral revolutionary stance. Therefore, that part of them that is passed along with the gifts is not firmly attached to the object but to the process of giving. In the relation between politicians and the Warao electorate, the moral obligation to reciprocate is not linked with particular objects but particular actions whose histories can be talked about. It is not a particular thing that is reciprocated but an action of a certain kind. When in the Delta politicians distribute gifts, they attach their names and their personas discursively to things so that people remember the action.

This is a process that starts as the mobilization of speech and talk, which is followed by distribution of gifts, which in turn is followed by further talk and speech about past gifts. As is the case in many other forms of reciprocation, discursive support is not measured or expected to be given in any specific form. The quality, quantity, and frequency of this support cannot be predicted by the form, quality, quantity, and frequency of the gift received. This creates a window of opportunity for making contrasting interpretations about how much and what form of reciprocation must be received. Here, I concentrate on the gap between gifts given to the Warao and the talk about those gifts. I contend that the solidarity created by gift giving is counteracted by the multiple narratives about the gift and by linguistic inequalities at play (Hymes 1996). More generally, I want to show how the distribution of state resources is not a predictable process that creates political support. I want to show the amount of work required to create the magic of the state and its particular instantiation as revolutionary. This is a semiotic process at its core, not a mere response to economic stimuli. The Warao of course do not just support whomever gives them things, although this is part of how many people in Venezuela still imagine the situation to be. The Warao engage in processes of interpretation with their own moral and semiotic ideologies at stake.

Promises from populist politicians are also not a straightforward means of creating social bonds with their audience. First of all, promises uttered in public are always received with suspicion. The creation of public political relationships often depends on what Albro (2001) calls "truthful indexicality"—or, the means by which politicians create a connection between the signs displayed in their public performance and the regimes of truth used to evaluate and interpret them. They also need to stay on message in order to become politically recognizable to certain kinds of political publics (Silverstein and Lempert 2012). This process makes the use of gifts and discourse useful only so long as truthful indexicality is created. On the other hand, the creation of regimes of truth depends on forms of narrative and discursive inequality. Who evaluates the connection between a politician's intentions and the signs that he or she displays as truthful? In other words, who is in control of the narrative means to create that connection and in which context?

I argue that the transduction of oil into state resources is followed by a second transduction of state resources into speech and speech into state gifts and political support. The agonistic competition between local politicians depends on their idea that the indigenous vote can be won by straightforward distributions of gifts. And Warao semiotic ideologies about the gift also create the necessity of a new gift out of talk.

Bercovitch (1994) has challenged the idea that gifts are only important in an agonistic public space. He argues that paying attention to hidden exchange is important to account for the non-harmonious nature of human society (see also Beidelman 1989; Josephides 1985). Hidden exchanges are part of factionalism and the creation of hidden competition for valuable resources. It seems then that gift giving can create and undermine solidarity at the same time. Different from Bercovitch, I would argue that in the public political sphere gifts are never deployed in isolation from other forms of social action. Discursive accounts of gifts are necessary for the gift to be appreciated and interpreted as creating solidarity. Discursive polyphony (Bakhtin 1981, 1986) prevents any single dominant narrative about a gift to prevail as its only interpretation. Therefore, the chances of the gift to be interpreted as contentious increase as do the multiple possible discursive versions that can circulate about it. The powerful centrifugal force of the gift is not belied by the also powerful centripetal force of narrative polyphony. Multiple interpretations of gift-giving events are always at play in the public and private sphere at any given moment. Therefore, it is not the hidden character of the gift that makes it potentially disruptive, but the interaction between gifts and other social meaning-making practices

that produces the disruption of social harmony. In what follows I show, with ethnographic examples, the process of constructing the revolutionary of magic of the Venezuelan state, and the production of social competition and disharmony in the Orinoco Delta.

The Generator

On the morning of July 7, 2008, a boat from the Antonio Díaz Municipal government (Alcaldía) arrived in the community of Morichito. A mechanic from the Alcaldía had come to evaluate the state of the town's electric generator to decide if it should be either repaired or replaced. Nobody in Morichito seemed to be expecting this visit. From a distance we saw the boat arriving in Barranquillas (a community across the river), and the crowd approached the boat in curiosity as is usual with all official commissions. Then the visitors crossed the river looking for Carlos, a respected *hoaraotu* (shaman) from Morichito.

That morning Carlos had left for Tucupita with his family and said that he would be back in a few days. Upon arriving at Carlos's house, the commission explained to some of his relatives that they were looking for him to talk about the community's electric generator. But Carlos was not there at the moment, and his relatives pointed the mechanics toward the place where the old generator was. Morichito's old busted generator was located a few meters behind Benito's house, where I was staying during my fieldwork. Benito was at the time the *plantero* (person in charge of the generator) appointed by the governor of the state. The commission soon arrived at the house looking for the machine, and a number of people gathered around them to listen to their conversation. Benito took the commission to a small hut where the generator was and let them test it. He explained that the community had been more than a year without electricity because the generator was old, rusty, and could not resist the stress of working long hours. After the inspection, the mechanics determined that instead of repairing it the *alcalde indígena* (indigenous mayor) Amado Heredia would give a new generator to the community. They told us that they had a number of machines in the town of Curiapo (capital of the Antonio Díaz municipality) waiting to be given away to communities in need. The catch was that they had no transportation to bring it to Morichito, and Carlos had taken the only *curiara* (boat) big enough to carry it.

Benito told them that we would try to find a *curiara* larger enough to go to Curiapo and fetch the generator. After they left, we discussed the situation

and Benito suggested going to neighboring towns to ask someone to lend us a boat for the task. His uncle Tito had an outboard motor and I had some extra gasoline and oil that we could use for the trip to Curiapo. In the afternoon a group of young men, the community's *neburatu* (workers or sons-in-law), came back from their daily work and gathered in Benito's house to ask about the issue.

The *neburatu* are the sons-in-law who come to live nearby conforming with the matrilocal postmarital rule (Heinen 1988, 1982, 1975; Suarez 1968, 1972; Turrado 1945; Wilbert 1993, 1996). They form a corporate group of men that undertakes the heavy communal work and forms the next generation of leaders. In Morichito, this group divides its alliance between the leadership of Carlos and Tito—the two most influential *aidamo-tuma* (elders/leaders) in town. That afternoon a number of relatives and supporters of both Carlos and Tito met in Benito's house but the *aidamo-tuma* were absent from the meeting. We had come empty-handed from Cocal in the Araguabisi River because the people there did not want to lend us the *curiara* mainly because of my presence. When we approached the owner of the canoe, he asked Benito for half a million bolivars (in old currency terms before the bolivar denomination was converted to *bolivar fuerte*) or gasoline, and Benito said that we had just the necessary gas to get to Curiapo and that he had no money for the trip. Without looking at me the owner of the canoe told Benito to ask me for seven hundred thousand and to split it with him. I responded in Warao *maraisa, ine estudiante ja, burata sanuka, ama-witu burata ekida* (my friend I am a student, I don't have lots of money, right now I have no money). Surprised and embarrassed he turned to Benito and asked him: *tamaja warao a-ribu naminaya* (this one speaks Warao?) Benito responded: *sanuka* (a little), and then he asked me in Spanish where I was from and what was I doing in the Delta. I tried to turn the conversation to the boat again but by now the boat was out of question. We returned to Morichito to meet the *neburatu*.

After hearing about our failed attempt to bring the boat, Fidel and others asked me if I had gasoline and oil. I told them that I had offered a barrel of gasoline plus a box of oil for the trip. Then they stood up at once and Fidel told me: *entonces conseguimos bote* (then we will find a boat). They asked Benito for his *curiara* and left for España, a community downriver. They came back with a big boat, borrowed for free, and gathered again at Benito's house to plan how to load the old generator in the boat. It was a complicated task because the lower Delta is a swampland with almost no firm ground along the riverbanks. But the tide was high and it helped the boat to get a little closer to the old generator. Then a walkway made of discarded tree trunks and some boards was improvised to provide a path to bring the 400-kilogram machine to the boat.

After some ten men helped to bring the old generator to the boat and tied it up in front of Benito's house, we agreed on leaving at 1:00 a.m. sharp in order to arrive in Curiapo at 7:00 or 7:30 a.m. just before the Alcaldía opens. At dawn we arrived at the mouth of the Rio Grande and stopped in one of the turns of the river to freshen up and wash our faces before getting into town. We got in town earlier than we thought (around 6:45 a.m.). Everything was closed and some of the neighbors informed us that the Alcaldía opens at 8:30 a.m. Since that was the first time in Curiapo for many of us, we decided to walk around the town and see what it had to offer. At around 7:45 a.m. some of the Alcaldía's employees started to get to the building and saw us waiting at the main door. The two mechanics who had visited Winikina were among them and asked if we had brought the old generator with us. We said yes, and then he told us that we were lucky because they were about to take two generators to another town.

They advised us to talk to the person in charge, Albenis Eurea, to convince him to reassign the machines to us. They asked if we had transportation because they could help us with finding him in town right away before he could give the order to send the generators somewhere else. We went in the boat to the warehouse where they store the machines and talked on the phone with Albenis. Some thirty minutes later he arrived and announced that the *alcalde indígena*, Amado Heredia, was very worried about the well-being of the communities and then asked if we would support Amado (politically). Benito took the lead and said that we were all with Amado following Carlos, even though all the *neburatu* knew that he was not a supporter of Amado or Carlos. He knew that sincerity was not what was required at the moment but a decisive pledge to the candidate. The sincerity of the pledge was beside the point after all the effort to come to Curiapo, and Benito actually told me later that he performed the pledge in the belief that the young men from Winikina would support his statement at that particular moment regardless of his actual political affiliation with another candidate.

The first internal election of the newly created Partido Socialista Unido de Venezuela (PSUV) was getting close and Amado, who was in contact with Carlos, wanted to know if he could count on the votes from Morichito. Amado wanted to run for governor of the state, but he was competing against Lizetta Hernandez and Pedro Rafael Santaella (Governor Yelitza Santaella's brother) for this position, which created a very competitive environment for political gift giving. Since Benito had taken Carlos's place representing the community on this trip, he assured the municipal authorities of our political support. Albenis then turned to me and said that the only problem was that they had no form to

give away the generator without having something as proof of the deal. I said I could take pictures, and he replied that only if I could leave a copy in the mayor's office. Luckily, I was carrying the USB cables to transfer pictures and data to my computer and offered to leave copies of the pictures with the officials. This proof, of course, was not for official purposes but to demonstrate to local media the generosity of Amado toward the people of Winikina and to create a sense of obligation in his constituents.

We went to the office and waited until the paperwork was ready. Then Benito as *plantero* signed the documents receiving the generator. We left the old generator on the deck and loaded the brand-new machine in the boat. It was almost noon and Albenis asked if we had eaten anything. Benito said he was very hungry, and Albenis took us to a *fogón communitario* (communal kitchen), a program run by the government to help underserved and impoverished populations with one meal a day. We had the option of eating either chicken or fish with rice and plantains. We all asked for fish, but I was given chicken because fish was the most sought-after meat and probably because I was the only criollo face at the table. My presence was a little odd for the ladies serving the food since this was a place for poor, hungry, mainly Indian clients. I smiled at them and asked for fish, and they gave me an extra big piece of chicken, telling me that I was too big for the pieces they usually serve.

After eating our meal, Albenis took us to his office and we sat around his desk. He took his *cuatro*, the four-string Venezuelan version of the guitar, and sang a couple of songs that he had written for us. We drank coffee as is typical in Venezuela—small, and with lots of sugar. We talked about music but slowly changed the topic to politics, and he asked us again about our political affiliation. We all answered saying *con el proceso* (with the process), which is the common way in which people from the revolutionary PSUV identify. *Con el proceso* means to be in accord with the revolutionary changes underway in Venezuela for the last seventeen years. Followers of the PSUV identify the Bolivarian revolution with an ongoing process of change whose goals Chávez has loosely identified with the development of a full socialist system.

Albenis asked us if we had gasoline to go back to Winikina. Benito said no, a statement I did not contest since it was my gasoline that we were using. Benito said that we needed two barrels of gasoline mixed with oil to go back. Albenis opened his drawer and wrote an order for the gasoline station. He told us to take the order with us and fill up the two barrels. Amado Heredia would pay for it. Albenis looked at us and said, "I know you only need one barrel but take two in the name of Amado and the revolution." Benito told me later that

it would be enough to replace my barrel to go back to Morichito, and since we would go with the current we would have an extra tank (a fraction of a barrel) to sell in Winikina. In the lower Delta the price of gasoline is much higher than in Barrancas del Orinoco, Volcan, or Tucupita. The gift of extra gasoline was greatly appreciated by everybody, including myself. We went back to Morichito that night and decided to wait until next morning to put the generator in its place. Next morning at around 7:00 a.m. there was great commotion in the community. Everybody wanted to see the new machine, and everybody had different ideas about its installation and maintenance. Benito told the people who had gathered around that they had to wait until the mechanics from the Alcaldía arrived because they knew how to proceed. Most people went back to their daily activities, but a group of men stayed with us. Benito asked me to help him reading the manual because it was in Spanish and English. We sat in front of his house and went over it, but I recommended waiting for the mechanics to proceed since I was not sure that the cables and electric infrastructure in the community were properly installed (Figure 11).

After some morning work a group of men returned to town and decided to move the generator to its place. Using the same strategy used to load the old machine in the *curiara*, they carried the generator to land. Meanwhile the

Figure 11 Young men carrying the old generator (picture by Juan Luis Rodríguez).

mechanics arrived in town and a big crowd gathered around the small hut. The mechanics explained how to fill up the tanks and what proportion of oil to gasoline must be used. They also taught us how the indicators worked and how long the generator could work at a time. Then they installed all the cables and put everything in place. Since I was helping gathering information and translating the manual, Benito asked me to start the machine for the first time. I turned the ignition key and as the machine started roaring, a woman from the crowd shouted, referring to me as "jotarao plantero carajo!!" (nonindigenous generator's operator, damn it!!!), and everybody started laughing and shouting.

The Return of Carlos

That night Morichito had electricity for the first time in more than a year. The opportunity called for a party with music from radios and *equipos de sonido* (CD and cassette players). Beer and rum were bought in Araguabisi, and some of the *bongueros* (boat vendors) that heard the gossip about the generator came to town to sell the local rum, which is sold at the equivalent of 50 cents per liter. The mechanics had left enough gas for the generator to work for a couple of months and everybody was eager to get drunk, sing, and have a good time. As the night progressed and people talked about the trip to Curiapo, I started to realize that the gift of the generator was a lot more than the source of happiness and cohesion. I was about to discover the polyphonic and unequal narrative that this political gift was creating in Morichito (Figure 12).

The gift had arrived at an odd moment. Amado Heredia's main supporter, Carlos, was not in the community when the mechanics were sent. That called for Benito, who was a supporter of Lizeta Hernandez (the other aspiring candidate in the PSUV), to receive the generator and bring it to the community. In the group that I was with that night, the gossip was that Carlos wanted the generator to serve only his part of town unless people joined the cause of Amado Heredia. It was claimed that Carlos had said that the generator was only for Amado's people. Those who supported Lizettica, as they called her during the campaign, had to pledge alliance to Carlos if they wanted electricity. Another item of hearsay was that Carlos had threatened to stop curing those who supported Lizettica. He was the only one with shamanic training in the community and therefore the first person to be asked for *hoa* curing songs if someone falls ill or injured.

After hearing the gossip, I realized the deep division that this particular gift could cause in Morichito. Carlos was out of town, but he would soon come back

Figure 12 *Neburatu* receiving the gift from Amado Heredia (picture by Juan Luis Rodríguez).

and he would see that the generator that was supposed to be under his control had already been received and was working for the entire community. I then also realized that Benito had been avoiding going to Curiapo in the first place. That is why after one rejection in Cocal he never suggested going to España to find a boat, even though his in-laws are from that town. Clearly, he knew he could borrow a big *curiara* for free there. But the *neburatu* who are not in positions of leadership did not care about this conflict of interest and were eager to go to España and happy to have the generator in the community as soon as possible (Figure 13).

Next morning, I asked Benito: *maraisa Carlos se va a arrechar?* (My friend, is Carlos going to be mad?). He responded: *no sé* (I don't know). He then said: "I think I will call a meeting with the whole community to discuss this issue. When Carlos comes back, I will talk to him." In the afternoon, Carlos came back to town. We saw the big canoe that was a gift from Governor Santaella to the community crossing the river in front of us and stopping in front of Carlos's house. Almost immediately, his relatives and friends came to greet him and talk to him. The *curiara*, as usual, continued on its way dropping other people around the town in front of their houses.

Figure 13 With the new generator in Morichito (picture by Juan Luis Rodríguez).

After a couple of hours, we saw a *curiara* approaching Benito's house. It was Carlos and some of his sons-in-laws. They had come to see the new generator. He greeted us with a friendly smile. I thought he was taking the situation very diplomatically since I also was involved, and I had given him gifts of tobacco and was supposed to bring him some bells from Caracas that he wanted to add to his shamanic paraphernalia. We sat in front of the house and told the story of the mechanics and the trip to Curiapo. Then he asked to see the machine and we went to the back of the house and showed him all the details of its functioning and maintenance. Carlos wanted to reassert that it was *Amado y su gente* (Amado and his people) who brought the machine. He said to me in Spanish: "I am friends with Amado I have the list of people who are going to vote for him." Then he asked Benito: "Are you with us?" And Benito responded: "Yes, I will vote for Amado." He asked us to stop by his house later to talk a little

more. His nephew wanted to be *plantero* and he wanted to discuss the situation with Benito.

When Carlos left, Benito came to me and told me: *yo quiero hacer reunión con la comunidad* (I want to have a meeting with the whole community). He wanted to meet with the whole community because he was the *plantero* and there was only one generator. He was worried that the election of Amado Heredia would cost him the job that has been his main source of income for almost twenty years. So, the next day we went to Carlos's house. Benito praised Carlos for being the most knowledgeable *aidamo* in Morichito and for being a very intelligent man who has training as a *hoarotu* and learned Spanish by himself since he had almost no schooling. Carlos asked us again about our trip to Curiapo and asked me about how my work in the community was going. Then he brought out some of his papers, some certificates that demonstrated that he had participated in government-sponsored performances in Caracas and invitations by the Ministry of Education to travel abroad to perform Warao folk songs. Among his latest appearances was at the Pan-American Meeting of Anti-Imperialist Indigenous Peoples of the Americas held in Cumana and Puerto la Cruz in eastern Venezuela. He told us about the food, the accommodations, and more importantly, about all the different indigenous people that were there. With great pleasure he told us about all the Brazilian, Venezuelan, and Colombian indigenous representatives. But he complained about the presence of some North American Indians who did not speak like true Indians; they were always speaking English, they were like gringos. Of course, in an anti-imperialist congress all English speakers became metonymic signs of imperial power.

After the greetings and exchange of stories Carlos brought out another set of papers. The papers were handwritten lists and signatures. He said: "So you brought the generator, are you with Amado?" We both said yes again. His question was directed also at me, which brought to my attention that doing ethnography about political life did not exempt me from my voting duties. And since I was involved in bringing the generator, I was also responsible for voting and participating politically. This broke the illusion of hiding behind my position of academic researcher. Despite my coming from an American institution, my Warao friends always reminded me that I am a criollo and could also vote. Unlike the ethnographers, botanists, and geographers from the United States who had gone to Delta, I had a different positioning. The rules of not participating in local political issues did not apply to me.

Carlos showed me the list and said, "Here are the people that will vote for Amado, do you have a pen?" I said yes, and he asked me to write down my name

and Benito's and then asked Benito how many of his people were supposed to vote. He said: *mi mujer y yo solamente* (only my wife and I). Obviously, the list was not official; it was a document between Carlos and the people of Amado Heredia. Carlos explained to us that during the last election Yelitza Santaella had given away 100,000 bolivars for each person voting for her. But Carlos would give 200,000 bolivars for those in the lists who voted for Amado to become candidate for governor. The list was the only text-like instrument that linked people to this form of underground gift giving. I asked if I would receive the money too, and he smiled and said, "Yes of course now you are in the list." Most people related to Carlos desired to be on the list to pledge alliance and get the gift after voting. Other people like Benito and I were included on the list because of circumstances beyond our control. These circumstances made clear to me that we had no alternative in that context. We had to sign, which made us by virtue of these specific discursive inequalities the indebted receiver of an unexpected political gift. Carlos, the rightful receiver, did not allow us to construct alternative narratives of the gift, at least in that particular context. By the same token, in Curiapo Albenis talked about Amado's generosity and we had to agree in the public display of this discourse because we were in no capacity to contest his speech in front of the *neburatu* (Figure 14).

Figure 14 Politicians distributing piles of money to gain political favors (picture by Juan Luis Rodríguez).

The list was Amado's attempt to count who was with him but also to reassure his political base that more gifts would come after his election and make them feel indebted to him. The list was his main instrument of communication in the agonistic process of offering more and better gifts than other candidates and for making the people in general become *compañeros* or *camaradas* as they are called in the internal structure of the PSUV. Putting your name on the list creates a sense of obligation and commitment even though everybody knows that the list is not binding, and nobody can prove whether you voted for a given candidate or not. It is only an attempt to strengthen and make more truthful the indexical power of the political gift. These lists have a long history in Venezuelan politics going back to the beginnings of the 1960s party houses (*casas del partido*) where people found their names in lists of political supporters who could receive gifts from winning candidates. Nevertheless, these lists are not a coercive mechanism and do not prevent the promised gifts from being interpreted in multiple ways by different political actors. The lists are more a moral contract put on paper than political leverage to be used against voters.

After writing down our names we started discussing the more pressing issue of who will become the *plantero* for the new generator. Benito had been the *plantero* for the last two decades. However, in the last couple of years he has been living in Barrancas because of internal fights in the community involving his daughter and wife, and because he became the president of the communal council as well, requiring him to be in touch with government institutions. Nevertheless, Benito's unintended move to pick up the generator gave him the upper hand since he signed all the documentation to receive it. Carlos then wanted to reach an agreement with Benito to share the position of *plantero* with his nephew. Benito in a bold move told Carlos that if Amado wins he must be able to offer his nephew a position through the Alcaldía. Benito's contract is with the governor. Therefore, they would be working for different branches of the government. Carlos agreed that it could be a good solution and we left.

That night Benito and I sat on the dock in front of his house, and he told me that he still did not feel safe about his position as *plantero*. He wanted to raise the issue in a discussion with the whole community to talk about the situation and settle who was to be in charge of the generator. I said that we should talk to Carlos about such a meeting. Next morning, we went to talk to him, and he agreed on a meeting for late in the afternoon that same day. He said that we needed to wait until the people (mainly the young men, the *neburatu*) returned from work to meet in his house. In the late afternoon we took Benito's *curiara* to

Carlos's house passing in front of many houses, so people saw us traveling to the site of the meeting. Little by little people who were interested started to show up.

In the beginning, people gathered around Carlos and Benito who were sitting in the front house (which is in fact the nurse's office) chatting about the communal council's upcoming projects and the payments for the government workers. When Carlos thought that there were enough people, we moved to the interior of the house, leaving the women behind and creating two de facto groups separated by gender. The men were supposed to discuss the issue of the *plantero* while the women had their own unspecified agenda. The women were not supposed to participate directly in the meeting, but it was obvious that they gathered close enough to overhear the conversation. This is a typical strategy used by Warao women who do not participate directly in public political issues but influence their husbands in private conversations. In this case the women were passive participants of the event, and most likely after overhearing the meeting they discussed it with their husbands and family members in private.

Carlos then took the first turn and explained to the audience the motive for the meeting. Aware of my presence he also said to the audience that I was there to record the event and bring the words to Caracas with me. In a way, the fact that the meeting was recorded gave it legitimacy. Carlos then explained the issue about the *plantero* position and told the audience that the best solution was to have two *planteros* paid by different branches of the government so that when Benito was in town, he would be in charge, and when Benito is in Barrancas, Carlos's nephew would be in charge. Then it was Benito's turn to talk and he explained how he wanted to share responsibilities only if Carlos's nephew was on the Alcaldía payroll and not with the governor. It would also allow Benito to take care of the communal council issues in Tucupita with no worries about the functioning of the generator in his absence. This meeting repeated in essence the private talk between Carlos and Benito, but this time in the public arena constructed by the event. The meeting was more about the public presentation of the issues and the social positioning of the political actors than about actually resolving any problem (Myers 1986). It was not actually meant to be a deliberation, but a public affirmation of the discussion previously held by the two community leaders.

In the discussion about this issue, the community not only dealt with the multiple versions of the gift but also created the necessity for a second gift, for example, a new position for a *plantero*. This position did not exist yet, but after both parties agreed that they needed a second *plantero*, Carlos decided that they should ask Amado Heredia for it. In the past this position was a political gift that

the AD party had given Benito. It had consolidated Benito's position within the community. On multiple occasions he had narratively linked this gift with the rise and fall of one of the most prominent politicians in the Delta's recent political history, Emery Mata Millán. By asking Amado for a new position, Carlos would be expecting a similar treatment for his nephew. In the next section, to understand how a job position is constructed as a gift, I will use Benito's narrative accounts linking his position as *plantero* with the political career and the construction of the public political self (Duranti 2006) of ex-governor Emery Mata Millán.

Emery Mata Millán

In July 2004, I was doing fieldwork in Barrancas del Orinoco between the Orinoco Delta and the State of Monagas in eastern Venezuela. After a few days of interviewing people in front of the town's old church, I heard Benito relating the story of his appointment as *plantero*. The first thing that caught my attention was that in order to talk about his appointment, he related also the full story of the rise and fall of ex-governor Emery Mata Millán. Benito's narrative about Emery was a narrative account of a political gift (Benito's position as *plantero* in Winikina) that linked his life story with the development of the political public sphere in the Orinoco Delta. Furthermore, the narrative was delivered with some poetic characteristics typical of traditional narrative genres such as constant repetition and parallelism, and accounts of movements through the geographical space of Delta in steps to describe how different activities took place over time. In narrating the rise and fall of Emery Mata Millán, Benito recounted how a political gift produced in him a sense of obligation and a particular form of subjectivity that can be associated with a wider process of building political publics in the Delta.

Revisiting this narrative from 2004 clarified for me the importance of the discussion between Carlos and Benito in 2008. In talking about the generator and the position as *plantero*, they were talking about received gifts and the duty of reciprocation but also about political subjectivity and identity. The relation between these two gifts had turned complicated. What connects these two gifts in 2004 and 2008 is the poetic and discursive work of framing the gift as such, and the role of this framing in creating a certain political subjectivity oriented toward a competitive agonistic public sphere. This has lately turned into a revolutionary, socialist process. In order for us to understand how a political gift is talked about, it is useful to turn to the narrative example provided by Benito.

That July in Barrancas del Orinoco, I asked him to tell me the story of Emery Mata Millán. Here is a translation from Spanish to English of his account. In this transcription JL refers to Juan Luis (the author), T refers to Benito. All text in brackets, for example, [text], shows commentary about the poetics and broader context of the narrative:

1. JL: Ok Benito tell me the story of Emery Mata Millán
2. T: Ok, from the beginning?
3. JL: yes because I was not recording.
4. T: Ok.
5. T: you know that when there is an election then there is campaigning.
6. T: the campaign in Winikina,
7. T: since there are no roads,
8. T: well,
9. T: there are big boats with two engines that can carry twenty people
10. T: or twenty-five people
11. T: or some carry thirty people.
    [Note the parallelism of lines 9–11]
12. T: Then, there are some three or four boats.
13. T: You know that [referring to the author's knowledge of local politics]
14. T: They are from the Acción Democrática party, COPEI and MAS.
15. T: Well then,
16. T: each one has its candidate.
17. T: Then I was with Acción Democrática.
18. T: Of course, we campaigned for them.
19. T: And, the election was on December 3rd.
20. JL: that was in nineteen eighty…
21. T: Ok that was in nineteen eighty-eight.
22. T: Well,
23. T: Emery Mata Millán won in [nineteen] ninety-eight.
    [Note the parallelism in lines 21–23]

24. T: In January, I came from there [Winikina] to here [Barrancas].
    [Benito moves the narrative across space from the Winikina Rivers to a port at the fringes of the Delta]

25. T: I got to Barrancas in January.
26. T: And then I made an errand.
27. T: And, I got to Tucupita.

28. T: I went into the party house.
29. T: Well,
30. T: Acción Democrática party.
     [Lines 25–30 repeated the same move from Winikina to Barrancas and
     Tucupita adding some poetic parallelism]

31. T: There they looked up my name in the forms.
32. T: Well,
33. T: it showed up.
34. T: I was with Acción Democrática.
35. T: Then they told me:
36. T: "It is true.
37. T: You are with us"
     [Lines 36–37 are the first example of quoted speech referring to the
     granting of a political gift. The quoted speech legitimizes the gift and is
     an index of the truthfulness of a past promise]

38. T: Then they nominated me.
39. T: They gave me a nomination.
40. T: They sent me to Obras Públicas.
41. T: In Obras Públicas there was an engineer who they called Farquimer.
     [Lines 38–41 move the narrative from the party house to the Obras
     Públicas's building where the political gift is given]

42. T: Well then,
43. T: He gave me a nomination.
44. T: He told me:
45. T: "Ok I will nominate you for a job
46. T: Go back [to Winikina] and work there"
     [Lines 40–43 move the narrative back to the rivers, from Barrancas and
     Tucupita to Winikina. The quoted speech in lines 45–46 is an index of the
     truthfulness of the promised gift coming from a state representative]

47. T: Then,
48. T: Since there was no *plantero* then I was given a position as *plantero*.
49. T: Well,
50. T: That is how in the month of March then I listened on the radio.
51. T: They were paying the workers,
52. T: the *planteros*,
53. T: the new ones,

54. T: Those who were nominated.

    [Lines 50–54 refer to hearsay events. Although not a direct quote from the radio, it describes how the knowledge of the realization of the gift was obtained. Note also the poetic parallelism in lines 51–54.]

55. T: Then I came from there [Winikina].

56. T: I got here to Barrancas.

57. T: I went to Tucupita.

58. T: I went into the governor's office.

    [Note the three-step movement from Winikina to Barrancas and to Tucupita]

59. T: Well,

60. T: Where the payroll is,

61. T: where they show the payroll

62. T: The name of the workers.

63. T: Well,

64. T: They searched for my name.

65. T: It was there:

66. T: "Benito Rivero."

    [Line 66 shows quoted speech legitimating the delivery of the gift]

67. T: Here it is [his name written down],

68. T: You are going to be paid a month,

69. T: one entire month.

70. T: Well,

71. T: Then they paid me.

72. T: Half month was two thousand two hundred and fifty.

73. T: A month was four thousand five hundred.

74. T: Ok,

75. T: Emery Mata Millán was still with Acción Democrática.

76. T: Well,

77. T: his term was I don't know how many years.

78. T: It seems it was four years.

79. T: After that,

80. T: When an election was getting closer then Emery Mata Millán quit Acción Democrática.

81. T: Then he joined COPEI.

82. T: Then Emery also founded a party.

83. T: It is the Meri party.
84. T: Then, me too,
85. T: I was with Acción Democrática.
86. T: Then since Emery gave me that job
87. T: I also quit Acción Democrática and joined COPEI.

[Lines 67–87 describe how after the delivery of the political gift Benito became Emery's supporter and indebted to him. He then constructs a parallel movement of Emery and himself from one political party to another]

88. T: Well, ok like that.
89. T: Then there were elections again and he [Emery] won.
90. T: He won again.
91. T: Emery Mata Millán with COPEI.
92. T: Then Emery governed for four more years.
93. T: Then four years Emery worked
94. T: Four more years of Emery.

[Lines 89–94 show repetition of the same information with different grammatical formations for emphasis]

95. T: Then there again
96. T: Emery ran for governor.
97. T: But this time it was an alliance,
98. T: Acción Democrática, COPEI and some other party.
99. T: Then he won the elections again.
100. T: Emery Mata Millán won the election for governor three times.
101. T: Well,
102. T: after working for two years.
103. T: Then I don't know how he was behaving.
104. T: Maybe he was stealing money.
105. T: I don't know how.
106. T: Then, you know that the politicians
107. T: This Yelitza Santaella was like a council woman for MAS.
108. T: Well,
109. T: Then Emery Mata Millán
110. T: Maybe he was stealing money from the state.
111. T: Then in the press it appeared:
112. T: "Look Emery Mata Millán is stealing one thousand million bolivars from the people of the Delta."

113. T: Therefore, we needed to sack him.

[Lines 95–113 describe how Emery Mata was removed from office. This section shows Benito's use of the adverb "maybe" in lines 104 and 110 to mark his uncertainty about the events. Then in line 112 he quotes the newspaper's headline to assert the certainty of Emery Mata's guilt and move safely in line 113 to describe how he was removed rightfully from office]

114. T: Well,

115. T: Already since Hugo Chávez

116. T: I think that he already was president

117. T: It was in the month of December.

118. T: I think that well already this council woman,

119. T: This woman,

120. T: governor Santaella

121. T: took over the state.

122. JL: Did you vote for her?

123. T: Yes, but later.

124. T: She took over without elections.

125. T: She took over Emery Mata Millán without elections.

126. T: Well then

127. T: When she took over,

128. T: After I think like a year already it was time for elections.

129. T: And Emery ran again for governor.

130. T: But no way, he lost the State.

131. T: Now yes, this woman Yelitza Santaella won.

132. T: She is the governor, right.

133. T: Then Emery was left out.

134. T: Well, I don't know.

135. T: That was last year.

136. T: We [the Waraos] heard that Emery was in jail

137. T: He was caught in Maturin.

138. T: That appeared in Notidiario.

139. T: In the press:

140. T: "Emery Mata Millán captured."

[Lines 114–139 describe how Yelitza Santaella won the state elections and how Emery Mata got out of jail. He was then captured again and put back in prison. This section shows how Benito uses "I don't know" in line 134

to show his lack of firsthand knowledge of the events and how in line 140
he resorted to quoting from the newspaper to express the certainty of the
capture of Emery Mata]

141. T: He was in jail.
142. T: After spending some three days there in the cell
143. T: The doctors said he was sick.
144. T: Then they took him out
145. T: They sent him to the hospital
146. T: Well, then the doctors said he was sick
147. T: But anyway, he was convicted.
148. T: He is in jail.
149. T: When they let him out from the hospital
150. T: They sent him to jail again.
151. T: They always said in the press:
152. T: "Emery is corrupted, a thief."

[Line 152 shows a quote from the newspaper asserting the knowledge of
Emery Mata's guilt]

153. T: Well Emery is not in jail anymore.
154. T: He is now on the streets.
155. T: He came here to Barrancas, too.
156. T: He came here to Barrancas saying:
157. T: "I am going to run for governor again."

[Note the parallelism of lines 154–156 and the start of quoted speech in
line 157]

158. T: "I want you to vote for me
159. T: because I want to be governor again,"
160. T: He said:
161. T: "I will be the one who you want me to be.
162. T: I will be governor for everybody in the Delta," Emery Mata Millán said.
163. T: Then for this election I think:
164. T: who am I going to vote for?
165. T: I still don't know.
166. T: I don't know.

[Lines 158–162 present a series of quotations from Emery Mata after
being released from prison. The quotations refer to promises of political
gifts. These quotations are different from those from the newspaper

because they do not index certainty about the information. On the contrary, Benito proceeds to establish in lines 164–166 his uncertainty about the truthfulness of Emery's promises.]

167. T: I have to see who goes to Morichito.
168. T: Then for me to,
169. T: you know how it is to vote like,
170. T: to be able to vote,
171. T: to know how to vote.

[Finally, in lines 167–171 Benito makes an appeal to the broader context in which this promise is made, pointing to the possibility that it will be followed by other meaningful signs that he expects to see in Winikina. In other words, Benito appeals to the trans-semiotic process and its continuation in time through more discursive and material signs to establish the possible truthfulness of Emery's promises]

172. T: That is it.
173. T: It is already it.

[Benito then finished this narrative with a typical Warao closing statement that can also be found in genres such as *dehe hido* (stories of recent times) and *dehe nobo* (or stories of ancient times)]

Example 14

This narrative starts with a description of how political elections are conducted in the lower Delta, using big boats with twenty to thirty people, going from town to town with party-like music and recruiting people with promises of *puestos* (positions) in the government payroll and other gifts. Then Benito moves to the story of how Emery got to be governor. In this part of the narrative, he introduces his own experience of getting involved with Emery's AD. He draws a parallel between the emergence of Emery in the ranks of the party with his own personal involvement in politics. Once Emery Mata established himself as governor, the same party structure that brought the boats to the lower Delta started to identify fellow members of the party and make the promises of political gifts. Benito had given his support to the candidate. He had campaigned for Emery, and voted in the election. Therefore, he had fulfilled his part of the deal. When he visited the party house in Tucupita, he was pleased to know that his name was in the list (note that this is the same kind of list used by Carlos during the controversy about the generator). This completed the cycle of promises and material exchanges that he established with Emery Mata.

Through his involvement with the party structure, he was nominated for the job as *plantero* in his community of origin in the Winikina River. His travels back and forth from Winikina to Barrancas and Tucupita are repeated in the narrative and have the same structure. This is a rhetorical strategy that allows Benito to move the narrative from the interior of the river to urban places and back into the rivers. Benito comes from there (Winikina), gets to (here) Barrancas, he goes to Tucupita and enters the party house or a government office. This journey is an integral part of collecting the benefits of government programs that all Warao that I know go through. Going back and forth to Tucupita is encoded as part of both the lived experience and the narrative strategy about collecting the gifts.

This narrative constructs the image of Emery Mata Millán as a giver politician. The narrative is an explanation about the cause of Emery's rise as the most successful politician in the recent history of the Delta. The strategy of using the boats to deliver face-to-face promises in the lower Delta started in the 1980s, and Emery Mata was one of the first politicians to use it effectively. Furthermore, he linked the strategy of making promises with a system of delivering the gifts. These were delivered to people on lists that ensured that people who endorsed the party could be identified for the distribution of gifts after every election.

Emery Mata's public political self is therefore constructed through indexical text-like signs (lists of people and promises) and the actual delivery of gifts that speak of the truthfulness of his promises. As has been mentioned before, typical interpretations of populism argue that state officials distribute both gifts and political favors in order to create a patron-client relation with their constituents. Nevertheless, these analyses miss what Benito establishes at the beginning of his narrative. The giving of political gifts is preceded by promising discourses and actions that must be depicted as truthful and that will be later narrativized and constructed as truthful. The linguistic work of framing and narrating the gift is just as important as the act of delivering the gift.

Benito then moved the narrative to the political space of national politics. For this he mentions the arrival of Hugo Chávez as president of Venezuela. The arrival of Hugo Chávez brought an investigation into Emery Mata's performance as governor in 1999. At this point Benito introduces the audience to the complexity of the political situation in the Delta, and Emery becomes part of the old political establishments in this turn of the narrative. Benito makes his own narrative more multivocal, introducing quotations from Emery Mata and the press, especially the newspaper *Notidiario*. This part of the narrative addresses how Yelitza Santaella became the governor without being elected and that implies the tacit support of Hugo Chávez in the investigation of Emery Mata.

Then Benito explains the whereabouts of Emery and quotes him multiple times, adding Emery's voice to his own narrative. In this fashion the new political revolutionary turn in the country is linguistically intertwined with Benito's own life trajectory.

Finally, when he relates the return of Emery from prison, he relies even more on quoted speech to exemplify the kind of promise that Emery made just fresh out jail. In Benito's narrative Emery was resorting to the same promises that created a moral link with him back in 1988. But this time the entire country was undergoing a vast political change: the Bolivarian revolution was in its first years, and Benito shows a high degree of political awareness in this regard. He understands the arrival of Yelitza Santaella as the sign of a profound change that would replace the old hegemony of AD in the state with the now-powerful structure of the PSUV. For him it was a moment of confusion. He did not know how to vote after Emery was released from jail and was back in town making the same kind of promises. The power of the PSUV was already well established and Chávez, who was now the president, was backing Yelitza Santaella, which meant a huge advantage in regard to access to resources. When I left the Delta in 2004, Benito was undecided about his political affiliation. He was still feeling some attachment to his old party structure, but the corruption and disappointing behavior of Emery Mata was something he did not want to be affiliated with. When I came back for my dissertation research in 2007, he had already left AD completely and joined the PSUV, but this time the internal struggles of the PSUV were taking a toll on the communities around the Delta along the lines that I described earlier in this chapter.

Conclusions

In the PSUV internal elections of 2008, Lizetta Hernandez became the candidate to run for governor of the Delta Amacuro state and eventually became the governor of the state. She defeated both Amado Heredia and Pedro Santaella, the two closest contenders for this position. During the campaign, Benito was involved in a circle of gift circulation coming from the Antonio Díaz municipality. Our names were in the list to receive money, and we had received the electric generator that was supposed to be a gift for the supporters of Carlos in Morichito. Benito was also afraid that he could lose his position as *plantero*, which had been a gift from the corrupt government of Emery Mata Millán. But in spite of all this political pressure, he voted for Lizetta Hernandez. I was surprised. All the

literature on populism in Venezuela would have predicted that Benito would change his mind following the latest gift from the politician that offered more money. But Benito showed me a more complicated process of political alliance based on his interpretation of truthful promises—the complicated process of framing the generator not as political gift for him but for Carlos. When I asked why he had voted for Lizetta, he told me that in spite of all the money and gifts that Amado had given, he did not believe that he would make good on his promises. He had been unreliable as *alcalde* and had always favored the Carlos's people. Amado had done poorly not on his political gift-giving strategy but on the more important dimension of framing the gift by performative and linguistic means. Faced with the uncertainty of the gift, Benito preferred to follow his uncle Tito and vote for a candidate that looked better positioned within the structure of PSUV. The fact that Governor Santaella favored Lizetta even above her own brother Pedro had a tremendous impact. It guaranteed that Lizetta would win the election, and he wanted to be with the winner so he could create a more stable relationship. So, his political positioning was not determined as a blind response to an immediate economic stimulus. It was a process of semiotic interpretation in which the promises and talk about politics—as well as the construction of the candidates' future careers and public political stances—had a tremendous impact in his decisions. In the end, Benito ended up being better positioned than I thought. Lizetta won the internal election. Amado decided to run with the Communist Party and ultimately lost the election for governor. The political situation changed dramatically in Morichito. Carlos, who was the one controlling the gifts, ended up fearing that he could lose his position in the Alcaldía, as well as the big boat that he controlled because it was a gift from the loser Governor Santaella.

Through this ethnographic example I have shown that the political alliance between the Warao and regional political leaders follows a complicated semiotic process. It also shows that the political gifts that are central to the construction of the magic of the revolutionary government in the Orinoco Delta depend on local regimes of truth and specific semiotic ideologies. My analysis also goes against interpretations in which the political position of the Warao is merely due to their impoverished conditions and lack of access to education. The Warao stances regarding political gifts depend as much on linguistic inequalities and control of public discourse as on calculations about which politician gifts the most during an election.

6

Revolutionary Messaging

Since the beginning of my fieldwork in the Delta, I saw people going through the pages of *Notidiario*—the only local newspaper in the state—searching for information regarding government plans, deferred salary payments from the government, and information more generally about political life in Tucupita. I often heard references to this newspaper when discussing politics. Sometimes these discussions became stories, such as my friend Benito's in Chapter 5 in which he quoted *Notidiario* as his main source of information. The constant reference to the news made me aware of the influence of the newspaper in the region and compelled me to collect it whenever it was possible. I usually bought it in the morning and gave it away to friends and acquaintances after taking pictures of the pages that interested me.

Although I have no official data on literacy rates among the Warao, I found that most men under thirty were able to read in Spanish. Older men were less likely able to read, but it was not uncommon. Among women I found the same pattern, but older women had less command not only of reading but also of speaking Spanish. Reading *Notidiario* was never a solitary activity. Usually there were groups of people gathered around a single newspaper reading out loud and commenting on every news item. Not all Warao have money to buy the newspaper every day, so whenever there was a copy available it was common to see people passing it around to see the pictures and read or reread the news. This fluid circulation allowed even those who did not know how to read to keep up with the news and what politicians were saying. The news from *Notidiario* was also the subject of many conversations when the newspaper was not even around. Among the Warao it is not uncommon to spend the afternoon visiting with family and friends. Oftentimes the topic of these conversations is news items from *Notidiario*. The news from this particular media outlet is then central to political and social life in any Warao community.

During my fieldwork two regional elections were scheduled. Talk about local candidates was unavoidable. *Notidiario* was heavily influential in the

construction of the public perception of these candidates running for office. Articles from this newspaper filled the public imagination with images of the personality and qualities of the candidates. From my point of view these articles formed in fact a corpus of naturally occurring discourse (Sherzer 1987) that I could use to delve into how local politicians construct their public persona. After following the news for a few months, I realized that there were politicians whose images appeared often and were closely followed by the Waraos I knew. Here I present some of these politicians who used *Notidiario* to construct and inhabit their political message (Lempert and Silverstein 2012) with the help of journalists and the press services of government agencies. All of them were candidates, or rather pre-candidates as they were then called, in the 2008 primary elections of the PSUV (United Socialist Party of Venezuela). They used extensively the press services of their government offices to create their political image and spread their message as revolutionary leaders. They were helped by a common set of journalists, editors, and press owners to mediate (Gershon 2010; Mazzarella 2003, 2004, 2006; Kunreuther 2014) the circulation of their message and spread the image of the magical revolutionary state in the Delta. *Notidiario* is notorious for providing quotes from politicians creating texts central to the constitutions of publics and forms of self (Warner 2002). In a small newspaper like *Notidiario* press notes about local politicians help constitute localized discursive practices with a heavy impact on the mediated constitutions of local publics (Figure 15).

Paying attention to situated practices has always been part of the craft of ethnographic description. Most of us go to the field searching for local practices in order to unpack their layers of signification. We spend a great deal of our time trying to get around the micro-politics of everyday events. We often aim at some sort of Geertzian thick description, very often associated with detailed accounts of social life. Most of the ethnographic facts commonly pursued for ethnographic thick description are obtained in a process of cultural/linguistic immersion in which we are "granted access" to cultural logics. What we consider the typical ethnographic materials is then different from the public and open archival material of the historian. But as Gupta (1995) very aptly argues, local print journalism can also be a form of situated practice that we can engage ethnographically not only by attending to the local archive but by finding archival material in the field (see also Graham 2011; Arndt 2010; Bate 2002; Cody 2009; Jackson 2008). It was by building my own newspaper archive that I gained insight into the public message of these politicians. I collected the newspaper and in doing so I built a linguistic corpus of public political speech that gave me a window into the public personae of these politicians.

Figure 15 Women's gathering to read *Notidiario* (picture by Juan Luis Rodríguez).

Here I use this corpus of discursive materials to analyze the construction of what Lempert and Silverstein (2012) call "message." A message here is understood as "the characterological aura of a persona, much like a character in realistic literature, who has not only said and done things, but who has the potential, in the fictive universe of a plot, to be imaginable as acting in certain ways in situations still unrealized in plot spacetime—the character's plot-framed 'future'" (Silverstein 2011: 204). This message is constructed in relation to the Habermasian public sphere and its "commentariat" (Lempert and Silverstein 2012). I show here that one of the most prominent rhetorical strategies in the Orinoco Delta is to inhabit the message of the politician/giver that can be reached at an affective level by their constituents. This rhetorical strategy is in essence a process of transduction since it performs a transformation of state resources into multiple forms of political discourse and everyday talk. In what follows I show four cases in which this process develops in the pages of *Notidiario* and in the context of the 2008 PSUV primaries.

Yelitza Santaella

On November 14, 2007, Mrs. Joséfina Moreno from the rural community of Rastrojos and Rastrojitos visited the editorial office of *Notidiario*. Journalist

José Angel Gascón recorded her visit and later recounted it for his readers. Mrs. Moreno had come to the office in full *chavista* gear (red shirt, red baseball cap, button with President Chávez's image on it) to talk about her love for Governor Yelitza Santaella. She also wanted to voice her complaint about a public employee who offended her during a recent visit to the governor's office. Mrs. Moreno's visit did not take the journalists by surprise since they often receive people from all over the state who have complaints. Usually, they record the conversations in order to have direct quotes from the source and to be able to write press notes based on the events as described by the visitor. These press notes bring community issues to the attention of the authorities and the general public. More importantly, the notes are instruments of praise and blame for political personalities and government agents, and therefore are instruments to talk about the personal qualities of the politicians.

Mrs. Moreno was in Tucupita that day to pay a visit to Governor Santaella. This was not the first time that the two had met. They had crossed paths in the past during political campaigns in the lower Delta. The governor knew who Mrs. Moreno was, although they were not friends. Mrs. Moreno went to the governor's office without an appointment and decided to wait for the governor to have a moment with her. As she waited, a new employee walked in and told her that the governor was not granting government assistance of any kind that day. In the Delta it is common for people in need to wait outside the governor's office in the hope that the governor will hear their request and grant some form of economic or bureaucratic help. The assumption of this new young employee was that Mrs. Moreno was one of those people in need. Mrs. Moreno took offence to the employee's assumption and decided to go to *Notidiario* to make public her discontent. She recounted to the journalist how she corrected the young women to make clear that Mrs. Moreno was there because she knew the governor personally and just wanted to say hello to her. Mrs. Moreno not only wanted to make sure this was public in the newspaper but also wanted to praise the governor because she acted magnanimously to correct the incident. She was helped by journalist Gascón, who recorded their conversation and wrote the following note the next day. Texts in brackets, for example, [text], are comments and clarifications:

> I [Mrs. Moreno] love Yelitza like my own daughter because she has been very good to us in the towns of Rastrojos and Rastrojitos, where she has visited on several occasions extending her friendly hand to us and worrying about the poor, and contributing with solutions for our community, where now we breathe calm and hopeful winds in an area that for years remained in silence and anonymity and at the mercy of being forgotten by past governors. Such were

the statements of Mrs. Joséfina Moreno when she visited our editorial office yesterday morning, very happy and showing great optimism, dressing all red, with a red baseball cap and wearing a button with President Chávez's image on her shirt, who she said will support forever because Chávez through PDVSA and Yelitza [the governor of the state of Delta Amacuro] brought well-being to those communities because now they can count on MERCAL [an state-owned chain of supermarkets], electricity, water, and the expansion and improvement of the local clinic, among other benefits—added Mrs. Joséfina Moreno who by the way has always been worried about the betterment of that neighborhood as well as the communities of the middle Delta.

One incident that cannot be repeated is the one that Mrs. Joséfina told us pointing out that when she got to the governor's office last Monday in the afternoon, and sat waiting for the governor, a young lady who works there, seeing her so humble, the first thing that she told her was: "Mrs. there is no government assistance here, so forget about it!" to which I [Mrs. Moreno] said "no young lady I am not here to ask for any help," an incident that she disregarded because she was there to said hello to the governor, who a few minutes later received Mrs. Moreno with affection and the same love as always, and to whom they [the elderly] will be forever grateful for giving them access to the social security through the Social Security Institute, for which they [the elderly] will be forever grateful, because she is the only governor that has noticed them in the whole existence of these communities of the middle Delta. Among other manifestations that have awoken in her [Mrs. Moreno] great feelings of love and appreciation for governor Yelitza Santaella was the gift of a purse that the governor brought her from Cuba, and a cellular phone which she showed us with the affection of a child who receives a gift in a good Christmas. What has awoken in Mrs. Joséfina an immense love and affection for Governor Yelitza Santaella, who she said loves as her own daughter. (Gascón 2007a: 4)

Example 15

This text starts with a direct quote from Mrs. Moreno in an effort to assert the authenticity of the claims made in the note. The strategy here is to present Mrs. Moreno's first-person account of the incident and her personal closeness to Governor Santaella. Mrs. Moreno is quoted as praising the governor and expressing her love for the "only" politician who has visited her community (Rastrojos and Rastrojitos), the only one that has worried about her problems, and the one who brought hope to her town. These expressions of feelings are conveyed using the image of bringing fresh air and hope to the community and personal presence in the community.

Then Gascón goes on to describe what Mrs. Moreno looks like. She was a typical *chavista* dressing in red and wearing signs of her affiliation with President Chávez and the Bolivarian revolution. Her revolutionary affiliation is not only established verbally but also all over her body. These become her personal, physical, and moral attributes as a devoted *chavista*. This level of commitment and support is then interpreted as the results of the material support that Chávez channels to the Delta Amacuro through the governor and PDVSA (Petroleos de Venezuela Sociedad Anonima). This statement could not be a more direct articulation of the process of transduction that I have tried to present throughout this book. The implication here is that Santaella's direct access to President Chávez and the Bolivarian revolution helps her to channel resources to the people of the middle Delta, who are grateful to the governor for not forgetting about them in these times of high oil prices. The governor becomes the mediating factor in the process—an overt process of transduction in which the money produced by oil exports in PDVSA is transformed into political gifts that people receive from Chávez through the governor. This makes the governor a magnanimous benefactor with whom the public can create a personal, emotional connection.

But those who see it as mere clientelism, such as the new worker in the governor's office, challenge that connection. The new worker had "mistaken" Mrs. Moreno as one of the countless people from all over the state who lobby in front of the governor's office to ask for personal favors. What this junior member of the staff did not understand is that Mrs. Moreno just "wanted to meet with the governor and give her a hug." Mrs. Moreno does not see herself as a client of the governor. She sees their relationship as moral and affective. She then decided to go to *Notidiario* to publicly scold this young lady but also to show that her support for Santaella was based on affection. She decided to make public the personal gifts that she has received from the governor to show this affection. The purse from Cuba and the cellphone that Mrs. Moreno received become the signs of a generous governor. The message here seems to be that some instances of this generosity might be mistaken as populism, but they are "really" coming from a caring leader and beloved politician/giver. These instances are indexical of the feelings of this governor for the people. In the rhetoric of this press note the governor becomes a grandiose giver who makes sure that everybody understands that the relationship between "the people," as the social body of the nation, and herself, as the personification of the political body, is based on moral grounds expressed through material gifts. These gifts in turn are transformations of oil into money into purses and cellphones.

One of the most salient economic benefits depicted as political gifts in the Orinoco Delta is social security pensions—which are a legal right for all Venezuelan citizens. Access to this right is very difficult, especially in rural areas of the country. A governor who helps with the paperwork is regarded as a giver who really cares about his people. Thus, distributing what is a legal right can be framed as a gift when the politician is willing to reign on the bureaucratic red tape. Pensions are not things made or possessed by governors, but the act of easing the access to them is taken as a gift in itself. These acts of "easing bureaucracy" are then praised in *Notidiario* to make Yelitza to appear as a revolutionary magician who has come to make right all the wrongdoings of the past.

In 2008, as her term in office was coming to an end, Yelitza Santaella mounted a public relations campaign to become national treasurer of the PSUV. This required her to enhance her image as a woman of the people and as a caring and well-prepared leader. In her effort to inhabit this message, she again used official communications from the governor's office such as the following note published by journalist Apolinar Martínez in *Notidiario* on January 10, 2008:

> Radiant, beautifully dressed, with the confidence and security of a star making her entrance in a TV studio, the governor of the Delta Amacuro State Yelitza Santaella seemed to have learned the teachings of emperor Julius the Apostate: dignitaries must always look forward as if they were contemplating the majesty of infinity...
>
> ...For who has been at the front of the State for so many years, with achievements and frustrations, with things achieved and unfinished plans, it is difficult to choose what has pleased her the most, Yelitza thinks it over a little and goes to the heart of it—Of course we have concluded many material projects in all orders from health to housing solutions, schools, stadiums, roads, sewage, water service, etc. But there is an element that is paramount to me: the connection and support, I would almost say the love that the people have manifested...
>
> ...how can I forget- and the governor makes a recount[ing] that resembles a geography professor when she mentions the towns and villages- the love from the communities of Manacal, Los Tres Caños, Guayo, Nabasanuca, Curiazo, Tortola, Santa Catalina, Pedernales ... The people touched me and told me: "It is a pity that you cannot be elected again, but we will remember you for all eternity. I will not forget those gestures either.... (Martínez 2008a: 12–13)

Example 16

This press note presents Governor Santaella as an impressive leader with the demeanor of a Roman emperor. Moreover, and very appropriate for a country in which soap operas and TV dramas occupy a great deal of media space, she

is described as a TV star entering the studio. These are images that describe the politician as a magical figure. It is as if the journalist refuses to ground the political person in any form of reality that is not at the same time magical. Then the press note shifts to describe Santaella's term turning the narrative into a quoted first-person account in the voice of the governor. This voice describes her own achievements in terms of the construction of multiple infrastructural projects and the distribution of pensions, but she stresses that the most important achievement is the support and "love" that people around the Delta gave her. The press note describes people so in love with the magical politician that they are heartbroken because she cannot be reelected. Thus, we have two forms of quotation constructing the governor's political message: first, the journalist quotes the governor; second, the governor quotes the people. These two quotations stress the leadership qualities and the affective connection created between Santaella and her constituents. According to the journalist, the governor shows that she cares about the people by recounting one by one the towns and villages that she visited and where she delivered gifts. Then, the governor showed that the people care about her by quoting their profound love for her. All of this embellished with imagery of TV stardom and the magic of a Roman emperor. Yelitza inhabits the message of a magnanimous politician/giver.

Pedro Santaella

The second politician I want to present here is Pedro Santaella Hernandez. He presents himself as the candidate of *la mano amiga* (the friendly hand) which is the motto of his faction within the local branch of the PSUV. He was the mayor of the Casacoima municipality in the southeastern Delta during my fieldwork. Pedro came to power in 2005 with the endorsement of President Hugo Chávez. Given that Yelitza and Pedro are related, I was under the impression that the Santaella family was taking control of the revolutionary movement in the state. Very soon this assumption proved to be wrong. Pedro is Yelitza's half-brother, but there is a great deal of animosity between the two. The PSUV's 2008 primary elections brought about competitive factionalism within the party and divided it in a number of groups. Pedro Santaella, Lizetta Hernandez, and Amado Heredia headed the most prominent of these groups.

By the time the primaries were called in late 2007, the PSUV was a newly created political party born out of the MVR (Movimiento Quinta República). In

early 2008, with the regional elections rapidly approaching, the PSUV needed a strategy to counteract the loss of a constitutional referendum in December 2007. The constitutional referendum was the biggest electoral setback of the Bolivarian revolution until then. In order to give its candidates "democratic legitimacy," they decided to promote the first general primary elections ever held by a Venezuelan political party. This was an ambitious project that included the election of all candidates from the municipal level to the national assembly by the party base. This move was also part of a public relations strategy that allowed the PSUV to point the finger at the opposition for not having legitimate candidates elected by the people. In the Delta this election had even more significance given the absolute majority of the PSUV. Winning the PSUV's primaries meant that winning the governor's office was almost guaranteed. Since a primary election had never been held in the region, this strategy also helped the PSUV candidates to gain more visibility and news coverage than ever before. The future candidate's period of exposure to media coverage almost doubled because the law now allowed campaigning not only for the duration of the primaries but also for the time when they were running for office.

Pedro Santaella developed a strategy to construct his political image for this election using the resources at his disposal in the Casacoima municipality. Throughout the election he used the press office of the Alcaldía to build his message around three topics: (1) he wanted to be known as a politician/giver summarized in his motto the "friendly hand"; (2) he wanted to be known as the best administrator; (3) finally, he wanted to be known as a candidate chosen by the divine. This was in clear contrast to his sister who emphasized the affective connection with the public. Pedro's press releases emphasized efficiency and good administration. This constituted a masculinized version of the politician/ giver. Pedro was the more "rational" candidate and the one favored by God.

By January 2008, all aspiring candidates released press notes making public their intentions to become the PSUV's candidates for governor. Pedro joined in launching his campaign with the following press release:

> Under the extraordinary management of the friendly hand's mayor, Pedro Santaella Hernandez, Casacoima now has a fruitful and successful administration characterized by more hits than misses, an administration that in only 3 years has brought great happiness and satisfaction to the inhabitants of this beautiful and paradisiacal place...
>
> ...Under this frame of reference, the communities of the southern Delta see with pleasure and celebrate the arrival to power of a hard-working and visionary mayor like Pedro Santaella, who totally changed the administration of

the municipality with projects of general interest and collective benefits for the inhabitants of Casacoima. Projects that will be remembered in history because never in the past two administrations were they completed, and they could not show this achievement that nobody ever thought could be possible with the start of local governments, today the sovereign people have an efficient bank that fits the development of this population, the people feel happy that for the first time in this locality they can access modern telecommunications with the activation of two antennas by Movilnet and Movistar which means that we are no longer in the shadows, social assistance can reach the dispossessed classes permanently, the national food plan MERCAL allows the people to buy food at low prices, also the elderly thank Santaella for allowing them to be secure at their age with their pensions, thinking about infrastructure projects for the exercise of good administration, the building for the municipal comptroller and civil protection and so many other projects were finished, so many that if we recount them all, there will be not enough lines in this press note…

…Now Pedro Santaella Hernandez, with the favor of the great architect of the universe, showing this extraordinary administration, is getting prepared to be governor of the State and surely the people who trust him will come out as a human tide to support a leader who does not have muddy feet and does not sell himself to the highest bidder, in this sense the 78% that is shown in the polls is not by chance or mere fabrication, but is part of the political and social work advanced by Santaella Hernandez to bring the most happiness to the Delta once he reaches the office of governor. (*Prensa Imataca* 2008a: 9; author's translation)

Example 17

This note, written by the official press agency of the Casacoima municipal government, starts by praising Pedro's successful administration for having more "hits than misses" and bringing a great deal of "happiness" to the people. Pedro is only the third mayor that this municipality had since the start of municipal elections in the early 1990s. Therefore, this comparison is a direct challenge to political actors that are recent in memory and are still very active in the political scene of the state. While his reference to happiness may seem inconsequential, it has profound implications for the recognition of Pedro as a revolutionary leader. It is a direct intertextual reference to the words and voice of President Chávez's motto that the best form of government is the "one that brings the most happiness to its people." This is a phrase that circulated widely in Venezuela's media at this time. Self-identified *chavistas* used it to describe what a good government is supposed to be. Therefore, the use of "happiness" is an inter-discursive reference indexing the *chavismo* that Pedro embraces.

The next part of the press note presents Pedro's specific achievements. First, he is praised for bringing a bank to town, which implies access to credit. He is referring here to the new branch of the *Banco Nacional de Credito* inaugurated shortly before his campaign in Casacoima. The BNC is a state-owned bank that aims to distribute credit for small-scale initiatives. This is depicted as "his plan" for development. He is also praised for bringing two telecommunication antennas from Movistar (the state-owned company) and Movilnet (a private company owned by Telefónica, Spain), the two main cellular companies in Venezuela at that time. These two companies, as the author of the note puts it, have taken Casacoima "out of the shadows." Other gifts that Pedro is "bringing" to the municipality are MERCAL (a state-owned supermarket chain) and the distribution of pensions for the elderly. These plans are presented as the personal achievement of a hardworking politician with vision and concrete development plans. But these achievements are part of national plans that are in constant expansion regardless of who is in charge at the municipal level. The trick here is to frame them as Pedro's "achievements" and to make them appear as products of his hard work. He needs to translate the expansion of the infrastructure of state-owned enterprises and services into his plan to make the magic of the state his own, and to line up his political message with the revolution. He becomes a magnanimous local revolutionary leader in the pages of *Notidiario* by appropriating the state, and by making the magic of the revolution his own. This is clear in the next few lines when the elderly are described as thanking Pedro for his generous acts.

Another interesting dimension of the construction of Pedro's political persona is that he is represented as predestined by the "great architect of the universe" to become governor. This religious imagery appears repeatedly in press notes describing his qualities and is used by other politicians as well. In Pedro's case the religious reference presents his election as inevitable because he has a form of divine blessing. A more dramatic example of this religious imagery is the following note full of references to the apocalypse and the inevitability of Pedro's election:

…Santaella Hernandez, confirmed an old compromise that he made with his people when he was working in the municipal council in Tucupita, experience that gave him wisdom and prepared him politically to face the challenges that the future would bring him, and what better experience when in odd conditions he had to compete for the Casacoima municipality and fairly defeated his contenders demonstrating that we were in the presence of a charismatic and virtuous leader that little by little, by means of his good administration, would be strongly projected on the regional political stage. A stage that has begun to

open up its doors and smile to him so that he becomes its new governor, so that he can continue serving the people who trust his great administrative capacity and dedication, requirements sine qua non to succeed in the new responsibilities that the great architect of the universe will put on his hands, because whatever should happen under this sun will happen, and there could be a thousand riders of the apocalypse that would try to oppose the signs of the divine will, but nobody can stop the march of the carriage of history that will support that great army of men and woman that will rise in the Delta to take THE FRIENDLY HAND to the office of governor. (*Prensa Imataca* 2008: 6; author's translation)

Example 18

Contrary to his sister, who wanted to show her soft nurturing and caring side, Pedro shows himself as chosen leader. His image is mediated by gender ideologies that prompt him to complement his image of giver with that of the strong and efficient leader chosen by Chávez and the divine "great architect of the universe."

Another very interesting aspect of Pedro's political message is his awareness that becoming a gift giver is regarded as a form of corruption. As a revolutionary leader, Pedro aims at breaking with the practices of parties such as AD and COPEI which have been depicted as deceiving the people with populist traps to gain control of the government for the parties' own benefit. He must balance his own depiction as politician/giver with the promise that he is not going to betray the people in the same way as past politicians. This is why the journalists supporting him try to differentiate Pedro's gift giving through meta-discursive exercises such as the following:

Today the people of the Delta won't fall in the same trap of the gifts and false promises of these politicians who are the same, who yesterday tricked us with false promises, that is why we are with Santaella Hernandez, a man of humble origins and son of this land that saw him grow, and that during his time in this city's Municipal Council demonstrated with courage what he is capable of doing for the people, a very convincing reason to ask the sovereign Warao people not to give up because there is hope and a firm path supporting Pedro Santaella for governor of the State and Rene Ramonis for the Municipality of Antonio Diaz to move our communities forward. (Prensa Imataca 2008: 9)

Example 19

Here he is presented as different from other politicians who use gifts as open political bribes. Even though Pedro struggles to show his "friendly hand," he

is capable of delivering goods and services that the Warao people are thankful for. This is part of the complexity of framing national programs such as the social security pensions as gifts. Pedro, Yelitza, and others are well aware that outside of the Delta gift giving is seen as populism, which is also connected with corrupt forms of governance. Their effort to become politician/givers must be counterbalanced with meta-discursive strategies that state their awareness and "rejection" of these very practices.

These writers do not find any incoherence in blaming other politicians for being corrupt and populists while at the same time they make Pedro the Delta's "friendly hand." In this logic the gifts from Pedro are truthful indexicals. For him the problem is not so much breaking the cycle of gift giving for votes but presenting his gifts as legitimate promises. This is only possible through extensive linguistic framing and by making his promises and gifts part of a newly imagined revolutionary ethic and message.

Lizetta Hernandez

During the PSUV's 2008 primaries the only aspiring candidate that held a position not elected by popular vote was Lizetta Hernandez. She was the head of the regional health system in Delta Amacuro. As such, she was also in close contact with Governor Yelitza Santaella and with the highest ranks of the revolutionary movement in the state. It was no surprise when in early January 2008 she announced her intention to be the candidate of the PSUV. Since the very beginning, her campaign had the support and public endorsement of Governor Yelitza Santaella (against her own brother) who was very frequently in her company during public ceremonies and social activities. Lizetta's campaign was run by the same people in charge of the governor's public image. It was natural then that they would emphasize the closeness and similarities between Lizetta and Yelitza. With Lizetta the programs and social policies of Yelitza were guaranteed and the progress of the revolution in the state was safeguarded. In the pages of *Notidiario*, Lizetta's political image and message pivoted around three topics: (1) continuity of Yelitza's work, (2) her image as a caring physician, and (3) her affective connection with the public.

Journalists supporting Lizetta constantly highlighted her explicit recognition of Yelitza's achievements as governor in order to assure her constituents of the continuity with Yelitza's administration. They praised and acknowledged Yelitza's achievements using embedded quotes in press articles such as the following:

… [Lizetta Hernandez] Recognized publicly that when Yelitze Santaella became governor, the rescue began, the excluded people's total participation, because before many became rich taking advantage of the Warao masses, and that is a reality that cannot be hidden, regardless of whom might be affected, once Yelitza became governor the indigenous people felt assisted. Likewise, the Warao communities were strengthened, but we need to continue working to take them out of poverty and that can only be achieved by giving them participation in their own production system, because our land is rich, because we cannot continue teaching the people not to work…. (Leon 2008: 3)

Example 20

This passage appeared at the end of a press note describing a political rally in Petion Street, Tucupita, supporting Lizetta's candidacy. Toward the end of the note the journalist embedded this indirect quote from Lizetta "publicly recognizing" the regard that Governor Santaella has for the Warao population, which had been "abandoned" by administrations of the past. "Past administration" is a code word for "pre-Chávez" administrations. Yet, different from Pedro, who presents himself as a technocrat, both Yelitza and Lizetta emphasize the caring and nurturing character of their own selves. Pedro wants to change to a more efficient form of government. Instead, Yelitza and Lizetta want to change to a more humanistic and caring form of socialism. The continuity between Yelitza and Lizeta is expressed in the form of an emotional likeness. They are both caring, socialist politicians linked with the humanistic agenda of the revolutionary government. This is also a topic that President Hugo Chávez has emphasized in many of his discourses in which he describes the Bolivarian revolution as humanistic in nature. Yelitza, Lizetta, and Pedro share the revolutionary rhetorical disgust with the pre-1998 political parties. They understand the Delta as a marginal land with a large dispossessed indigenous population. But they imagine differently the way out of this poverty and therefore the way in which they have to construct their public message.

Connection with the "Warao masses" can be achieved, in the words of Lizetta, by "giving the Warao participation in their own production system." The poverty of the Warao is explained by the exploitation of those who became rich at their expense. In order to change this situation, "we must teach them how to work" to become productive individuals within the economic socialist system but without abandoning their traditional form of production ("their own production system"). The Waraos' "own production system" seems to be self-evident, and neither the journalist nor Lizetta need to explain what it is or how

it will be incorporated into the socialist policies of the state, a topic that other politicians such as Amado Heredia emphasize (see next section).

An interesting example of the rhetorical strategy connecting both Lizetta's and Yelitza's messages as humanistic and caring revolutionary leaders are the following press note passages:

> Once again, the pre-candidate Lizetta Hernandez aimed at the use of politics for humanitarian and social attention that she said had developed in her professional career and the activities carried out with the Delta's Maximum Revolutionary Leader [Yelitza Santaella].
>
> [Lizetta was visiting Warao communities and giving free medical check-ups] …. According to what she reported, the visit resulted in the more than 300 check-ups….
>
> In regard to the support that her staff has measured among the Delta's collectivities, Lizetta Hernandez emphasized that she feels very satisfied with the unconditional support that various sectors have professed in favor of her pre-candidacy and her peer in battle, Alexis Hernandez, pre-candidate for the Tucupita Municipality. (Leon 2008: 3)

Example 21

The image of the caring physician giving free checkups to 300-plus patients at a time is not only a reference to the humanistic character of Lizetta but also an indirect reference to one of Venezuela's most pervasive religious images, Dr. José Gregorio Hernandez. He was a physician in Caracas at the beginning of the twentieth century and a professor in the school of medicine at the Universidad Central de Venezuela. He was famous for taking care of numerous patients for free in a time when access to medicine was scarce and too expensive for the poor. In most Venezuelans' imagination, Dr. José Gregorio Hernandez not only took care of these patients in their own homes but also gave away medicines, alleviating his patients' suffering and helping them when they were unable to afford treatment. His deeds are held as the ultimate standard of professional behavior for Venezuelan physicians, and he is nowadays worshiped in the Catholic Church as almost a saint, and in the Maria Lionza cult as part of its pantheon. José Gregorio Hernandez partakes in the religious and moral world of Venezuelan academic and religious institutions.

Lizetta Hernandez's comments about her own dedication to service and her willingness to take more than 300 patients at a time is a deep dive into the cultural imagination of those whom she sees as the poorest of the poor, the Indians of the Delta. She tries to link her image with the ultimate standards of ethical and

moral behavior within her discipline, showing a connection with the humanism of the socialist revolutionary government and the image of the physician/giver constructed around José Gregorio. Her caring action is a token of the standard established by a saint. This image strengthens her emotional link with the poorest constituents in the state to whom she is devoted and who are morally indebted to her in the same way in which they are indebted to José Gregorio. In her campaign, the magic of the Catholic Church and the Maria Lionza cult is mixed with the magic of a revolutionary ethics to produce the image of a sensible politician who would take care of Warao bodies as well as their social well-being. Lizetta is a revolutionary leader who takes advantage of not only the magic of the revolutionary state but also the magic of her biomedical training and Venezuela's religious imaginary.

Amado Heredia

The fourth and final politician that I want to present is the indigenous mayor Amado Heredia. In 2008, for the first time in the Delta's political history a Warao politician aspired to become governor of the state. Amado Heredia, the first Warao-elected mayor of the Antonio Díaz municipality (the area with the largest Warao population in the state), announced his intention to become the PSUV's candidate for governor. He is a very well-known teacher who in the early 2000s became one of the founders of the revolutionary government in the state. His coming to power in Antonio Díaz coincided with the 1999 constitutional reform and with the development of the Ministry of Indigenous Affairs. Following these developments, Amado joined the MVR (Movimiento Quinta República), whose ranks were open to new indigenous representatives in ways that parties such as AD and COPEI never allowed in Delta Amacuro.

Since his election as mayor, Amado's political image has pivoted around his indigenous roots and his loyalty to Hugo Chávez. In the 2008 primary elections, he was the only pre-candidate recognized as indigenous and, as such, he claimed to be the "legitimate" representative of the Waraos. He was born in the rivers of the lower Delta and speaks both Spanish and Warao with equal fluency. He is very proud of the fact that he can navigate the world of regional politics, at ease in Warao communities as well as in Tucupita. Amado always stresses this ability, and many of his media appearances highlight his command of Spanish and his knowledge of the nonindigenous world. For example, in November 2007 the radio station La Sureña del Delta selected him as the outstanding mayor of 2006.

He was presented with an award and journalist José Angel Gascón published the
following note in *Notidiario*:

> Due to his outstanding governmental performance which makes him the 2006
> most notable mayor in the State of Delta Amacuro, Sureña del Delta, directed
> by journalist Epifanio González Serra, gave a recognition plaque to the mayor of
> the Antonio Díaz Municipality Prof. Amado Heredia, who deserved the award
> given to him after an evaluation of his performance [that puts him] over the
> mayors in the other four municipalities conforming the State of Delta Amacuro,
> where the decision favored mayor Heredia.
>
> This deserved recognition, given in a very selective way, was awarded in an
> apotheosic act that took place recently in the Warao Aoriwakanoko auditorium,
> and later was given in the office of the known public servant because of his
> intention to comply with the assumed obligations with the inhabitants of the
> Antonio Díaz municipality and with the rest of the dwellers in the Delta's region,
> who have seen in mayor Heredia an open, easy-going and humble person with
> characteristics of probity and honesty who understands the hardships of poverty
> and the needs that during years have made prisoner the hopes of progress in the
> State of Delta Amacuro.
>
> On this occasion, Heredia pointed out that this gesture was not beyond
> what can be given assuming the responsibility as public servant, undertaking
> public work as is demanded, where he has done nothing more than trying to
> accomplish the promises and responsibilities contracted because he accepted
> and assumed them, so in this way he acted. Therefore, all this work and all these
> results from the actions carried out in 2006 deserved this award –he said-.
>
> Likewise, he added that this plaque is not only for Amado Heredia but also
> for all his staff working in the municipality, all the people of the Antonio Díaz
> municipality and all the people in the State of Delta Amacuro. (Gascón 2007: 2;
> author's translation)

Example 22

In the narrative of the press note, Amado performs better than any of the other
three (criollo) mayors of the state. He is the best mayor measured by the "standards"
of "professional journalists." Moreover, he has accomplished this outstanding
performance because he can understand the hardships of poverty (supposedly for
being Warao himself). Most people know where Amado is from and understand
the reference to his humble origins as a reference to his Indianness.

Amado's use of his Warao identity to enhance his political position is a new
phenomenon in the Delta. Unlike the indigenous coalitions such as ORPIA,

CONIVE, and other similar organizations in the State of Amazonas in southern Venezuela, Warao political leaders have not participated in electoral processes and have been kept out of Venezuelan traditional party structures. The surge of Amado Heredia is a product of the increasing awareness about indigenous rights within the PSUV as the newest political party in the country. Amado explicitly links his rising in regional politics to this process and to wider transnational political developments that give legitimacy to his political message. In his speeches and interviews, he makes constant references to the rising indigenous leadership in Latin America and to his capacity to move between the indigenous and criollo worlds. For example, on February 22, 2008, journalist Apolinar Martínez invited Amado for an interview in *Notidiario*'s main office in Tucupita. In an article based on this interview, Martínez started by warning his readers:

> It is necessary to know Mayor Amado Heredia well enough not to be confused about his condition as descendant of the Warao world. His gestures, language and way of expression coincide in all respects with what we associate as *criollo*. (Martínez 2008b: 12–13; author's translation)

Example 23

Amado has the disposition of a criollo politician. He not only navigates the criollo world very well but also his appearance "makes" people mistake his identity. Amado's flawless Spanish and demeanor allow him to participate in the public sphere avoiding most of the time the deep racial ideologies of the Delta. Nevertheless, in the new political environment post-1999, he can let his Indian self be seen because it has become an asset in his political career. It is with the Bolivarian revolution that Amado has been able to use his Indianness to gain political ground. He establishes this connection very explicitly in statements such as the following:

> Apolinar Martínez: There are speculations that your candidacy is well regarded at the level of the High Government and that even they will see with sympathy that you end up being the candidate of the PSUV in the region. What do you think of such consideration, is it only gossip or does it have some real ground?

> Amado: In the first place it should be clear that I do not have any support other than the one that the people can give me. Of course, I am part of a whole in the struggle carried out by the indigenous people of Latin America to win a respectable place in all aspects of the conduction of a process that has not stopped since the time of the conquest until our days. In that wave is inscribed the presidency of our friend Evo Morales in Bolivia and the coming of different

indigenous candidacies throughout our continent. I am very proud for deserving the respect and recognition of not only president Chávez and the fundamental leaders of our organization, but all that would be in vain if it did not have the support and solidarity of our results. It is not true that the vote numbers in Antonio Díaz were manipulated and handled speculatively [he is referring to the results of the 2007 constitutional referendum]. The numbers obtained by me are serious and reflect a grateful community.... (Martínez 2008a: 12–13; author's translation)

Example 24

Amado traces his political network not only to the Bolivarian revolution in Venezuela but also to the rise of indigenous political leaders in the continent. Of all aspiring candidates in the PSUV's primaries, he is the only one constructing his political image in direct connection to transnational political forces. Other aspiring candidates can only link themselves with the struggle to overcome the political monopoly established by AD and COPEI. Amado is able to share that agenda in conjunction with his indigenous identity to legitimize his candidacy. Here is another example of this connection from the same interview:

Apolinar Martínez: Antonio Díaz turned out to be a curious case in the elections for the constitutional reform given the case that it had achieved one hundred percent of the votes in favor of the YES option. To what do you attribute the affinity with the principles of President Chávez?

Amado Heredia: Look, it is not so much that the people of Antonio Díaz, and indigenous communities in general, coincide with the president of the republic. It is exactly the contrary. It is that the National Head of Government is the first one to discover something that was already there. Socialism has always constituted the form of indigenous living. For us that is a way of living. We have conducted ourselves always in solidarity distributing our production whether it is fish, wood, agriculture or any other order of things among all the dwellers of a collectivity. The president only brought into the constitution something that was already a norm of existence. That is why it was logical that we followed Chávez in a proposal of such a nature. Trying to find any other explanation is simply not to know or understand the Warao communities' idiosyncrasy. (Martínez 2008b: 12–13; author's translation)

Example 25

In order to fully understand this press note, we need some context about the political circumstances in which it was written. In December 2007, one of Hugo

Chávez's political proposals (a constitutional reform) was rejected by popular vote for the first time since the start of his Bolivarian revolution. Nevertheless, in the entire state of Delta Amacuro the "yes" option in favor of the constitutional reform won by a large margin. In the Antonio Díaz municipality, this support reached "almost" 100 percent of the votes. Since this is the municipality with the largest Warao population, the overwhelming vote in favor of Chávez was taken as a sign of the Waraos' blind support for the figure of the president.

The local victory of the "yes" prompted Martínez to ask Amado about the cause of this overwhelming support. Amado then broke into a meta-cultural exercise in which he interprets Warao's political feelings and what he called their "idiosyncrasy." It seems, according to Amado, that the support that Chávez enjoys among the indigenous people in Venezuela is the product of his ability to understand a "fundamental cultural tenet." The Warao culture is socialist to begin with, and that explains why Chávez's proposal appeals to them so strongly. Amado uses his indigenous identity to give legitimacy to Chávez's proposal. At the same time, he uses the stereotype of the "naturally socialist society" as proof that he is an authentic Indian who understands better the "idiosyncrasy" of his own people.

The idea that indigenous cultures are examples of primordial socialism has been often repeated in Venezuela since the start of the revolution. Whether or not Amado is conscious of it, his statements about the socialist nature of Warao culture cannot be disconnected from early South American political thinkers such as José Carlos Mariátegui, who imagined a natural link between the forms of indigenous social organization and socialism. Mariátegui's work is deemed as the first formulation of a socialist theory in South America and is often invoked in activist's discourses of indigenous rights around the continent. Of course, we cannot attribute Amado's comments to a direct quote from Mariátegui. What we have here is a generalized idea of the socialist Indian circulating and providing explanations about the course of contemporary politics in Venezuela. Chávez has mentioned these beliefs multiple times, and even if Amado is unaware of the origins of these ideas, the topic is central to the construction of his own political revolutionary message.

With all the emphasis on the indigenous roots of his political views and his ideological link with the transnational rising of indigenous leaders in the Americas, Amado also shares the local political field and the semiotic ideologies that deem indigenous constituents as easily manipulated through gift giving. In Chapter 5 we have seen how he tried to win the favor of the people of Morichito in the Winikina River with the gift of a generator. He used this gift to form a political base, and like other aspiring candidates, he makes constant references to these gifts in his public performances and speeches. At the moment in which

he decided to become the PSUV's candidate for governor, he started to reach populations beyond Antonio Díaz with his gifts, making this practice a more public issue. As he was engaging in more widespread gift giving, he released press notes like the following:

> With a welcome that deserved applause full of gratitude, compliments, and positive comments, the people of Pedernales received yesterday morning the inauguration by the mayor of the Antonio Diaz Municipality, Prof. Amado Heredia, of a new and modern unit for fluvial transportation, the product of a project approved by President Chávez and executed by PDVSA-CVP and the Antonio Diaz Municipality, answering in this way the need for transportation that has been felt in a vast sector of the Delta. This is a boat with a capacity for 30 passengers, and a *peñero* boat with capacity for 28, *casco en pie*, with a closed cabin and two engines with 200hp, 4 speed Yamaha 400 with the name of Warao Anarunoko, constructed in the State by Nuicenter enterprise, represented by Mr. Orangel Lacourt. It was known that the number of boats built will be nine in total, identical to the one described, they will distribute 8 for Antonio Diaz municipality and 1 for Pedernales.... (Gascón 2007: 4; author's translation)

Example 26

This press note articulates in a few lines all the ideological and semiotic processes that I have been trying to flesh out in this book. Amado Heredia appears here as a mediator and gift giver, framing the natural resources of the state (in this case oil extracted by PDVSA) and articulating those frames in specific rhetorical and linguistic terms. Amado mediates the translation of oil from the natural body of nation (extracted by the national oil company) into money and from money into political influence over the social body represented by the Warao. In the process, he becomes a surrogate giver and leader mediating also between the political body of the nation, represented here by Hugo Chávez, and the newly constituted public of Warao voters. The entire process is therefore explicitly summarized in these press notes. The semiotic mediation is made explicit so that the Warao voters can recognize the kind of moral bindings produced under the magic of the revolutionary state.

Conclusion

The PSUV's primaries took place on June 1, 2008. The first poll results showed Lizetta Hernandez as the winner and future candidate for Governor. Nevertheless, for a few days after the election, Amado Heredia challenged the legitimacy of

the results in disbelief that he would not be chosen as the candidate and possibly first indigenous governor of the Delta. He appealed to Chávez and the high ranks of the PSUV for a recount, but the leadership of the PSUV confirmed Lizetta a few days later. Amado then faced two alternatives: to accept defeat and support Lizetta or to abandon the PSUV. Even in defeat he was always loyal to the central command of the party, so in order to maintain that support and avoid being left out of the revolutionary movement altogether, he moved his candidacy to the PCV. Amado, in view of the internal conflict in the PSUV, moved to a party equally loyal to President Chávez with very little opportunity to win the election but not out of the revolutionary movement. The results of these elections had more to do with healing the wound produced by the loss in the constitutional referendum of December 2007 and consolidating the structure of the PSUV than any other consideration.

Lizetta's victory seems not to be the result of an original rhetorical strategy (her image of caring physician) or the use of promises and distribution of gifts per se, but mostly of her position as the candidate who guaranteed continuity with the policies and programs of the previous governor Yelitza Santaella. Whenever I discussed her victory in the Delta, people seemed to agree that Amado was corrupt and dishonest and had done nothing for them. His distribution of gifts was probably too little too late, and in any case, these gifts were challenged by the people who did not support him. In other words, Amado's gifts were not true indexicals of a continuous relation with constituents. They felt that had Amado become governor, he would have forgotten his promises. Amado had failed to create continuity between the gifts and his discourse. This interpretation applies also for Yelitza's brother Pedro Santaella, whose dysfunctional relation with his sister made people doubt that he would have a real connection with the Bolivarian movement. Pedro's relationship with his sister/governor made his capacity to deliver on his promises unclear.

The image of the politician/giver is central to all the politicians that I have presented in this chapter. The common theme of being a politician/giver coincides with a pervasive semiotic ideology among them that regard the Warao as easily manipulated with gifts and promises. Even if they juxtapose other characteristics in their political messages, they all share the idea that the poor and the Indians can be prompted to vote with the right economic stimulus. Nevertheless, as the results of this election show, far from being merely manipulated subjects, the Warao enter into complicated semiotic plays looking for true indexical signs of possible semiotic connections between the here and now of political discourses and the there and then of future political gifts.

Now, if all politicians share the idea that the Warao can be manipulated, why bother attempting to create juxtapositions with other features of the political self? On the one hand, this is a response to the double articulation between local politics and the trans-local projection of a politician's image. Local politicians are well aware that the people in the Delta are not the only ones looking at them, and they want to link their images with broader and more cosmopolitan political agendas. On the other hand, the emphasis on other characteristics of their political personae, even if it does not help them win, is a constitutive part of the personal character of the candidate or politician. In the same way in which meetings in small-scale societies sometimes have no consequence other than constituting the polity itself (Duranti 1994; Myers 1986), we can also argue that in localized journalistic practices, the deployment of multiple sides of the politician's message is not aimed only at winning elections, but at constituting the candidate as a political being.

Conclusion

The Warao have experienced the transformation of the Orinoco Delta from a colonial frontier into a Venezuelan Federal Territory and finally into a state with full democratic representational rights. During this time, they witnessed the Venezuelan democratic public sphere developing around them. This was an exclusionary process that kept them apart from political participation and representation. This political and territorial transformation occurred in a moment in which Venezuela's economy became almost exclusively oriented toward oil exports. In the twentieth century, oil became the most important commodity in the country, and the Venezuelan government became dependent on controlling this natural resource to carry out their social programs and policies. The successes and failures of Venezuela's economy have been tied to this dependency regardless of the ideological orientation, or democratic commitment, of whoever is in charge of the government at the time. No president, political party, or social movement has ever seriously challenged the country's rentier economic model. Oil is the backbone of what Fernando Coronil (1997) called the magical state. The state is magical because the richness of oil is translated into uncontrollable forces that allow politicians to look like sorcerers who develop the country with tricks made possible by oil. Oil allows corruption to flourish, social spending to happen, and economic miracles to be performed. If Venezuelans want hospitals and health programs, schools and well-paid teachers, roads and transportation, sometimes even food on their tables, it all seems to depend on oil. The general fate of the country and its politicians is then tied to this natural resource. This is why political anxiety in Venezuela is high when oil prices are low, but also why the country becomes a carnival when prices are high.

This dynamic transduction of oil into development is also extended into its transduction into political communicative practices. The Venezuelan state has been transformed by oil not only in its economic infrastructure but also in the way in which politicians communicate with the social body of nation. To be a Venezuelan citizen with political rights means not only having civil rights and responsibilities but, additionally, sharing the bounty of oil richness. This puts the

politicians in the position of making sure that the distribution of such richness is understood as coming from the state—but also from them as the face of the state. Politicians need to know how to communicate this in performances of proper political oratory, and through appropriate distribution of material resources. In indigenous areas such as the Orinoco Delta, this also implies bringing a non-Spanish-speaking public into the sphere of influence of these performances. Translation of languages then parallels the transduction of oil into state magic. Only by translating Spanish into Warao and Warao into Spanish can a politician also produce the magic of the state in a remote area like the Orinoco Delta.

Venezuelan writer Jose Ignasio Cabrujas used to say that it is political suicide for a Venezuelan politician to not promise paradise. In this book I have shown that it is not just the promising but the delivery of these promises as gifts that save the politicians from political suicide. Venezuelan politicians are always precariously performing in front of a national public like dancing Jacobins, as Rafael Sanchez (2016) would put it. I proposed in the course of this book to look at this process as a triadic semiotic process. The Venezuelan magical state is a semiotic sign to Venezuelans standing for the oil richness of the country's subsoil. It forms a Peircean semiotic relationship standing for a bountiful nature, making Venezuelan citizens feel that they live in a wealthy country. The state takes nature as its semiotic object, and makes people believe that they are rich—or at least talk as if the nation and they themselves are rich. That is why Venezuelans say almost without hesitation that the country is rich in spite of its poverty. After all, the state is the guardian and mediator between the people and a bountiful, seemingly infinite, oil reserve. Venezuelans grow up knowing that Venezuela's oil reserves are so big that they could, and now do, surpass those of Saudi Arabia. The magic of the state depends on Venezuelans believing in such potential richness and in the capacity of the state to mediate between the people and the country's magical reserves.

All of Venezuela's political projects since the second half of the twentieth century seem to be a spin-off of this mediated process. Nevertheless, in this chapter I would like to take a different angle in this mediation between the state, oil, and the people, one that Coronil left unresolved for us after his untimely death in 2011. In 2008 he wrote:

> As if following the script of the great social revolutions of the modern period, Chávez is re-writing the nation's history through his prolific verbal production— as far as I know, he speaks publicly more than any national leader ever anywhere. Yet his words, perhaps because of their exuberant proliferation, serve not to just to reconstruct past history or to guide its new construction, *but to substitute for*

it. As they conjure up a world of their own, at times it is not clear whether one is living through a real or a rhetorical revolution, perceiving the initial flowering of human capacities in a freer society or the manicuring of a bonsai revolution, having a dream or a nightmare, or awakening to recognize history as both. (Coronil 2008: 3; emphasis added)

Chávez's verbal exuberance stands, then, for his Bolivarian revolution. He would broadcast his speeches for hours on end using all radio and TV stations at once, something we call in Venezuela "chaining," which can be appropriately interpreted as linking all channels but also keeping the audience captive. In those lengthy speeches he would explain his plans for the nation and try to educate the public about what it means to be a good socialists and patriotic Venezuelan. I take Chávez's prolific speech as a symptom of something more general. Chávez's overflow of explanations, complaints, and pedagogical speeches do not stand for the revolution—they are the revolution. I take Coronil's final clue about Chávez's speech to argue in this chapter that the Bolivarian revolution is a rhetorical revolution, but not only in the sense of a proliferation of speech. The latest instantiation of the magical state has not just the capacity to turn oil into state magic. Its trick is to make Venezuelans believe that they are in the presence of a changing nation while the state is doing nothing of the sort. The trick of the Bolivarian revolution has been making people believe in change, inclusion, and social justice without actually changing the basic functioning principles of state formation and reproduction in the country. The state remains a rentier magical state. Oil remains the only source of real income for Venezuela as a country. Yet, for twenty years this magical state presented itself as if it were changing in front of us. How does the Bolivarian revolution accomplish this feat? The ethnography I have presented in this book gives us a clue about this process. Chávez's trick is not just making the state represent the richness of the country but also making the state into a semiotic object to be represented by a proliferation of revolutionary signs. The Bolivarian trick has been to take control of the signs and linguistic practices that stand for the state, and to promise that those changing signs will change the nature of the nation itself. The Bolivarian revolution imagines itself as inclusive, socialist, anti-imperialist, and more. It imagines the nation as being refounded through the new 1999 constitution. But this revolutionary change requires only new linguistic and performative practices to represent it. This is why it requires an overabundance of rhetoric. Chávez needed to explain, to teach, to exemplify. He spent hours every week in front of TV cameras trying to get through to the general public about what the revolution meant. All this explaining, and all the exuberant signs that we have

seen appear in front of indigenous peoples in the course of this book, happens without doing anything about the economic structure of the country. Chávez promised socialism and hoped that his words and his performances would produce revolutionary consciousness without ever changing the economic infrastructure in which the state lies.

In Venezuela the revolution has been performative and rhetorical in a Peircean semiotic sense. In a Peircean sense, rhetoric does not mean just persuasive or pleasurable language but the capacity of signs to overdetermine interpretants (Colapietro 2007). What this means is that rhetoric analyzes not the relationship of representation between signs and objects, but how signs produce affective, physical, or logical reactions to them. In Peircean terminology, speculative rhetoric is the branch of semiotics that studies how signs affect interpretants, not how signs stand for objects. Considering rhetoric in this sense helps us understand why state agents in a revolutionary state concentrate their efforts on the production and control of linguistic practices in the hope of compelling people to feel and think about a sense of change without necessarily changing anything but signs. In Venezuela this rhetorical sense of change is possible, thanks to the oil revenue that sustained revolutionary dreaming. To accomplish this dreaming, the state only has to provide people with verbal and material evidence that everything is changing. In an oil-producing country like Venezuela, the easiest way to achieve this rhetorical overabundance of signs is to use processes of translation and transduction. By infusing state revolutionary plans with oil money, the state changes from being a sign representing the nation to a semiotic object which we are compelled to judge by the signs it provides for us. Talking about revolution, promising revolution, and more importantly here, translating revolution has overdetermined revolutionary thinking in Venezuela. The Bolivarian revolution is not substituted for Chávez's speech. Chávez's speech is the revolution. There is no confusion between real revolution and rhetorical revolution because they are one and the same.

This rhetorical strategy depends on a history of linguistic practices also overdetermined by the structural conditions of state formation inherited by the Bolivarian revolution. It can only make Venezuelans feel a part of a revolutionary process for as long as it has the oil money to continue producing the rhetorical signs that compel those feelings and thoughts. But the Bolivarian revolution has not changed the magical illusion of the state, and it all comes crashing when oil fails to deliver. Revolutionary magic is an absolute faith that the performative power of signs and symbols could change the country for good. Immense oil reserves perpetuate the idea that it is possible to do so.

How then did the Warao get caught in the middle of this magical rhetorical revolution? Historically, this process reached its peak in the mid-twentieth century with the arrival of democracy and political parties to the lives of the Warao. Under this new democratic rule, political parties started to compete to gain the support of areas of the country that were disregarded by the centralized power of the nation-state. The first political parties of the democratic era (AD and COPEI) developed the strategy of creating direct links with their constituents by distributing state resources as political gifts and making promises on behalf of their political leaders in Caracas. In the Orinoco Delta, this process accelerated in the 1990s when it became a state because its citizens gained the right to vote at all levels of public administration. Voting meant becoming the target of the signs of the magical state. With the expansion of the public sphere and party politics, the Warao started having expectation about how politicians should perform political discourses and how these discourses have to refer to future and past distributions of state resources, which are usually represented as gifts on behalf of political leaders.

Oftentimes this process of gift giving is plagued with semiotic hazards (Keane 1997) and does not occur as expected by the Waraos and the politicians involved. During the performance of political discourse, politicians and indigenous leaders are not always able to make promises or link their discourse in any other way with processes of political gift giving. We have seen this happen in Chapter 3 through the examples of two Warao leaders who were unable to make promises during their speeches. By contrast, in this same chapter, we found a Ye'kuana politician who used the strategy of framing state policies as political gifts from the central government. The reaction of the Warao audience to these two events was very different. In the case of the two Warao politicians, their speeches did not satisfy the aspirations of local leaders. Many of those who attended were disappointed and even abandoned the meeting to pursue other activities. Moreover, the meeting was transformed into a *monikata*-style meeting by other Warao leaders who saw the opportunity to show their leadership and complain about the abuses of the National Guard. This transformation of genres drew attention away from other aspects of the proceedings and left unresolved the gap between this discursive event and any other involvement of the politicians with Warao communities.

When a political gift is given, it is expected that some political talk, discourse, or promise precedes it. Nevertheless, the distribution of gifts does not always conform to this pattern. In Chapter 4 I showed an example of this aspect of the process. The gift of a generator for the community of Morichito in the Winikina

River turned into a competition over the legitimacy of this object as a gift. When this gift was delivered to the community, the rightful receiver was out of town. Being a very high-priced item, the young men of the community organized the collection of this political gift in spite of the resistance of older community leaders. After the person who was supposed to receive the gift returned to the community and realized that someone else had received his gift, he promptly called a mediation meeting. This gift had been delivered without any previous promise, and those who actually received it did not feel obligated to recognize it as a gift to them. Moreover, they did not feel obligated to support the political faction of Amado Heredia, the politician who gifted the generator to the town of Morichito. Paulino, the shaman who was supposed to receive the gift, also felt betrayed since the gift was given randomly. He tried to deal with this situation by enrolling Tirso on the list of people who were supposed to vote for Amado. This is an example of a failed gift which was not appropriately linked to a particular rhetorical strategy. No promise was made directly to Tirso or the people who picked the gift up. Paulino, who had talked about this gift with Amado Heredia, lost the opportunity to depict the generator as a proper political gift to the community.

The examples in Chapters 3 and 4 form the core of my explanation of how a translation of state resources into political performances semiotically links political discourse and political gift. Both of these chapters show different aspects of the same semiotic process. This is a clear example of how the history of the Delta created the conditions for the creation of an ideological connection between sign systems, that is, discourse and material exchange. By postulating this semiotic relation, I propose that these systems of political gifts and political discourse are constitutive of each other and establish a dialectic relation that develops in time and space. I also described the historical conditions in which this particular relation between discourse and political gift emerged. In other words, I do not consider this relationship to be something intrinsic to Warao culture, but rather the product of a particular historical process. The Warao position within Venezuela's political dynamic is a historical product, not the product of an intrinsic cultural way of perceiving the world or an ontological perspective.

This ideological relation between discourse and gift is an integral part of the relationship between the Warao and local politicians. In Chapter 5, I showed that after a gift is delivered it becomes the engine behind the production of more political discourse. I use the example of the only newspaper in the Delta to illustrate this process. In the pages of *Notidiario*, I found reliable sources

of rhetorical practices linking promises and political discourse with the self-presentation of specific politicians. In these journalistic narratives, the relation of the politician with gifts is also variously constructed. The newspaper presents narratives about the personal qualities of the politicians that link them with images of generosity and their specific abilities to distribute state resources. For example, the past candidate and current governor of the state Lizetta Hernandez used the narrative of the dedicated doctor to imply a parallel with the religious imagery of the Venezuelan saint José Gregorio Hernandez. Like him, she was willing to perform selfless acts of generosity by attending to large numbers of patients and distributing medicine to the poor. On the other hand, I showed how Amado Heredia, the only indigenous candidate during that election, connected his own image to ideas of primordial indigenous socialism and his ability to distribute gifts beyond the borders of his municipality; and how Pedro Santaella, the mayor of the Casacoima municipality, presented an image of a good administrator based on his supposed ability to bring services to the people. All these are examples of how political gifts pervade the narratives that help politicians to construct their public self.

I concluded by exploring the consequences of this study. First, I proposed that the connection with this form of politics has brought the development of a new form of leadership among the Waraos. Previous to the development of the Bolivarian revolution in the early 2000s, we find two traditional forms of dealing with hierarchy and coercive power among the Warao. The first one is the capacity to enroll as many sons-in-law as possible to control their labor. The second is the hierarchical structure of shamans who are the owners of ritual and symbolic means of production. To this form of power, we can now add forms of hierarchical relation introduced by agents of the nation-state. The figures of *kobenahoro, borisia,* and *kabitana* were introduced by the missionaries to create leaders who would control the newly formed communities that moved to the shores of the rivers between the 1930s and 1970s. Finally, the new constitutional reform of 2000, introduced by Hugo Chávez, helped to produce a new generation of Warao leaders appointed this time by the central government. These are elected and unelected indigenous leaders who are connected with national and international discourses and ideas. Often, these leaders, through their endeavors to deal with the demands of transparency and good governance, collide with Warao expectations and demands of a semiotic link between their discourses and expected political gift giving.

Many times, political leaders in these situations are accused of populism and of transforming the Warao into political clients. I argue that these

interpretations do not pay enough attention to the effect of the so-called populist policies on their subjects. By neglecting this side of the equation, they miss deep semiotic play that the process of distribution of state resources implies. This has the effect of negating the agency of the subjects of the so-called populist regimes and the capacity for interpreting the political situation around them. The concept of populism is probably more an obstacle than a theoretical tool in our understanding of how political ideologies pervade the relation between indigenous peoples and the nation-state. I propose that a semiotic approach to this situation renders a more powerful depiction.

The development of the Bolivarian revolution in Venezuela has caused profound changes in how indigenous people participate in national politics. A deep transformation in the way in which indigenous leadership is elected and legitimized is underway in Venezuela. A future avenue of research is the specific performative strategies that these new leaders use to navigate their involvement with national and international audiences and their indigenous constituents. Graham (2002) has shown that we need ethnographic analysis of the specific strategies that these indigenous leaders use to be successful in different cultural contexts and with different audiences that demand accommodation to their own political agendas. Thus, one of the main questions that need to be explored is the relationship between this process linking gift giving and rhetorical strategies with broader global forms of circulation of information and images. How is the semiotic relation between gift giving and discourse played out in the circulation of Warao images and political agendas outside the Delta? I can only provide a limited answer to this question in this book.

More research is also needed about the transformation of gender ideologies that is underway among the Warao in relation to the formation of new indigenous leadership. As we have seen, most of the Warao leaders linked to the Bolivarian revolution are women. This contrasts with traditional forms of political leadership and with the conformation of political structures in communities of the lower Delta. During my fieldwork it was clear that most leaders of communal councils were men, while most high-ranking leaders in other offices were women appointed by the PSUV or government structures. This requires more ethnographic attention.

Finally, the magical revolution that started twenty years ago is now not only translating oil into political tricks but also fundamentally changing the way in which the state is reproduced among the Warao. As I showed in Chapters 2 and 3, practices of translation have changed direction so that now it is Spanish texts that are translated into Warao and not the other way around.

The translation of the national anthem and other texts into Warao is supposed to signal a change of attitude in the government, but the sustainability of this change depends on the revolution staying in power to continue the process of social inclusion. As Venezuela has entered one of its most profound crises in recent history because of low oil prices, it is unclear whether translations of oil into revolutionary magic and of Spanish texts into Warao will continue in that direction. Lack of oil money in Venezuela often means the end of inclusive policies, the end of translation of oil into political well-being for indigenous peoples, and the halt of linguistic translations from Spanish into Warao. This is not just an end of translation of oil reserves into political gifts but a breakdown of the state's rhetorical capacity in general. The current economic crisis means that it is no longer possible to create signs of the Bolivarian revolution that people would believe in. The Warao live in one of the most loyal *chavista* states in the country. They have voted and supported Hugo Chávez and the PSUV in every single election since 1999, even those the *chavistas* lost. But now the state has lost its capacity to produce the signs of political and economic inclusion that this support relied on. It is now time to see if the rhetorical capacity of the state will survive the international crisis of oil prices. Only time will tell if this is a definite blow to Venezuela's magical state or if the crisis will result in a new iteration of its political magic tricks.

Notes

Introduction

1 For an ethnography of patronage and clientelism in northern Brazil similar to the Venezuelan case, see Ansell (2014).
2 For a recent discussion of populism in Venezuela, see Samet (2019).
3 For an analysis of the semiotic co-naturalization of language and race, see Rosa (2019).
4 For an anthropological analysis of state violence in Venezuela, see Coronil (1994), Coronil and Skurski (1991).

Chapter 1

1 See Hill (1994b) for an analysis of state formation and discursive inequality linked to international politics in southern Venezuela.
2 Gupta (1995) has shown that state formation and the development of civil society cannot be separated, even though in Western thought it is a dual process.
3 The idea of encouraging immigration from Europe, North America, and Asia—due to the alleged superiority of these peoples over local indigenous peoples or national criollos—was very widespread in Latin America during the late nineteenth century (Hill 1999).

Chapter 2

1 Webb Keane (1997) has shown how language ideologies work in the production of marginality in Indonesia.
2 For a detailed description of Gomez's religious and territorial policies, see Arcaya (1936); Carrocera (1953); Coronil (1997);; Gilmore (1964); Rourke (1937); Yarrington (2003).
3 Olea does not provide the exact words that he used to translate these lexical items.
4 In this conversation "A" will stand for the "rational Warao" and "B" for Lavandero.

5 Heterotopies are "Real places—places that do exist, that can be pointed out on a map, lived in, visited, or empirically experienced in an obvious fashion. But heterotopias are very special kinds of places because (and here I depart from Foucault's formulation) they mediate, in a mirror like fashion between utopias and ideological subjects. In other words, heterotopias enable—incite, compel, invite— people to see them reflected in some utopia. They function as an ideological hinge, linking social subjected (people) with a possible political-moral identity (utopia) that they assume (inhabit)" (Deshpande 1998: 250).

6 A *Hoa* is conceived symbolically as an arrow thrown to produce illness or death.

7 Hill (2003) proposed that Shamanic discourses like the *hoa* presented here are forms of creating and controlling imagined communities similar to those described by Anderson (1991).

Chapter 3

1 There have been local attempts at translating the national anthem to indigenous languages during the twentieth century, but these translations, done by indigenous intellectuals, never had government support and did not circulate widely in the country (see, for example, Graham and Palmar Barroso 2014). Here I am referring to recent attempts by the current socialist revolutionary government at giving indigenous languages official status, which made possible a wider circulation for these texts.

2 Here I identify two publics organized around the translated anthem as a text: (1) Warao indigenous leaders and Warao speakers and (2) nonindigenous, Spanish-speaking, Venezuelans. These are publics in the sense that Michael Warner gives the term: "The kind of public that comes into being only in relation to texts and their circulation" (2002: 413).

3 For a recent treatment of the importance of qualia in semiotic analysis, see, for example, Chumley (2013), Chumley and Harkness (2013), Hankins (2013), Harkness (2013), Lemon (2013), Gal (2013).

4 https://www.YouTube.com/watch?v=7l5ylT7bTrE&index=1&list=PLGSOKWvPJPy3 -5NzkrCtmf4vr2oRgM40M.

5 https://www.youtube.com/watch?v=7dxYjDnM3dQ&list=PLGSOKWvPJPy3-5N zkrCtmf4vr2oRgM40M&index=3.

6 https://www.youtube.com/watch?v=rvgGjZkdQKQ&list=PLGSOKWvPJPy3-5N zkrCtmf4vr2oRgM40M&index=2.

7 https://www.youtube.com/watch?v=gqVLZ-Rzpf4&list=PLGSOKWvPJPy3-5NzkrCt mf4vr2oRgM40M&index=5.

Chapter 4

1 These "new indigenous leaders" are those either elected or appointed after 2000, when a new constitution and set of laws granted new political rights to indigenous peoples in Venezuela.

2 Although I argue that failing to make promises makes political discourses less relevant for establishing a relation with other semiotic events, this does not affect the discourse's poetic, phatic, and indexical effectiveness. I recognize with Jakobson (1960) the multiplicity of functions of any given utterance.

3 See, for example, Urban (1986, 1988), Riviere (1971), Sherzer (1983, 1999), Basso (1985), Briggs (1992, 1993, 1994, 1998), Hendricks (1988, 1993), Hill (1993, 1994), Graham (1993, 1995, 2005), Surralles (2003).

4 For a post-functionalist view of the role of passionate speech and deliberative language in political meetings, see Bailey (1983), Bilmes (1976), Bloch (1975), Borgström (1982), Bowen (1989), Brenneis (1988), Brenneis and Myers (1984), Paine (1981).

5 In January 8, 2007, President Hugo Chávez announced the Simon Bolivar National Project, which included what he called five revolutionary engines: (1) enabling laws (passed by the congress to give the president special powers over legislatures or issues of national interest); (2) constitutional reform; (3) education and values; (4) a new geometry of power; (5) an explosion of popular power, especially of communal power in the form of councils.

6 Most likely these interactions remained in Spanish for my benefit.

7 Fundacomunal is the Venezuelan national institution in charge of channeling the money for the communal councils.

8 The spelling of this auditorium's name (Auriwakanoko) is an alternative spelling of the Warao word *oriwakanoko* which can be translated as "a place to speak or talk to each other." I opted to keep the spelling as it appears in the banners and the press notes that refer to this place.

References

Agha, Asif. 2007. *Language and Social Relations*. Cambridge: Cambridge University Press.

Ahlers, Jocelyn C. 2006. "Framing Discourse: Creating Community through Native Language Use." *Journal of Linguistic Anthropology* 16, no. 1: 58–75.

Albro, Robert. 2000. "The Populist Chola: Cultural Mediation and the Political Imagination in Quillacollo, Bolivia." *Journal of Latin American Anthropology* 5, no. 2: 30–88.

Albro, Robert. 2001. "Reciprocity and Realpolitik: Image, Career, and Factional Genealogies in Provincial Bolivia." *American Ethnologist* 28, no. 1: 56–93.

Allard, Olivier. 2010. "Morality and Emotion in the Dynamics of an Amerindian Society (Warao, Orinoco Delta, Venezuela)." Ph.D. diss., University of Cambridge.

Allard, Olivier. 2013. "To Cry One's Distress: Death, Emotion, and Ethics among the Warao of the Orinoco Delta." *Journal of the Royal Anthropological Institute* 19, no. 3: 545–61.

Anderson, Benedict. 1991. *Imagined Communities: Reflections on the Origin and Spread of Nationalism*. New York: Verso.

Ansell, Aaron. 2014. *Zero Hunger: Political Culture and Antipoverty Policy in Northeast Brazil*. Chapel Hill: University of North Carolina Press.

Appadurai, Arjun. 1986. *The Social Life of Things: Commodities in Cultural Perspective*. New York: Cambridge University Press.

Appadurai, Arjun. 1996. *Modernity at Large Cultural*. Minneapolis, MN: University of Minnesota Press.

Aragon, Lorrain V. 1996. "Twisting the Gift: Translating Precolonial into Colonial Exchanges in Central Sulawesi, Indonesia." *American Ethnologist* 23, no. 1: 43–60.

Arcaya, Pedro Manuel. 1936. *The Gomez Regime in Venezuela and Its Background*. Washington, DC: Sun Printing Company.

Armellada, Cesareo de. 1954. *Fuero Indígena Venezolano, Parte II*. Caracas: Ministerio de Justicia.

Arndt, Grant. 2010. "The Making and Muting of an Indigenous Media Activist: Imagination and Ideology in Charles Round Low Cloud's 'Indian News.'" *American Ethnologist* 37, no. 3: 499–510.

Austin, J.L. 1962. *How to Do Things with Words*. London: Oxford University Press.

Bailey, F.G. 1983. *The Tactical Uses of Passion: An Essay on Power, Reason, and Reality*. Ithaca, NY: Cornell University Press.

Bakhtin, M. 1981. *The Dialogic Imagination: Four Essays*. Austin: University of Texas Press.

Bakhtin, M. 1986. *Speech Genres and Other Essays*. Austin: University of Texas Press.

Basso, Ellen. 1985. *A Musical View of the Universe: Kalapalo Myth and Ritual Performances*. Philadelphia, PA: University of Pennsylvania Press.

Bastenier, M.A. 1989. La 'Coronación' de Carlos Andrés Pérez. El Pais. Accessed Septiembre 25, 2019. https://elpais.com/diario/1989/02/05/internacional/602636405 _850215.html.

Bate, Bernard. 2002. "Political Praise in Tamil Newspaper: The Poetry and Iconography of Democratic Power." In *Everyday Life in South Asia*, edited by Diane P. Mines and Sarah Lamb, 308–25. Bloomington, IN: Indiana University Press.

Becker, A.L. 2000. *Beyond Translation: Essays Towards a Modern Philology*. Ann Arbor, MI: University of Michigan Press.

Beidelman, T. O. 1989. "Agonistic Exchange: Homeric Reciprocity and the Heritage of Simmel and Mauss." *Cultural Anthropology* 4, no. 3: 227–59.

Bercovitch, Eytan. 1994. "The Agent in the Gift: Hidden Exchange in Inner New Guinea." *Cultural Anthropology* 9, no. 4: 498–536.

Bilmes, J. 1976. "Rules and Rhetoric: Negotiating the Social Order in a Thai Village." *Journal of Anthropological Research* 32, no. 1: 44–57.

Birth, Kevin. 2008. *Bacchanalian Sentiments: Musical Experiences and Political Counterpoint in Trinidad*. Durham: Duke University Press.

Bloch, Maurice, ed. 1975. *Political Language and Oratory in Traditional Society*. London: Academic.

Borgström, Bengt-Erik. 1982. "Power Structure and Political Speech." *Man* 17, no. 2: 313–27.

Bourdieu, Pierre. 1977. "The Economics of Linguistic Exchanges." *Social Science Information* 16, no. 6: 645–68.

Bourdieu, Pierre. 1991. *Language and Symbolic Power*. Cambridge, MA: Harvard University Press.

Bowen, John R. 1989. "Political Duels and Political Change in the Gayo Highland of Sumatra." *American Anthropologist* 91, no. 1: 25–40.

Brenneis, Donald. 1988. "Language and Disputing." *Annual Review of Anthropology* 17: 221–37.

Brenneis, Donald L. and Fred R. Myers, eds. 1984. *Dangerous Words: Language and Politics in the Pacific*. New York: New York University Press.

Briggs, Charles. 1988. *Competence in Performance: The Creativity of Tradition in Mexicano Verbal Art*. Philadelphia: University of Pennsylvania Press.

Briggs, Charles. 1992. "'Since I Am a Woman, I Will Chastise My Relatives': Gender, Reported Speech, and the (Re)Production of Social of Relations in Warao Ritual Wailing." *American Ethnologist* 19, no. 2: 337–61.

Briggs, Charles. 1993. "Personal Sentiments and Polyphonic Voices in Warao Women's Ritual Wailing: Music and Poetics in Critical and Collective Discourse." *American Anthropologist* 95, no. 4: 929–57.

Briggs, Charles. 1994. "The Sting of the Ray: Bodies, Agency, and Grammar in Warao Curing." *Journal of American Folklore* 107, no. 423: 139–66.

Briggs, Charles. 1996a. "The Politics of Discursive Authority in Research on the 'Invention of Tradition.'" *Cultural Anthropology* 11, no. 4: 435–69.

Briggs, Charles. 1996b. "Conflict, Language, Ideologies, and Privileged Arenas of Discursive Authority in Warao Dispute Mediation." In *Disorderly Discourse: Narrative, Conflict, and Inequality*, edited by Charles Briggs, 204–42. New York: Oxford University Press.

Briggs, Charles, ed. 1996c. *Disorderly Discourse: Narrative, Conflict, and Inequality.* New York: Oxford University Press.

Briggs, Charles. 1998. "'You're a Liar-You're Just Like a Women!': Constructing Dominant Ideologies of Language in Warao Men's Gossip." In *Language Ideologies: Practice and Theory*, edited by Bambi B. Schieffelin, Kathryn A. Woolard, and Paul V. Kroskrity, 229–55. New York: Oxford University Press.

Briggs, Charles. 2000. "Emergence of the Non-indigenous Peoples: A Warao narrative." In *Translating Native Latin American Verbal Art: Ethnopoetics and Ethnography of Speaking*, edited by Kay Sammons and Joel Sherzer, 174–96. Washington, DC: Smithsonian Institution Press.

Briggs, Charles. 2005. "Communicability, Racial Discourse, and Disease." *Annual Review of Anthropology* 34: 269–91.

Briggs, Charles. 2008. *Poeticas de Vida en Espacios de Muerte: Genero, poder y estado en la cotidianidad Warao.* Quito: Abya-Yala.

Briggs, Charles. 2016. *Tell Me Why My Children Died: Rabies, Indigenous Knowledge, and Communicative Justice.* Durham and London: Duke University Press.

Briggs, Charles and Clara Mantini-Briggs. 2003. *Stories in the Time of Cholera: Racial Profiling During a Medical Nightmare.* Berkeley, CA: University of California Press.

Briggs, Charles and Richard Bauman. 1992. "Genre, Intertextuality, and Social Power." *Journal of Linguistic Anthropology* 2, no. 2: 131–72.

Britto García, Luis. 1989. *El Poder sin la Máscara: de la Concertación Populista a la Explosión Social.* Caracas, Venezuela: Alfadil Ediciones.

Caballero, Manuel. 2000. *La Gestación de Hugo Chávez: 40 años de Luces y Sombras en la Democracia Venezolana.* Madrid: Libros de la Catarata.

Cabrujas, José Ignacio. 1987. "El Estado del disimulo." *Estado & Reforma, Edición Especial,* 5–35.

Calello, Hugo. 1973. *Poder Político y Populismo: Del Peronismo a la Subversión y otros Ensayos.* Caracas: Ediciones de la Biblioteca, Universidad Central de Venezuela.

Carrocera, Cayetano de. 1953. "El Delta del Orinoco y las Misiones." *Boletín de la Academia Nacional de la Historia,* 141: 28–45.

Cavanaugh, Jillian R. and Shalini Shankar, eds. 2017. *Language and Materiality: Ethnographic and Theoretical Explorations.* Cambridge, UK: Cambridge University Press.

Celis Parra, Bernardo. 1986. *Masificación y Crisis.* Mérida: Editorial Venezolana.

Chumley, Lily Hope. 2013. "Evaluation Regimes and the Qualia of Qualia." *Anthropological Theory* 13, no. 1/2: 169–83.

Chumley, Lily Hope and Nicholas Harkness. 2013. "Introduction: QUALIA." *Anthropological Theory* 13, no. 1/2: 3–11.

Ciccariello-Maher, George. 2013. *We Created Chávez: A People's History of the Venezuelan Revolution*. Durham: Duke University Press.

Clastre, Pierre. 1977. *Society Against the State: The Leader as Servant and the Humane Uses of Power Among the Indians of the Americas*. New York: Urizen Books.

Cody, Francis. 2009. "Daily Wires and Daily Blossoms: Cultivating Regimes of Circulation in Tamil India's Newspaper Revolution." *Journal of Linguistic Anthropology* 19, no. 2: 286–309.

Colapietro, Vincent. 2007. "CS Peirce's Rhetorical Turn." *Transactions of the Charles S. Peirce Society* 43, no. 1: 16–52.

Conklin, Beth A. 1995. "'Thus Are Our Bodies, Thus Our Custom': Mortuary Cannibalism in an Amazonian Society." *American Ethnologists* 22, no. 1: 75–101.

Conklin, Beth A. 1997. "Body Paint, Feathers, and VCRs: Aesthetics and Authenticity in Amazonian Activism." *American Ethnologists* 24, no. 4: 711–37.

Conklin, Beth A. and Laura R. Graham. 1995. "The Shifting Middle Ground: Amazonian Indian and Eco-Politics." *American Anthropologists* 97, no. 4: 695–710.

Coronil, Fernando. 1994. "Listening to the Subaltern: The Poetics of Neocolonial States." *Poetics Today* 15, no. 4: 643–58.

Coronil, Fernando. 1997. *The Magical State: Nature, Money, and Modernity in Venezuela*. Chicago: University of Chicago Press.

Coronil, Fernando. 2000. "Magical Illusions or Revolutionary Magic? Chavez in Historical Context." *NACLA Report on the Americas* 33, no. 6: 34–42.

Coronil, Fernando. 2008. "Chávez' Venezuela: A New Magical State." *ReVista: Harvard Review of Latin America* Fall: 3–4.

Coronil, Fernando and Julie Skurski. 1991. "Dismembering and Remembering the Nation: The Semantics of Political Violence in Venezuela." *Comparative Studies in Society and History* 33, no. 2: 288–337.

Cusack, Asa K. 2019. *Venezuela, ALBA, and the Limits of Postneoliberal Regionalism in Latin America and the Caribbean*. New York: Palgrave Macmillan.

Deshpande, Satish. 1998. "Hegemonic Spatial Strategies: The Nation-Space and Hindu Communalism in Twenty-Century India." *Public Culture* 10, no. 2: 249–83.

Dix, Robert H. 1978. "The Varieties of Populism: The Case of Colombia." *The Western Political Quarterly* 31, no. 3: 334–51.

Dix, Robert H. 1985. "Populism: Authoritarian and Democratic." *Latin American Research Review* 20, no. 2: 29–52.

Duranti, Alessandro. 1994. *From Grammar to Politics: Linguistic Anthropology in a Western Samoan Village*. Berkeley, CA: University of California Press.

Duranti, Alessandro. 2003. "The Voice of the Audience in Contemporary American Political Discourse." In *Linguistics, Language, and the Real World*, edited by Deborah Tannen and James E. Alatis, 114–34. Washington, DC: Georgetown University Press.

Duranti, Alessandro. 2006. "Narrating the Political Self in a Campaign for U.S. Congress." *Language in Society* 35, no. 4: 467–97.

Errington, Joseph. 2001. "Colonial Linguistics." *Annual Review of Anthropology* 30: 19–39.

Federici, Silvia. 2004. *Caliban and the Witch: Women, the Body and Primitive Accumulation*. New York: Autonomedia.

Fernandes, Sujatha. 2010. *Who Can Stop the Drums? Urban Social Movements in Chávez's Venezuela*. Durham: Duke University Press, 2010.

Firth, Raymond. 1972. "Verbal and Bodily Rituals of Greetings and Parting." In *The Interpretation of Ritual: Essays in Honour of A.I. Richards*, edited by J. S. La Fontaine, 1–38. London: Tavistock.

Foucault, Michel. 1977. *Discipline and Punish: The Birth of the Prison*. New York: Vintage Books.

Fraser, Nancy. 1985. "What Is Critical About Critical Theory?: The Case of Habermas and Gender." *New German Critique* 35: 97–131.

Fraser, Nancy. 1990. "Rethinking the Public Sphere: A Contribution to the Critique of Actually Existing Democracy." *Social Text* 25/26: 56–80.

Friedrich, Paul. 1986. *The Language Parallax: Linguistic Relativism and Poetic Indeterminacy*. Austin: University of Texas Press.

Gal, Susan. 1989. "Language and Political Economy." *Annual Review of Anthropology* 18: 345–67.

Gal, Susan. 2013. "Tastes of Talk: Qualia and the Moral Flavor of Signs." *Anthropological Theory* 13, no. 1/2: 31–48.

Gal, Susan and Judith Irvine. 1995. "The Boundaries of Languages and Disciplines: How Ideologies Construct Difference." *Social Research* 62, no. 4: 968–1001.

Gal, Susan and Judith Irvine. 2019. *Signs of Difference: Language and Ideology in Social Life*. Cambridge: Cambridge University Press.

Gal, Susan and Kathryn Woolard, eds. 2001. *Languages and Publics: The Making of Authority*. Manchester: St. Jerome Publishing.

Garcia, Argimiro. 1971. *Cuentos y Tradiciones de los Indios Guaraunos*. Caracas: Universidad Católica Andrés Bello.

Gascón, Jose Angel. 2007a. En los Rastrojos y Los Rastrojitos la Gobernadora Ha Cumplido. Notidiario, November 14: 4.

Gascón, Jose Angel. 2007b. La Sureña del Delta Otorgó Reconocimiento al Alcalde Amado Heredia. Notidiario, November 1: 2.

Gascón, Jose Angel. 2007c. Moderno Transporte Fluvial Puso en Marcha el Alcalde Heredia. Notidiario, Noviembre 28: 4.

Gershon, Ilana. 2010. *The Breakup 2.0: Disconnecting over New Media*. Ithaca: Cornell University Press.

Gibson, James J. 1986. *The Ecological Approach to Visual Perception*. London: Lawrence Erlbaum Associates, Publishers.

Gilmore, Robert. 1964. *Caudillism and Militarism in Venezuela, 1890–1910*. Athens: Ohio University Press.

Goffman, Erving. 1959. *The Presentation of Self in Everyday Life*. Garden City, NY: Doubleday.

Goffman, Erving. 1974. *Frame Analysis: An Essay on the Organization of Experience*. New York: Harper & Row, Publishers.

Graham, Laura. 1993. "A Public Sphere in Amazonia? The Depersonalized Collaborative Construction of Discourse in Xavante." *American Ethnologist* 20, no. 4: 717–41.

Graham, Laura. 1995. *Performing Dreams: Discourses of Immortality Among the Xavante of Central Brazil*. Austin, TX: University of Texas Press.

Graham, Laura. 2002. "How Should and Indian Speak? Amazonian Indians and the Symbolic Politics of Language in the Global Public Sphere." In *Indigenous Movements, Self-Representation, and the State in Latin America*, edited by Kay B. Warren and Jean E. Jackson, 181–228. Austin, TX: University of Texas Press.

Graham, Laura. 2005. "Language and Instrumentality in a Xavante Politics of Existential Recognition: The Public Outreach work Etènhiritipa Pimentel Barbosa." *American Ethnologist* 32, no. 4: 622–41.

Graham, Laura. 2011. "Quoting Mario Juruna: Linguistic Imagery and the Transformation of Indigenous Voice in the Brazilian Print Press." *American Ethnologists* 38, no. 1: 164–83.

Graham, Laura R. and Flor Angela Palmar Barroso. 2014. "Yaletüsü Saaschin Woumain (Glory to the Brave People): Flor Angela Barroso's Creative Strategies to Indigenize Education in Venezuela." In *Indian Subjects: Hemispheric Perspectives on the History of Indigenous Education*, edited by Brenda J. Child and Brian Klopotek, 229–66. Santa Fe: SAR Press.

Gregory, C. A. 1980. "Gifts to Men and Gifts to God: Gift Exchange and Capital Accumulation in Contemporary Papua New Guinea." *Man* 15, no. 4: 626–52.

Gregory, C. A. 1982. *Gifts and Commodities*. London: Academic Press.

Gupta, Akhil. 1995. "Blurred Boundaries: The Discourse of Corruption, the Culture of Politics, and the Imagined State." *American Ethnologist* 22, no. 2: 375–402.

Habermas, Jurgen. 1989. *The Structural Transformation of the Public Sphere*. Cambridge: The MIT Press.

Handman, Courtney. 2007. "Access to the Soul: Native Language and Authenticity in Papua New Guinea Bible Translation." In *Consequences of Contact: Language Ideologies and Sociocultural Transformations*, edited by Miki Makihara and Bambi B. Schieffelin, 166–88. Oxford: Oxford University Press.

Handman, Courtney. 2010. "Events of Translation: Intertextuality and Christian Ethnotheologies of Change among Guhu-Samane, Papua New Guinea." *American Anthropologist* 112, no. 4: 576–88.

Handman, Courtney. 2014. *Critical Christianity: Translation and Denominational Conflict in Papua New Guinea*. Berkeley, CA: University of California Press.

Hankins, Joseph Doyle. 2013. "An Ecology of Sensibility: The Politics of Scents and Stigma in Japan." *Anthropological Theory* 13, no. 1/2: 49–66.

Hanks, William F.. 1999. *Intertexts, Writings on Language, Utterance and Context*. Denver: Rowman and Littlefield.

Hanks, William F. and Carlo Severi, eds. 2014. "Translating Worlds: The Epistemological Space of Translation." Special issue, *Hau: Journal of Ethnographic Theory* 4, no. 2.

Harkness, Nicholas. 2013. "Softer Soju in South Korea." *Anthropological Theory* 13, no. 1/2: 12–30.

Harkness, Nicholas. 2014. *Songs of Seoul: An Ethnography of Voice and Voicing in Christian South Korea*. Berkeley: University of California Press.

Hawkins, Kirk A. 2009. "Is Chávez Populist?: Measuring Populist Discourse in Comparative Perspective." *Comparative Political Studies* 42, no. 8: 1040–67.

Hawkins, Kirk A. 2010. *Venezuela's Chavismo and Populism in Comparative Perspective*. Cambridge: Cambridge University Press.

Heinen, H. Dieter. 1975. "The Warao Indians of the Orinoco Delta: An Outline of Their Traditional Economic Organization and Interrelation with the National Economy." *Antropológica* 40: 25–55.

Heinen, H. Dieter. 1982. "Estructura social y mecanismos de desintegración en la sociedad Warao." *Acta Científica Venezolana* 33: 419–23.

Heinen, Dieter. 1985. *Oko Warao: We are Canoe People*. Wien, Fohrenau: Acta Ethnologica et Linguistica.

Heinen, H. Dieter. 1988. "Los Warao." In *Los Aborigenes de Venezuela: Etnologia Contemporanea*, Vol. 3, edited by W. Coppens, B. Escalante, and J. Lizot, 585–689. Caracas: Instituto Caribe de Antropología y Sociología, Fundación La Salle de Ciencias Naturales.

Heinen, H. Dieter. 1992. "The Early Colonization of the Lower Orinoco and its Impact on Present Day Indigenous Peoples." *Antropológica* 78: 51–86.

Heinen, Dieter and Alvaro Garcia-Castro. 2000. "The Multiethnic Network of the Lower Orinoco in Early Colonial Times." *Ethnohistory* 47, no. 3–4: 561–79.

Heinen, Dieter and Paul Henley. 1998–1999. "History, Kinship and the Ideology of Hierarchy Among the Warao of the Central Orinoco Delta." *Antropológica* 89: 25–78.

Heinen, Dieter, Roberto Lizarralde, and Tirso Gomez. 1994–1996. "El Abandono de un Ecosistema: El Caso de Los Morichales del Delta del Orinoco." *Antropológica* 81: 3–36.

Hellinger, Daniel. 1984. "Populism and Nationalism in Venezuela: New Perspectives on Acción Democrática." *Latin American Perspectives* 11, no. 4: 33–59.

Hellinger, Daniel and David Smilde, eds. 2011. *Venezuela's Bolivarian Democracy Participation, Politics, and Culture under Chávez*. Durham, NC: Duke University Press.

Hendricks, Janet W. 1988. "Power and Knowledge: Discourse and Ideological Transformation Among the Shuar." *American Ethnologist* 15, no. 2: 216–38.

Hendricks, Janet W. 1993. *To Drink of Death: The Narrative of a Shuar Warrior*. Tucson: The University of Arizona Press.

Herrmann, Gretchen. 1997. "Gift or Commodity: What Changes Hands in the U.S. Garage Sale?" *American Ethnologist* 24, no. 4: 910–30.

Hill, Jonathan D. 1993. *Keepers of the Sacred Chants: The Poetics of Ritual Power in an Amazonian Society*. Tucson: University of Arizona Press.

Hill, Jonathan D. 1994a. "Musicalizing the Other: Shamanistic Approaches to Ethnic-Class Competition in the Upper Rio Negro Region." In *Religiosidad y Resistencia Indígenas Hacia el Fin del Milenio*, edited by A. Barabas, 105–28. Quito: Abya-Yala.

Hill, Jonathan D. 1994b. "Alienated Targets: Military Discourses and the Disempowerment of Indigenous Amazonian Peoples in Venezuela." *Identities: Global Studies in Culture and Power* 1: 7–34.

Hill, Jonathan D. 1999a. "Nationalisme, Chamanisme et Histoires Indigenes au Venezuela." *Ethnologie Française* XXIX, no. 3: 387–96.

Hill, Jonathan D. 1999b. "Indigenous Peoples and the Rise of Independent Nation-States in Lowland South America." In *The Cambridge History of Native Peoples of the Americas: South America, Vol. III, Part 2*, edited by F. Salomon and S. Schwartz, 704–64. Cambridge: Cambridge University Press.

Hill, Jonathan D. 2000. "Colonial Transformation in Venezuela." *Ethnohistory* 47: 747–54.

Hill, Jonathan. 2003. "Shamanizing the State in Venezuela." *Journal of Latin American Lore* 21, no. 2: 163–77.

Hill, Jane H., and Irvine, Judith T., eds. 1993. *Responsibility and Evidence in Oral Discourse*. New York: Cambridge University Press.

Hymes, Dell. 1996. *Ethnography, Linguistics, Narrative Inequality: Towards an Understanding of Voice*. London: Taylor and Francis.

Inoue, Miyako. 2002. "Gender, Language, and Modernity: Toward and Effective History of Japanese Women's Language." *American Ethnologist* 29, no. 2: 392–422.

Inoue, Miyako. 2006. *Vicarious Language: Gender and Linguistic Modernity in Japan*. Berkeley, CA: University of California Press.

Irvine, Judith T. 1989. "When Talk Isn't Cheap: Language and Political Economy." *American Ethnologist* 16, no. 2: 248–67.

Jackson, Jennifer L. 2008. "Building Publics, Shaping Public Opinion: Interanimating Registers in Malagasy *Kabary* Oratory and Political Cartooning." *Journal of Linguistic Anthropology* 18, no. 2: 214–35.

Jakobson, Roman. 1960. "Language and Poetics." In *Style in Language*, edited by Thomas Sebeok, 350–77. Cambridge, MA: MIT Press.

Jakobson, Roman. 1970. "Language in Relation to Other Communication Systems." In *Selected Writings, Vol 2*, edited by Stephen Rudy, 697–710. The Hage: Mouton.

Jones, Bart. 2007. *Hugo: Hugo Chávez Story from Mud Hut to Perpetual Revolution*. New Hampshire: Steer Forth Press.

Josephides, Lisette. 1985. *The Production of Inequality: Gender and Exchange among the Kewa*. London: Tavistock.

Keane, Webb. 1994. "The Value of Words and the Meaning of Things in Eastern Indonesian Exchange." *Man* 29, no. 3: 605–29.

Keane, Webb. 1997. *Signs of Recognition: Powers and Hazards of Representation in an Indonesian Society.* Berkeley: University of California Press.

Keane, Webb. 2006. "Subjects and Objects." In *Handbook of Material Culture*, edited by Christopher Tilley, Webb Keane, Susanne Kuchler, Michael Rowlands, and Patricia Spyereds, 197–202. London: Sage.

Keane, Webb. 2007. *Christian Moderns: Freedom and Fetish in the Mission Encounter.* Berkeley: University of California Press.

Keane, Webb. 2013. "On Spirit Writing: Materialities of Language and the Religious Work of Transduction." *Journal of the Royal Anthropological Institute* 19: 1–17.

Keane, Webb. 2014a. "Affordances and Reflexivity in Everyday Life: An Ethnographic Stance." *Anthropological Theory* 14, no. 1: 3–26.

Keane, Webb. 2014b. "Rotting Bodies: The Clash of Stances toward Materiality and Its Ethical Affordances." *Current Anthropology* 55, no. S10: S312–21.

Kroskrity, Paul V. 2000. "Regimenting Language: Language Ideological Perspective." In *Regimes of Language: Ideologies, Polities, and Identities*, edited by Paul V. Kroskrity, 1–34. Santa Fe, New Mexico: School of American Research Press.

Kunreuther, Laura. 2014. *Voicing Subjects: Public Intimacy and Mediation in Kathmandu.* South Asia Across the Disciplines Series. Berkeley: University of California Press.

Lauer, Matthew. 2006. "State-led Democratic Politics and Emerging Forms of Indigenous Leadership among the Ye'kwana of the Upper Orinoco." *Journal of Latin American Anthropology* 11, no. 1: 51–86.

Lavandero Perez, Julio. 1991. *Ajotejana I: Mitos.* Caracas: Hermanos Capuchinos.

Lavandero Perez, Julio. 1992. *Ajotejana II: Relatos.* Caracas: Hermanos Capuchinos.

Lempert, Michael, and Michael Silverstein. 2012. *Creatures of Politics: Media, Message, and the American presidency.* Bloomington: Indiana University Press.

Leavitt, John. 2014. "Words and Worlds: Ethnography and Theories of Translation." *Hau: Journal of Ethnographic Theory* 4, no. 2: 193–220.

Lemon, Alaina. 2013. "Touching the Gap: Social Qualia and Cold War Contact." *Anthropological Theory* 13, no. 1/2: 67–88.

Leon, Freddy Jr. 2008. Marea Roja se Desbordo en Calle Petion. Notidiario, January 10: 3.

Lizarralde, Roberto, ed. 1956. *Los Guaraos del Delta Amacuro: Informe de una Investigación de Campo Efectuada con Fines Pedagógicos.* Caracas: FACES-Universidad Central de Venezuela.

Lomnitz, Claudio. 1995. "Ritual, Rumor and Corruption in the Constitution of Polity in Modern Mexico." *Journal of Latin American Anthropology* 1, no. 1: 20–47.

Lomnitz, Claudio. 2001. *Deep Mexico, Silent Mexico: An Anthropology of Nationalism.* Minneapolis, MN: University of Minnesota Press.

López Maya, Margarita. 2003. "The Venezuelan *Caracazo* of 1989: Popular Protest and Institutional Weakness." *Journal of Latin American Studies* 35: 117–37.

Malavé Mata, Héctor. 1987. *Los Extravíos del Poder: Euforia y Crisis del Populismo en Venezuela.* Caracas: Universidad Central de Venezuela, Ediciones de la Biblioteca.

Marcano, Christina and Alberto Barrera Tyszka. 2007. *Hugo Chávez: The Definite Biography of Venezuela's Controversial President*. New York: Random House.

Marin Rodríguez, Cruz José. 1977. *Estampas Deltanas*. Tucupita.

Marin Rodríguez, Cruz José. 1981. *Historia del Territorio Federal Delta Amacuro*. Caracas: Ediciones de la Presidencia de la República.

Martin, Elias. 1977. *En las Bocas del Orinoco: 50 años de los Misioneros Capuchinos en el Delta Amacuro*. Caracas: Ediciones Paulinas.

Martínez, Apolinar. 2008a. El Delta Dara un Salto Gigantesco hacia el Futuro. Notidiario, January 10: 12–13.

Martínez, Apolinar. 2008b. El Mundo Warao Está Listo para Asumir la Gobernación del Estado. Notidiario, February 22: 12–13.

Mauss, Marcel. 1967 [1925]. *The Gift: Forms and Functions of Exchange in Archaic Societies*. New York: Norton.

Mauss, Marcel. 1990. *The Gift: The Form and Reason for Exchange in Archaic Societies*. New York: W.W. Norton.

Mignolo, Walter D. 1992. "On the Colonization of Amerindian Languages and Memories: Renaissance Theories of Writing and the Discontinuity of the Classical Tradition." *Comparative Studies in Society and History* 34, no. 2: 301–30.

Mintz, Sidney W. 1985. *Sweetness and Power: The Place of Sugar in Modern History*. New York: Penguin Books.

Myers, Fred. 1986. "Reflections on a Meeting: Structure, Language, and the Polity in a Small-Scale Society." *American Ethnologists* 13, no. 3: 430–47.

Oakdale, Suzanne. 2004. "The Culture-Conscious Brazilian Indian: Representing and Reworking Indianness in Kayabi Political Discourse." *American Ethnologist* 31, no. 1: 61–75.

OCEI. 1993. *Censo Indígena de Venezuela*. Caracas: Oficina Central de Estadística e Informática.

Olea, Bonifacio. 1928. *Ensayo Gramatical del Dialecto de los Indios Guaraunos*. Caracas: Emp. Gutemberg.

Orinoco Company LTD. 1899. *Representation to the Minister of Agriculture, Industry and Commerce by the Orinoco Company Limited: Respecting its Property of the So Called "Imataca" Mine*. Caracas: Imprenta Federacion.

Paine, R., ed. 1981. *Politically Speaking: Cross-Cultural Studies of Rhetoric*. Philadelphia: ISHI.

Parmentier, Richard. 1994. *Signs in Society: Studies in Semiotic Anthropology*. Bloomington, IN: Indiana University Press.

Passes, Alan. 2004. "The Place of Politics: Powerful Speech and Women Speech and Women Speakers in Everyday Pa'ikwené (Palikur) Life." *Journal of the Royal Anthropological Institute* 10: 1–18.

Pierce, Charles Sanders. 1955. *Philosophical Writings of Pierce*. New York: Dover Publications.

Pierce, Charles Sanders. 1998. *The Essential Pierce: Selected Philosophical Writings*. Bloomington, IN: Indiana University Press.

Pineda, Nelson. 1992. *Petróleo y Populismo en la Venezuela del Siglo XX*. Caracas: Fondo Editorial Tropykos.

Pineda, Nelson. 2000. *El Ocaso del Minotauro o la Declinación de la Hegemonía Populista en Venezuela*. Mérida: Universidad de los Andes, Consejo de Publicaciones, Facultad de Ciencias Económicas y Sociales.

Prensa Gobernación Delta Amacuro. 2008. Gobernación Entregó más de 300 Pensiones del Seguro Social. Notidiario, April 7: 3.

Prensa Imataca. 2008a. Casacoima Cuenta con Obra de Gobierno Exitosa. Notidiario, January 9: 9.

Prensa Imataca. 2008b. Santaella Continua Contacto Directo con las Comunidades. Notidiario, February 5: 6.

Prensa Imataca. 2008c. Juramentado Comando de Campaña en Antonio Díaz. Notidiario, January 12: 9.

Rafael, Vicente L. 1993. *Contracting Colonialism: Translation and Christian Conversion in Tagalog Society Under Early Spanish Rule*. Durham: Duke University Press.

Ramos, Alcida Rita. 1998. *Indigenism: Ethnic Politics in Brazil*. Madison: University of Wisconsin Press.

Riviere, Peter. 1971. "The Political Structure of the Trio Indians as Manifested in a System of Ceremonial Dialogue." In *The Translation of Culture: Essays to E.E. Evans-Pritchard*, edited by T.O. Beidelman, 293–311. London: Tavistock.

Robbins, Joel, Bambi B. Schieffelin, and Aparecida Vilaça. 2014. "Evangelical Conversion and the Transformation of the Self in Amazonia and Melanesia: Christianity and the Revival of Anthropological Comparison." *Comparative Studies in Society and History* 56, no. 3: 559–90.

Rodríguez, Juan L. 2008. "The Translation of Poverty and the Poverty of Translation in the Orinoco Delta." *Ethnohistory* 55, no 3: 417–38.

Rodríguez, Juan Luis. 2011. "Rhetorical Strategies and Political Gift Giving in the Orinoco Delta." Ph.D. diss. Southern Illinois University, Carbondale.

Rosa, Jonathan. 2019. *Looking Like a Language, Sounding Like a Race: Raciolingusitic Ideologies and the Learning of Latinindad*. New York: Oxford University Press.

Rourke, Thomas. 1937. *Tyrant of the Andes: The Life of Juan Vicente Gomez*. London: Michael Joseph LTD.

Sahlins, Marshall. 1994. "Cosmologies of Capitalism: The Trans-Pacific Sector of 'The World System'." In *Culture/Power/History: A Reader in Contemporary Social Theory*, edited by Nicholas B. Dirk, Geoff Eley, and Sherry B. Ortner, 412–54. Princeton: Princeton University Press.

Salas, Miguel Tinker. 2009. *The Enduring Legacy: Oil, Culture, and Society in Venezuela*. Durham: Duke University Press.

Samet, Robert. 2019. *Deadline: Populism and the Press in Venezuela*. Chicago: Chicago University Press.

References 197

Sánchez, Rafael. 2016. *Dancing Jacobins: A Venezuelan Genealogy of Latin American Populism*. New York: Fordham University Press.

Schieffelin, Bambi B., Kathryn A. Woolard, and Paul V. Kroskrity, eds. 1998. *Language Ideologies: Practice and Theory*. New York: Oxford University Press.

Schiller, Naomi. 2018. *Channeling the State: Community Media and Popular Politics in Venezuela*. Durham: Duke University Press.

Sherzer, Joel. 1983. *Kuna Ways of Speaking: An Ethnographic Perspective*. Austin, TX: University of Texas Press.

Sherzer, Joel. 1987. "A Discourse-Centered Approach to Language and Culture." *American Anthropologist* 89, no. 2: 295–309.

Sherzer, Joel. 1999. "Ceremonial Dialogic Greetings Among the Kuna Indians of Panama." *Journal of pragmatics* 31, no. 4: 453–70.

Silverstein, Michael. 2003a. "Indexical Order and the Dialectics of Sociolinguistic Life." *Language & Communication* 23, no. 3/4: 193–229.

Silverstein, Michael. 2003b. "The Whens and Wheres -As Well As Hows- of Ethnolinguistic Recognition." *Public Culture* 15, no. 3: 531–57.

Silverstein, Michael. 2003c. "Translation, Transduction, Transformation: Skating Glossando on Thin Semiotic Ice." In *Translating Cultures: Perspectives on Translation and Anthropology*, edited by P. Rubel and A. Rosman, 75–105. Oxford, UK: Berg Publishers.

Silverstein, Michael. 2005a. "The Poetics of Politics: 'Theirs' and 'Ours.'" *Journal of Anthropological Research* 61, no. 1: 1–24.

Silverstein, Michael. 2005b. "Axes of Evals: Token versus Type Interdiscursivity." *Journal of Linguistic Anthropology* 15, no. 1: 6–22.

Silverstein, Michael. 2006. "Old Wine, New Ethnographic Lexicography." *Annual Review of Anthropology* 35: 481–96.

Silverstein, Michael. 2011. "The 'Message' in the (Political) Battle." *Language and Communication*. 31, no. 2: 203–16.

Silverstein, Michael and Greg Urban, eds. 1996. *Natural Histories of Discourse*. Chicago: Chicago University Press.

Singer, Milton. 1986. *Man's Glassy Essence*. Delhi: Hindustan Publishing Corporation.

Smilde, David, and Daniel Hellinger, eds. 2011. *Venezuela's Bolivarian Democracy: Participation, Politics, and Culture Under Chávez*. Durham: Duke University Press.

Suarez, Maria Matilde. 1968. *Los Warao: Indígenas del Delta del Orinoco*. Caracas: Departamento de Antropología, Instituto Venezolano de Investigaciones Científicas.

Suarez, Maria Matilde. 1972. *Terminología, Alianza Matrimonial y Cambio en la Sociedad Warao*. Caracas: Universidad Católica Andres Bello.

Surralles, Alexandre. 2003. "Face to Face: Meaning, Feeling and Perception in Amazonian Welcoming Ceremonies." *Journal of the Royal Anthropological Institute* 9, no. 4: 775–91.

Thomas, Nicolas. 1991. *Entangled Objects: Exchange, Material Culture, and Colonialism in the Pacific*. Cambridge: Harvard University Press.

Thurber, O.E. 1907. *The Venezuelan Question Castro end the Asphalt Trust: From Official Records*. New York: Noble Press.

Tsing, Anna L. 1994. "From the Margins." *Cultural Anthropology* 9, no. 3: 279–97.

Turner, Terence. 1991a. "Representing, Resisting, Rethinking: Historical Transformation of Kayapo Culture and Anthropological Consciousness." In *Colonial Situations: Essays on the Contextualization of Ethnographic Knowledge*, edited by George Stocking, 285–313. Madison, WI: University of Wisconsin Press.

Turner, Terence. 1991b. "The Social Dynamics and Personal Politics of Video Making in an Indigenous Community." *Visual Anthropology Review* 7, no. 2: 68–76.

Turner, Terence. 1992. "Defiant Images: The Kayapo Appropriation of Video." *Anthropology Today* 8, no. 6: 5–15.

Turner, Terence. 1995. "Representation, Collaboration, and Mediation in Contemporary Ethnographic and Indigenous Media." *Visual Anthropology Review* 11, no. 2: 1–5.

Turner, Terence. 2002. "Representation, Polyphony, and the Construction of Power in a Kayapo Video." In *Indigenous Movements, Self-representation, and State in Latin America*, edited by Kay B. Warren and Jean Jackson, 229–50. Austin, TX: University of Texas Press.

Turrado Moreno, Angel. 1945. *Etnografía de los Indios Guaraunos*. Caracas: Tercera Conferencia Interamericana de Agricultura.

Ugalde, Luis. 1994. *Mentalidad Económica y Proyectos de Colonización en Guayana en los Siglos XVIII y XIX: El caso de la compañía Manoa en el Delta del Orinoco, Tomo II*. Caracas: Academia Nacional de Ciencias Económicas.

Urban, Greg. 1986. "Ceremonial Dialogues in South America." *American Anthropologist* 88, no. 2: 371–86.

Urban, Greg. 1988. "Ritual Wailing in Amerindian Brazil." *American Anthropologist* 90, no. 2: 385–400.

Urban, Greg. 1991. *A Discourse-Centered Approach to Culture: Native South American Myths and Rituals*. Austin, TX: University of Texas Press.

Urban, Greg. 2001. *Metaculture: How Cultures Moves Through the World*. Minneapolis, MN: University of Minnesota Press.

Valencia Ramírez, Cristobal. 2005. "Venezuela's Bolivarian Revolution: Who are the Chavistas?" *Latin American Perspectives* 32, no. 3: 79–97.

Valencia Ramírez, Cristobal. 2008. "Hemos Derrotado al Diablo! Chavéz Supporters, Anti-Imperialism, and Twenty-First Century Socialism." *Identities: Global Studies in Culture and Power* 15, no. 2: 147–70.

Valencia Ramírez, Cristobal. 2015. *We Are the State!: Barrio Activism in Venezuela's Bolivarian Revolution*. Tucson: University of Arizona Press.

Vaquero, Antonio. 1965. *Idioma Warao: Morfología, Sintaxis, Literatura*. Tucupita: Estudios Venezolanos Indígenas.

Velasco, Alejandro. 2015. *Barrio Rising: Urban Popular Politics and the Making of Modern Venezuela*. Berkeley: University of California Press.

Vidal, Silvia. 2002. "El Chamanismo de los Arawakos De Rio Negro: Su influencia en la política local y regional en el Amazonas de Venezuela." *Serie Antropologia* 313: 1–20. Departamento de Antropologia Instituto de Ciências Sociais Universidade de Brasília.

Warner, Michael. 2002. "Publics and Counterpublics." *Public Culture* 14, no. 1: 49–90.

Webster, Anthony K. 2009. *Exploration on Navajo Poetry and Poetics*. Albuquerque: University of New Mexico Press.

Webster, Anthony K. 2014. *"Dif' G'one'* and Semiotic Calquing: A Signography of the Linguistic Landscape of the Navajo Nation." *Journal of Anthropological Research* 70, no. 3: 385–410.

Webster, Anthony K. 2015. *Intimate Grammars: An Ethnography of Navajo Poetry*. Tucson: University of Arizona Press.

Whitehead, Neil L. 1992. "Tribes Make States and States Make Tribes: Warfare and the Creation of Colonial Tribe and State in Northeastern South America, 1492–1820." In *War in the Tribal Zone: Expanding States and Indigenous Warfare*, edited by Brian Ferguson, and Neil Whitehead, 127–50. Santa Fe: School of American Research Press.

Whitehead, Neil L. 1996. "Ethnogenesis, and Ethnocide in the European Occupation of Native Suriname, 1499–1681." In *History, Power, and Identity: Ethnogenesis in the Americas, 1492–1992*, edited by Jonathan Hill, 20–35. Iowa: University of Iowa Press.

Wilbert, Johannes. 1972. *Survivors of El Dorado: Four Indians Cultures of South America*. New York: Praeger Publishers.

Wilbert, Johannes. 1993. *Mystic Endowment: Religious Ethnography of the Warao Indians*. Cambridge: Harvard University Center for the Study of World Religions.

Wilbert, Johannes. 1996. *Mindful of Famine: Religious Climatology of the Warao Indians*. Cambridge: Harvard University Center for the Study of World Religions.

Wilbert, Johannes. 1997. *Mindful of Famine: Religious Climatology of the Warao Indians*. Cambridge, MA: Harvard University Press.

Wilbert, Johannes. 2004. "The Order of Dark Shamans among the Warao." In *Darkness and Secrecy: The Anthropology of Assault Sorcery and Witchcraft in Amazonia*, edited by Neil L. Withehead and Robin Wright, 21–50. Durham: Duke University Press.

Wilbert, Johannes and Miguel Layrisse, eds. 1980. *Demographic and Biological Studies of the Warao Indians*. Los Angeles: UCLA Latin American Center Publications.

Wilbert, Werner and Cecilia Ayala- Lafee. 2001. *Hijas de la Luna: Enculturación Femenina entre los Warao*. Caracas: Fundación la Salle de Ciencias Naturales.

Wilbert, Werner and Cecilia Ayala- Lafee. 2008. *La Mujer Warao: De Recolectora Deltana a Recolectora Urbana*. Caracas: Fundación la Salle de Ciencias Naturales.

Wolf, Eric. 1982. *Europe and the People Without History*. Berkeley: University of California Press.

Yang, Mayfair Mei-Hui. 1989. "Gift Economy and State Power in China." *Comparative Studies in Society and History* 31, no. 1: 25–54.

Yang, Mayfair Mei-Hui. 2000. "Putting Global Capitalism in Its Place: Economic Hybridity, Bataille, and Ritual Expenditure." *Current Anthropology* 41, no. 4: 477–509.

Yarrington, Doug. 2003. "Cattle, Corruption, and Venezuelan State Formation during the Regime of Juan Vicente Gomez, 1908–1935." *Latin American Research Review* 38, no. 2: 9–33.

Index